TODAY'S MOMS

COLLINS LIVING

An Imprint of HarperCollins Publishers

To HANNAH +
Leia Wonderful
Enjoy this
first year!

TODAY'S MO·MS

Essentials for Surviving Baby's First Year

TODAY

Mary Ann Zoellner and Alicia Ybarbo

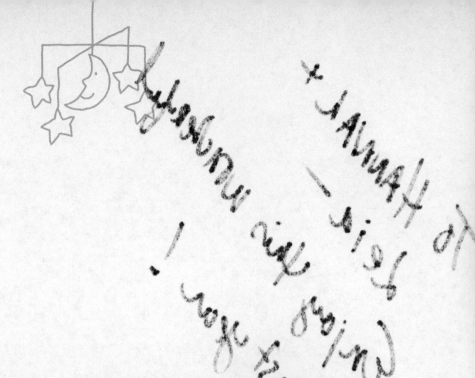

HarperCollins books may be purchased for educational, business, or sales promotional use. For information, please write: Special Markets Department, HarperCollins Publishers, 10 East 53rd Street, New York, NY 10022.

FIRST EDITION

Designed by Kate Nichols

Photo: © Gravicapa/Dreamstime.com

Library of Congress Cataloging-in-Publication Data
  Zoellner, Mary Ann.
    Today's Moms : essentials for surviving baby's first year / Mary Ann Zoellner
  and Alicia Ybarbo. — 1st ed.
      p. cm.
    ISBN 978-0-06-172185-4 (pbk.)
    1. Infants—Care. 2. Mother and infant. 3. Parenting. I. Ybarbo, Alicia.
  II. Today show (Television program) III. Title.
  HQ774.Z64   2009
  649'.122—dc22   2008053608

09 10 11 12 13   OV/RRD   10 9 8 7 6 5 4 3 2 1

t his book is dedicated to my precious little girls, **Zurielle** and **Arabella**, and to my husband, **Alexander**. Your humor, support, and love make each day better than the last.

—MARY ANN ZOELLNER

t his book is lovingly dedicated to my husband, **Mark**, and children **Jack** and **Lucy**. Mommy will be home soon!

—ALICIA YBARBO

CONTENTS

ACKNOWLEDGMENTS

A Big Thank-You
to All the Folks Who Helped Make
TODAY'S MOMS Possible

The Contributors, Who Shared Their Stories and Expertise: We Can't Thank You Enough

Tiki Barber (AJ and Chason's dad), *TODAY* National Correspondent

Joy Bauer, M.S., R.D., C.D.N. (Jesse, Cole, and Ayden Jane's mom), *TODAY* Contributor and Registered Dietitian/Nutritionist

Tanya Benenson, M.D., Medical Director, NBC Universal

Lloyd Boston, *TODAY* Style Editor

Rachel Burstein (Maya's mom), *TODAY* Producer

Jean Chatzky (Jake and Julia's mom), *TODAY* Financial Editor

Ann Curry (Mac and Walker's mom), *TODAY* News Anchor

Leslye Fagin (Jenna's mom), *TODAY* Stage Manager

Ada Famulari (Derek and Blake's mom), *TODAY* Program Manager/HR

Kathie Lee Gifford (Cody and Cassidy's mom), *TODAY* Co-Anchor, 4th Hour

Peter Greenberg, *TODAY* Travel Editor

Claudia David Heitler (Arlo and Lois's mom), Former *TODAY* Booker/Producer

Paul Hochman (Lily, Carter, and Oscar's dad), *TODAY* Gear and Technology Editor

Debbie Kosofsky (David, Jeffrey, and Pamela's mom), *TODAY* Producer

Matt Lauer (Jack, Romy, and Thijs's papa), *TODAY* Co-Anchor

Janice Lieberman (David and Judah's mom), *TODAY* Consumer Correspondent

Melissa Lonner (Noah and Jadon's mom), *TODAY* Senior Producer

Linda Mason (Farrell, Lucas, and Grace's mom), Bright Horizons Family Solutions/NBC Universal's Full-Service and Back-Up Child Care Centers

Elizabeth Mayhew (Madeleine and Charlie's mom), *TODAY* Contributing Editor and Lifestyle Expert

Natalie Morales (Josh and Luke's mom), *TODAY* National Correspondent

Joan Ortiz, R.N., B.S.N., C.L.C. (Kristina and Ashley's mom), Limerick, Inc./NBC Universal's Workplace Lactation Program

Eve Pearl (Joey's mom), *TODAY* Makeup Artist

Ruth Peters, Ph.D. (Lindsay and Chris's mom), *TODAY* Contributor and Clinical Psychologist

Amy Robach (Annalise and Ava's mom), *TODAY* National Correspondent/Weekend *TODAY* Co-Anchor

Al Roker (Courtney, Leila, and Nicholas's dad), *TODAY* Weather and Feature Reporter

Vanessa Rowson (Joshua's mom), *TODAY* Production Finance Coordinator

Gail Saltz, M.D. (Emily, Kimberly, and Tori's mom), *TODAY* Contributor and Psychiatrist

Robin Sindler (Charlotte's mom), *TODAY* Producer

Nancy Snyderman, M.D. (Kate, Rachel, and Charlie's mom), NBC News Chief Medical Editor

Dierdre Stadtmauer, *TODAY* Hair Stylist

Meredith Vieira (Ben, Gabe, and Lily's mom), *TODAY* Co-Anchor

Jen Wilson, NBC Senior Fitness Specialist

Cecilia Fang Wu (Christian's mom), *TODAY* Producer

Other NBC Folks Who Helped Us Along The Way

Jeff Zucker: For hiring us into the *TODAY* family eight years ago.

Phil Griffin: For making this three-year, three-hundred-plus-page dream a reality. Buddy, you're the best.

Jim Bell: For being such a great boss and fostering a workplace that supports working moms.

Dana Haller: For taking our calls and always greeting us with a smile.

Jaclyn Levin and Beth O'Connell: For listening to our idea.

Stuart Goldstein, Steve Chung, David McCormick, Cheryl Gould, and Marni Pedorella: For reviewing the book.

Mary Ann's Family and Friends

Alexander: The love of my life.

Zurielle and Arabella: My bean and pinky, I can't believe God gave me such great little girls.

John Zoellner: My father, a World War II hero, and the greatest dad in the world.

Jean Ann: For being such an important part of my family.

Ann and Bob Knight: Mama, thanks for being there at the births and for continuing to teach me how to be a parent.

Erik, Shamron, Robert, Carrie, Edward, Darci, Charles, Kendra, Philip, Darci, Roy, Jennifer, Titus, and Abigayle: Brothers and sisters words can't describe.

Kayleigh, Jacob, John, Noah, Christian, Allison, Bridget, Blake, Beau, Caleb, Hannah, Chloe, Sophia, Lilianna, Zeta, Zody, Henry, Caspar, Benedict, and Leila: Aunt May loves you!

Bruce, Elfride, Gigi, Erik, and Ollie: My amazing in-laws, thanks for all your kindness and support.

Christy: For providing me with my birthing team.

Barbara Sellers, Elizabeth Boyce: Midwives extraordinaire.

Amy Brown and Terry Richmond: My doulas.

My best friends: Marge, Vito, Margaret, Cristin, and Katrin for believing in the dream!

Ana: Yo te quiero mucho, gracias por todo.

Alicia: Clear as day . . . blood, sweat, tears and years, baby!

Alicia's Family and Friends

Markie: Thanks for letting me be *the flower* while I took the time to focus on this book. I promise that I will be *the stem* on our next adventure together. I love you.

Jack and Lucy: I love my monkeys and am so proud to be your mommy. My energy, drive, and enthusiasm come from you.

Mom and Dad: Thanks for showing me that life is worth slowing down for.

Grandma Alicia, The Steel Magnolia of Murrietta Place: One day I hope to have the wisdom and strength that you've shared for so many years.

Paul: Thanks for showing me that there's more than one way to see the world (and decorate it).

Kathryn: Do you think those stickers we spent years collecting are worth anything today? Un beso grande!

Rudy: Here's to saving the world, one diesel car at a time.

Logan and Amelia: Auntie Shosh loves you.

Ira and Edith: Big hugs to my biggest cheerleaders

Lisa: Thanks for loving my children as if they were your own.

To my gals **Lisa, Cindy, Sonia, Whit, Mill, Natalie, Kluger, Goodman, Kalika, Hebert, Cher, and Ginny**: The wrinkles are well worth the laughter.

To the original **New Mother's Luncheon/Little Maestros** mommy group, especially **Beth, Robin, Rosanne, Alison, Heather, and Isabel**: I could not have survived those first few months (heck, years!) without you.

Mary Ann: My writing partner, dear friend, and bosom buddy, thanks for everything.

To Our Book Family

Mary Ellen O'Neill: Three cheers for second chances.

Ruth Mannes: Thanks for helping make the connection.

Matthew Patin: For keeping us on schedule.

Lelia Mander: For copyediting the book.

Alrica Goldstein: For getting us started on the right foot.

Tracy Fisher, Eric Zohn, Suzanne Gluck, and Elizabeth Reed: The William Morris gang.

Mary Ann and Alicia Would Especially Like to Thank

Karen Moline (Emmanuel's mom), writer extraordinaire: We're so happy you decided to join us on this wild ride . . . while crossing our T's and dotting our I's along the way. Big bear hugs to Emmanuel for generously sharing you with us. We love you!!!!!!

INTRODUCTION

The concept of this book was born in a car seat. Not just any car seat, mind you, but the TriplePlay Sit'n'Stroll 4100 Travel System Stroller, to be precise!

Mary Ann: There was nothing that my baby girl, Zurielle, hated more than her car seat. All my experienced mom friends told me to just put her in the car seat and drive, and she'd soon calm down and fall asleep. Not my Zurielle. The screaming started the minute she was strapped in and didn't end until she threw up.

One night, when she was about three months old, we trotted off to Wal-Mart to remedy the situation. Being a producer at NBC's *TODAY* show, I'm used to leaving no stone unturned when it comes to research. My husband, Alexander, and I inspected every single car seat on the shelves to find one with the exact right reclining angle that we hoped would nip that carsickness in the bud. When we found one that seemed perfect, we were so excited. Well, Zurielle screamed when we strapped her in, but that was to be expected. It would be fine once we got moving. Nope; once again the shrieking was following by vomiting.

This led to many discussions with Alicia, my best friend at *TODAY*, with whom I had bonded a few years earlier when we both got engaged and were planning our weddings. We chat about everything, and this led to a discussion among many of our female colleagues about car seats and my desperate situation. That's when another producer at *TODAY* told me about the

Sit'n'Stroll, a stroller with retractable wheels that turns into a portable car seat. I promptly ordered it and prayed it would do the trick, which it did.

Fast-forward two months. Alexander, Zurielle, and I were on our way to Costa Rica for a family vacation. As I sat in the bathroom at the Miami airport breastfeeding, I realized that every mom who walked in there was asking me about the Sit'n'Stroll. I explained that my co-worker had recommended it, and it was the only car seat that kept my baby from screaming and puking in the car!

As I sat in the airport bathroom, I realized this situation was no different from those we have every day at *TODAY*. The other producers and staffers who juggle, schedule, and program the toughest and most successful four hours of network television every day manage to produce and raise babies, too. We produce segments that are meant to inform people about news, educate them about various topics, and entertain them. Talking to women in an airport bathroom about strollers while breastfeeding my infant certainly qualified for all three categories.

Alicia: As producers at *TODAY*, when we have a question about any topic at all, we go right to the experts. We go to Janice Lieberman, our consumer correspondent, about which stroller to buy; to Peter Greenberg, our travel ace, for the best place to head on a baby-friendly vacation; to Paul Hochman, our gear and technology guru, to learn the difference between a megabyte and a megapixel; or to Lloyd Boston, our style editor, to find a flattering outfit that will hide our postdelivery baby tummies without breaking the bank. And to all the other experts that appear daily on *TODAY* to help our viewers with their own child-rearing issues.

Even *TODAY*'s anchors share information with us. As Matt Lauer told us, "We talk about our kids all the time in the makeup room. It's one of the things we all have in common on the show. So it's not only a nice kind of comfort to know that you're not alone, it's a real resource to have Meredith, Ann, and Al tell me what to expect."

So here we are, almost four years, four babies, and countless diapers, stuffy noses, and sleepless nights later, full of love for our children and our jobs, and blessed to be working with so many incredible women at *TODAY* who freely share their hopes and joys, triumphs and failures, health scares and fertility problems, pregnancies and adoptions with each other. As working moms at the show, we've experienced all the ups and downs together. We're challenged at work to keep *TODAY* on top, and challenged at home to keep our marriages alive, all while trying to raise healthy, happy children. We've learned how to maintain that elusive balance, and that being a working mom does not mean putting one challenge on hold to meet the other, because you don't stop loving your children when you go back to work and vice versa.

As many new moms are, I was always online researching, even at three in the morning when my breasts were so engorged I thought I'd start levitating out of my bed. I found sites where I was able to chat with other sleep-deprived moms who had the same annoying, alarming, humorous, embarrassing questions. I realized that I was not alone, that other moms needed information and reassurance too. The more I listened to other women, the more confident I became as a mother.

TODAY's Moms is our fun yet informational take on our babies' first year. We hope all moms will think of this book as a surrogate girlfriend. It is not a substitute for straightforward parenting and medical advice, because we're not doctors. But we are experienced moms who have the power of the *TODAY* show's resources collectively behind us—moms who know best how to balance diapers and deadlines. We hope this book will help *all* mothers feel more confident about their first year of motherhood.

PART ONE

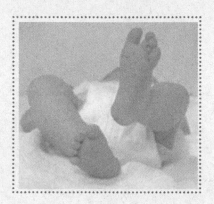

Baby Basics

CHAPTER ONE

Where's the Owner's Manual?

TOP TEN MYTH BUSTERS OF BABY'S FIRST YEAR

MYTH #1: When you see your baby for the first time, you'll experience *love* like you've never felt before.

BUSTER: Don't be fooled by those baby food ads. Some moms bond quickly; some don't bond for months. In either case, it's perfectly normal.

MYTH #2: All the moms I see leisurely strolling their babies are so much happier and better rested than I am.

BUSTER: They just fake it better than you do.

MYTH #3: Breastfeeding is a breeze.

BUSTER: For many new mothers it's difficult, complicated, and downright painful.

MYTH #4: A good mother always knows why her baby is crying.

BUSTER: Maybe. But even a well-fed, comfortable baby can cry for no real reason. (Sort of like some adults.)

MYTH #5: You'll never get your pre-baby body back.
BUSTER: Not easily or quickly. Slow and steady wins the weight-loss race.

MYTH #6: : More specifically, your breasts will never go back to their normal size.
BUSTER: Sadly, they will. And sooner than you think.

MYTH #7: You'll never have time for yourself again.
BUSTER: Not as easily or as cheaply as before, but you can. Hiring a babysitter for even a few hours a week can be a lifesaver.

MYTH #8: Sex? Yuck. Who would ever want that again?
BUSTER: You will, sooner or later. Trust us.

MYTH #9: My husband is lucky to escape to work every day.
BUSTER: Don't sit around feeling lonely. Get out there and make new friends. Mommy mixers are one of the best places to meet them!

MYTH #10: You always said you'd be cooler than your own mom.
BUSTER: She might not have been so uncool after all.

Alicia: It was ten days before my due date when, around 3 a.m. early one Sunday morning, cramps suddenly kicked in. I woke my husband, Mark, but he simply rolled over and went back to sleep.

He eventually woke up, as my pains grew in intensity.

While I was doubled over in the bathroom Mark called the doctor. I couldn't hear the doctor on the other end of the telephone, but by Mark's responses I could tell that she was telling him to wait a few more hours before heading to the hospital. I wasn't happy to hear that and he must have seen the look on my face, because the next thing I knew we were heading out the door. Already five centimeters dilated, we arrived at the hospital, where I immediately had an epidural.

The doctor said I was dilating quickly and we'd have the baby soon.

At that point, the nurses told me to go ahead and sleep for a few hours before we started pushing. I know what you're thinking. *Who could sleep at a time like this?* Trust me. You can. When I woke up, I saw my husband, who at the time was working for the NFL—and naturally, it was draft weekend, which was hugely important for him—sprawled out, his legs up on a table, staring at the TV and chowing down on a protein bar. I asked if I could get him anything else to make his stay more relaxing. As all women know, labor *is* all about the husband, right?

Anyway, after a few pain-free hours, I dilated to nine centimeters. Then something happened. I was taking too long to dilate to ten centimeters, which is when you can start pushing, so I was given a labor-inducing drug. However, after only a few minutes, the baby's heart monitor started to flat-line.

"Get onto your hands and knees," the nurses and doctors in my room said. "Let's try and get the baby to move around and increase his heart rate." It worked at first, but after a few more heart monitor scares, the doctor told me I needed a C-section. While doctors and nurses hurried about, one of them handed my husband a pair of operating-room scrubs. Once he'd put them on, he approached the nurses with a strange look on his face.

"Excuse me," he asked them, "do you think I could get another pair of scrubs? These don't really fit me that well and I'd like to look good for my baby."

The nurses found this highly amusing. Needless to say, I did not.

Although I'd had the epidural, I needed more anesthesia to numb me from my chest down. My arms were tied down to the gurney, and I felt like I was in a straitjacket. "Breathe normally," I was told. My baby's heart rate was jumping around like a Mexican jumping bean, I was getting prepped for surgery, my husband's scrubs didn't fit, and I was supposed to breathe normally? Fat chance!

I couldn't feel any part of my body and started hyperventilating in a panic. Then, mercifully, my doctor leaned over and told me the baby was coming out in a few seconds, but I was still in a complete state of panic. So the doctor did what any other sane person in her position would have done: She asked the anesthesiologist to put me out. In what felt like the blink of an eye, I woke up and my baby was placed in my arms. He was perfect, beautiful, and healthy.

At the time, it all seemed so traumatic, but looking back, it really wasn't that bad. That's what Mommy Brain does to you!

Mary Ann: I had a perfect pregnancy, without one day of morning sickness. I had gained just the right amount of weight—thirty-three pounds—and was determined to give birth naturally, without drugs. I had prepared myself mentally by taking a Bradley Method child preparation class and studying Hypnobirthing after we did a segment on it on the show (one of the mantras was *Trust your body, it will know what to do*); and physically by thinking of pregnancy as "training," and staying in the best shape possible. I'd opted for a midwife instead of an obstetrician, and had hired Amy, a doula (or birthing assistant), a calm and experienced person who could manage both my mother and my husband's tendency toward squeamishness.

But by the end, I was all raw nerves. In fact, my prelude to childbirth was a huge fight with my mother, who lives in Tulsa, Oklahoma. She has nine children (seven birth, two adopted); one of them was born at home (delivered by my then-thirteen-year-old brother!) and another in a taxi en route to the hospital, so she knows something about childbirth. Mama was so determined to be at my baby's birth that she showed up two weeks before my due date, convinced that I was going to pop that baby out early.

As a result, she spent those two weeks staring at me, analyzing me, looking for any sign that today was the day. Any time I spent a few extra minutes in the bathroom, she'd check me out and declare, "Mary Ann, I know today's the day." After two weeks of this, she told me that she'd have to leave soon if I didn't just have the baby already. I lost it, and cried and cried. Luckily, when I woke up the next day and puked my guts out, Mom got all excited that it was finally the day.

When I went into labor, I was walking around our tiny apartment like a caged animal, sucking on Popsicles, to no avail. Everything I ate came right back up. Amy the doula soon came over and told me to get on the bed on all fours. She was standing behind me doing a pelvic squeeze when my water broke. Mushy green goop gushed out all over my nice white bedspread.

"It's meconium," Amy said, and from the look on both her and my mom's faces I realized that it wasn't good—it meant my baby had passed its first bowel movement in utero and could be in distress.

When we got to the hospital, I was only dilated to three centimeters. I couldn't believe it. Thank God I didn't, or I would have asked for an epidural. And that was not part of the plan. I'm an athlete, part of the first group of women to box in the Golden Gloves in 1994, and having grown up with seven brothers, I'm a pretty tough cookie.

Instead, I focused on my mantra: *Trust your body, it will know what to do.*

Amy moved happily about the room, saying, "Let's light some candles and put on some good music," and my mom looked at her in disbelief, then ran off to find my midwife. She'd sensed what no one else could anticipate—that for someone who'd never given birth, I was about to set a record as I dilated from a three to a ten in only an hour.

It was already time to start pushing, and not long thereafter my beautiful baby girl was born.

That was a shock! Since I have so many brothers, I was positive I'd be having a boy. It never even occurred to me that I would have a girl, and such a *feisty* little girl at that. After they suctioned out the meconium to make sure it wouldn't get into her lungs, my little Zurielle already had her fists up in the air, starting a fight with the doctor.

Welcome to the World
By MEREDITH VIEIRA and AL ROKER

Meredith: I didn't even know who my son, Ben, was. I needed a C-section because he was a breech, and they took him from me to clean him up, and the next thing I knew they were bringing this Nordic-looking kid through the delivery room and I actually was offended. "Why are they bringing me someone else's kid?" I said to my husband, Richard. "I don't need to be looking at these babies." Richard said, "It's yours." "Oh, isn't he cute!"

Al: While planning for labor I made mix tapes and had the camera. My wife, Deborah, said "If you bring that video camera into the delivery room I will kill you," so I didn't. And then she needed a C-section at the last minute, and the doctors asked me to come over and cut the umbilical cord. I looked down and said, what is *that*? Oh! Her uterus! Oh! Wow! It was like "Hey Rocky, watch me pull a rabbit out of my hat!"

BE PREPARED

It might be hard to think this way when you're pregnant, but you really need to prepare yourself for what might happen, starting with your hospital stay:

> Be prepared for a C-section.
> Be prepared for how much childbirth hurts, even with an epidural.
> Be prepared for the baby not latching on to breastfeed.
> Be prepared for postpartum depression.

> Be prepared to be so tired that it can affect all your decisions.
> Be prepared to be a little freaked out!

from ➤ **CLAUDIA DAVID HEITLER**

What freaked me out most when the baby was born was the fact that I—who could barely take care of myself—was now responsible for this little-bitty, helpless, defenseless baby. Your freedom is instantly revoked (for something much, much better, mind you!). But once the Wonder of Life really took over, I realized how much I *love* the responsibility of giving my babies the best possible—a tight family, healthy foods, nature, and values, and an outlook on life that my husband and I feel proud to pass along.

STAY IN THE HOSPITAL AS LONG AS POSSIBLE

Mary Ann: I checked out of the hospital fewer than twenty-four hours after giving birth to my first daughter, which was a big mistake. I was just too exhausted and too overwhelmed. Try to stay in the hospital as long as you possibly can. And, I can't stress this enough, sleep, sleep, and SLEEP!

You might think that the bed is uncomfortable and the nurses are blunt, but your body needs to recover from labor, and you need time to adjust to the overwhelming idea that you're now a mom—where there are experienced nurses on duty 24/7 to answer any questions you might have.

Alicia: When my first child, Jack, was born, I thought I was supposed to have him in the room with me every minute so I could single-handedly change every diaper and soothe every cry. I learned my lesson quickly. When my second child, Lucy, was born, I wanted my rest before returning home. I promised myself not to feel guilty about getting a lot of sleep in the hospital.

One night the nurse brought Lucy to my room at midnight to breastfeed. I fed her and pushed the call button for the nurse to return Lucy to the nursery. No one came. Finally, with stitches in my stomach and an IV and epidural still attached to my arm, I dragged myself out of bed, entered the nursery, and added a very content, sleeping Lucy to the parking lot of crying babies. I smiled at the nurses and went back to bed. I've never slept better!

REMEMBER:

> We learned after baby number two that your newborn doesn't have to be in the same room with you 24–7. If you need a break, utilize the nursery.
> If you're going to be breastfeeding, don't let the baby be given a bottle. Ask the nurses to bring the baby to you when he or she is hungry.

- If you decided not to breastfeed, make it clear that your opinion will not be swayed and you do not want to discuss it.
- Take a shower as soon as the doctor says you can. You'll feel 100 percent better.
- If you have any problems or issues at all—from breastfeeding techniques to postpartum depression—now is the time to raise them. Hospitals have experts on staff to help you, and your time there is as much for you as it is for the baby.
- Don't worry about taking care of every infant detail—your goal in the hospital is to quickly recover from delivery.
- Everyone wants to see the baby, but ask them to wait until you're home. The only exception is if you've had a C-section and you're in the hospital for more than three days.
- Don't worry about handling the baby. They won't break.

THE NAME GAME

Choosing a name can be great fun, very emotional, and full of love and excitement. It can also drive you into despair once you realize that whatever name you choose, someone is going to criticize your choice.

Mary Ann: I wanted to see my baby before choosing a name, but I was so sure I was having a boy, we hadn't picked out girls' names. And then I was rushed, because a name had to be put on the birth certificate before we left the hospital. Luckily, we remembered a name we'd seen in a book— Zuriel, the angel of harmony—and we feminized it and loved it. Her entire name is Marisol Zurielle Kathryn. Kathryn is after my grandmother. Marisol means "sunny sea," which combines two of my favorite things.

When my second daughter was born, my husband and I liked two names: Avrielle (another angel) and Arabella. We placed eight pieces of paper into a hat: four for Arabella and four for Avrielle. Then two-year-old Zurielle drew more Arabellas than Avrielles. Our daughter's entire name is Zoe Arabella Ann-Elfride. Zoe is short for Zoellner. Ann is my mother's name, and Elfride is my mother-in-law's name, so we hyphenated them.

Alicia: We knew after our first ultrasound that we were having a boy. We decided on either Jack or Charlie, the latter for Mark's Grandpa Charlie. I've always loved the name Lucy for a girl, but we realized that if we had a second child who was a girl, we'd have a Charlie and a Lucy and then we'd have to get a dog named Snoopy, so we went with Jack. His middle name is Harris, in memory of Mark's late Uncle Harold.

Lucy's middle name is Rose. My sister was pregnant at the same time that I was, and when she found out she was having a boy at the same time that I found out I was having a girl, my mom said, "I'm going to have an older grandson and a younger grandson. This little girl of Alicia's is my rose between two thorns." And it stuck!

My Sons' Names: AJ and Chason
By TIKI BARBER

My wife, Ginny, and I debated about our first son's name for a while. She wanted a Junior, but I didn't. Then over dinner with Alicia and Mark, he made a good point . . . that no matter what we named our son, he would always be thought of as Tiki Jr. That convinced me, so we gave him my real name, Atiim Kiambu, Jr., or AJ, with the thought that he would get some mileage out of my unique name (which means "fiery-tempered king" in an African dialect) since I did not—everyone calls me Tiki.

With our second son, we wanted to incorporate my wife's name somehow, particularly her maiden name, Cha. We spent a lot of time going through names like Charlie (but we didn't like Charles), Chauncey, Chandler, and Chase (but we wanted two syllables). Eventually, we got literal . . . son of Cha. And there you have it: Chason.

ADJUSTING ONCE YOU'RE HOME WITH THE BABY

Even though both of us have been at *TODAY* for more than eight years and are confident in our skills, we still get butterflies when we work on big stories for the anchors. The pressure is intense, and accuracy is key. Well, after a few minutes as new moms, we realized that having a baby zoomed us right back to the way we felt our first day on the job: anxious, scared, sure we'd mess up but oh-so-eager to learn and do well. And then we realized we were preparing for the worst (not knowing what we were doing) yet hopeful for the best (quickly catching on).

We had to learn *not* to apply our work standards to what was going on with the baby at home. This was a very tough lesson: As television producers, we're used to meeting tough deadlines. If a segment has to be done, sometimes you have to stay up all night to finish it so it can go on the air in the morning. There we were, used to being able to accomplish whatever we set our minds to—used to having a million balls in the air at one time and juggling them well—and all of a sudden a new baby arrived that completely knocked our socks off.

As a result, we zoomed into overwhelm, going from accomplished professionals to rookies without a clue! We often felt like permanent residents of Loserville.

This wasn't helped when our hubbies got home from work and took one look at the pajamas we hadn't gotten out of all day, our wild-eyed stares, and the house in turmoil.

"What happened to you?" they asked. *What did you DO all day?*

Oh, how that drove us crazy! What did we do? We took care of a newborn, a nonstop feeding, pooping, peeing, spitting-up, crying machine, that's what! Picture this scenario: You have to take the baby to the pediatrician, and the baby poops all over you—okay, stay calm, change the outfit—then the doctor comes over and the baby pees and poops all over everything again, and of course you've got only one outfit which is now filthy and it's freezing cold outside and then you realize you used up all the diapers already and after bursting into tears they hand you some spares, which makes you cry even harder. Of course you feel like the doctor is looking at you as if you are the worst mom ever.

Bottom line: You're living a new life. It's really tough to learn mommy language, because there's no instruction manual. No matter how much advice you get, at the end of the day you've still got to figure it out yourself.

While a lot of people will give new mothers a break, you have to give yourself a break first. Forget about writing thank-you notes the minute you get baby gifts. What you need to do is get your strength back and sleep as much as possible.

YOU MEAN IT'S SAFE TO GO OUTSIDE WITH A BABY?

Alicia: Delivering my first child didn't happen quite the way I wanted it to, but adjusting to the fact that I had "a baby" was the bigger shock. After ten months of hoping and praying that I'd have a healthy baby boy, Jack still didn't seem real.

As a result, Jack and I had more of a business relationship in the hospital during those first few days. He needed food; I fed him. He needed a clean diaper; I changed it. Four days later I was told I could take him home. Huh? Take him *where*? How could you trust me to take this thing home when I didn't know how all the parts worked?

Fast-forward to the next day, when I was desperate for a coffee. My husband had already gone to work. My mom was out on an errand. How was I going to manage? How did the stroller work? Oh, no, forget that, the baby's too small for a stroller. How did that baby carrier thing strap on, and was my baby old enough for it? What if my baby got a cold—no, wait, what if my baby got pneumonia? And what if someone I know sees my big ol' after-birth belly?

And then the most taxing question of all hit me: *What if the baby poops?*

An hour later, I might as well have been going to the North Pole, the way I'd prepared for my expedition. At that point, I was too tired to go out, so I did what any sane new mom would do. I fell asleep.

Eventually, I got over my fears and ventured outside without the baby, because I had my mom to help me for five glorious weeks. After I finished a feeding, she took Jack and did the burping and the changing, and then put him down for a nap while I tried to catch some Z's or shower. She kept me sane. Thanks, Mom!

Life soon became ideal (aside from my breastfeeding woes, which I'll talk about in the next chapter). Mark's co-workers kept asking him, "Dude, is Alicia's mom still living with you?" and he kept telling them he'd never had it so good. He could sleep all night, he was well fed, his clothes were clean, and our apartment never looked more organized. Somehow my mom was not only single-handedly taking care of baby Jack, but also taking care of the two real babies in the house, Mark and me.

But when she left I had a whopping case of delayed nerves, as I hadn't realized all that she had done for me. After she said good-bye, I burst into hysterical sobs of pure panic, wondering what I was supposed to do (mind you, my mother had been gone at this point for about three minutes).

Jack was sleeping, blissfully unaware in his Moses basket. I looked at him and willed the panic away. Then I did the most logical thing I knew, I called my husband . . . every five minutes for the rest of the afternoon. "I need help!" I cried.

"But what do you need help *with*?" he asked. "The baby's *sleeping*!"

Bottom line: It is scary to be dealing with a newborn on your own, but once you take the plunge, you'll be fine. When my panic subsided, I realized a good cry was all I needed to get over my fears. And then I took Jack with me to get my cup of joe.

Trust Your Instincts
By MEREDITH VIEIRA

We all have an instinct. You should at least give yourself the option to not be afraid of it. I think that's the biggest thing—that fear of the unknown, that somehow you're going to be the parent that really messes up and years from now your kid will be on the psychiatrist's couch because you did something wrong the first day and it is imprinted on him forever.

You also need to learn to delegate. I'm somewhat of a control freak and I always felt, "I'm the mom, I know what to do." Especially when you're breast-feeding, you think that you're the only connection to the baby. I had to allow my husband, Richard, into the picture as an equal partner, and it took me longer than he would have liked. But it all works out in the end.

BABY TEAMS RULE!

BIRTH THAT BABY! B-I-R-T-H RIGHT NOW! Yay, team!

Okay, so Alicia was a high school cheerleader and Mary Ann wasn't, but we made up for it with our own baby teams. A baby birthing team is made up of however many trusted friends or family members you need, people you can depend on to see you through the birth process without fainting, and who'll show up once you get home to feed the pets, stock the fridge, take photos, kick out anyone who's not letting you get any sleep, and tell you that you look fabulous when you know you look like dog doo.

If possible, try to get friends and family on three baby teams: a birth team; a take-home team to help you through the adjustment shock; and a replacement team—friends who'll show up to vacuum, make you a cup of tea, and not point out that your hair looks like a rat's nest and your boobs and tummy are competing for the same space.

SLEEP WHEN THE BABY SLEEPS

With any luck, this is a lesson you learned when you were still in the hospital, but we've had the bags under our eyes to prove that the only way to get any rest is to sleep when the baby sleeps.

If there's a mess all over the floor, an overflowing diaper pail, and the dog just peed all over the kitchen floor, so what? When the baby goes down, so do you. Naptime is not your chance to catch up on housework or return all those phone calls, but to recharge your own batteries. Sure, the baby is your top priority, but it's also essential to take care of yourself. Besides, the mess you clean up today will miraculously reappear tomorrow.

DON'T PUSH YOURSELF RIGHT AFTER YOU HAVE THE BABY

Mary Ann: When Zurielle was about ten days old I decided to go out with my husband and return paint to the local hardware store, even though I'd woken up that morning with pains in my breasts and a weird feeling that something just wasn't right. I didn't have a fever, so I convinced myself everything was fine. Until I crossed the street, where I stumbled, fell down, and fainted. My husband carried me back home, and I grabbed the phone to call my midwife.

I had a whopping breast infection. It hurt as though someone was sticking me with needles, and my boobs were hard as rocks. For the next two days I was forbidden to leave my bed. I was told to drink tons of water and nurse like it was going out of style.

I thought I was invincible. This infection showed me otherwise. I was lucky it hadn't progressed to the type of problem that requires antibiotics or hospitalization.

Take it easy when you have a newborn. This is a really good time to sit back, (try to) relax, and get used to the fact that you're going to have to ask for help because you sure don't want to do all the child care on your own.

Be a Checklist Girl

Alicia: I am obsessed with lists. They keep me on track at work, where there are always a million details to attend to. So when Jack came along, I used a new notepad to make checklists for myself; not only was it a habit I'm good at doing, but it helped me keep track when I was too tired to find the keys, much less count the diapers I had left in the bag. As I went through the day, it became very satisfying to check *something* off, even if it was only a note to make a doctor's appointment.

It's Okay to Say No

As women we're conditioned to want to please our loved ones. That means we often swallow those "No's" rather than saying them.

Having a newborn gives you license to say "No." You can ask for help when needed, and you can also say "No" when you're just not up to doing something. That means you can say *Hasta la vista!* and push friends out the door if they're getting in the baby's face and driving you temporarily crazy!

> tip: *One way to get your girlfriends to visit at once is to have a Sip 'n' See. It's a Southern tradition where guests sip lemonade (or something stronger) while they see the baby. It's like a baby shower, but the baby is the guest of honor—and you get to rest! Let your friends plan one for you.*

As producers, we never miss our deadlines. But as moms, we finally got assertive and missed some new-mom deadlines. We canceled dates. We didn't answer the phone. We ignored our e-mail. Especially if the baby had been up screaming all night and we were still walking around with the same ol' droopy maternity pants.

How Does This Sling Work, Anyway?

Learn how to use the baby carrier before you need it. Believe it or not, they are more complicated than you think, so have one of your baby team members come over and give you a tutorial. Practice with a heavy bag of flour or a doll before you try it with the baby on your own. For more about great baby gear, see Chapter 7.

BABIES CRY—IT'S THEIR JOB

Babies cry. It's what they do. They cry when they're hungry, wet, tired, overstimulated, anxious, or bored. Sometimes they cry just because they feel like it.

Soothing your child can often seem like the toughest job you'll tackle all day. And many moms have felt like total failures because they couldn't stop (or endure) the crying.

Alicia: Jack and Lucy's wonderful pediatrician taught me three ways to soothe a crying newborn, and I've shared them with countless moms at work, on the bus, and in the playground: Use a pacifier, swaddle the baby like a burrito, and use the sound of running water.

The pacifier and swaddling made perfect sense, but my doctor also explained that in the first weeks of life, the sound of running water mimics what a fetus hears in the womb. There's no need to waste water—simply buy an inexpensive white-noise machine/clock radio that plays "Rain" or "Waterfall," or look for play-yards with soothing water and nature sounds built in.

Mary Ann: Zurielle cried all the time, so I cried too! To help soothe her, I'd put her in the BabyBjörn and carry her around with me, especially on long outdoor walks. She loved the sound of my heartbeat—it reminded her of the womb.

Sometimes one of our husbands would be holding the baby who was wailing away, and he'd want to do a quick handover, and we'd tell him to figure the problem out instead. "What do you mean? What do I figure out?" he'd ask in a panic. "How do I figure it out?"

Go through the checklist: Does the baby want the pacifier? No. Is she hungry? No. Did you hear that characteristic short cry followed by a howl that is code for "I just pooped and it's a whopper"? No. Is she wet? Yes. Fine, you change her.

If the baby keeps screaming after that, then you have to try the time-worn techniques of pacing around the house with the baby on your shoulder or sitting in the rocking chair with the baby until the crying stops.

> **tip**: *Next time your baby cries, don't immediately rush in. Sing "Twinkle, Twinkle Little Star" to yourself a few times. If your baby really needs you, the crying will intensify. If it stops, do not go in to check until a good few minutes have passed.*

If you run to your baby and instantly pick her up every single time she cries (or in that pre-wail stage where she scrunches up her face and is deciding whether to let 'er rip or not), trust us, the baby will have you trained in short order instead of vice versa. Pretty soon you'll have a little diva who's happy only when being held 24/7.

tip: If you've tried everything and your baby is still waking up a lot or crying inconsolably after a good feeding, make sure you rule out a physical problem. It may be reflux, or colic, or something else, and your pediatrician needs to do a thorough examination to rule out these conditions. Or your baby might just be a champion crier!

How to Cope When the Baby Won't Stop Crying
By RACHEL BURSTEIN

I had a fussy baby. I don't like to categorize children, especially my own. But Maya was fussy. Or "sensitive" or "slightly colicky" or "aware" (that was my mom's explanation . . . she's just so *aware* of her surroundings!). Once every twelve days, she would cry all day long. Nonstop. One night I finally gave in and called the doctor for some advice. She told me that some babies just don't sort themselves out until four to six months. Be patient, she said—this will pass.

It was useful information. Still, in those early months, when all of my new friends were cradling their angelic newborns at the local new moms' luncheons, I would be standing in the back swaying back and forth while Maya howled. My favorite incident was being thrown out of baby massage class because Maya was disturbing the other babies' massages.

But what goes around comes around, as I now have one of the most well-behaved, talkative, verbal, and non-tantrum-throwing kids around. Oh sure, this is probably just a phase, too, and a month from now she could be a little terror. But I'm so glad I learned early on that babies change. They are figuring themselves out and figuring the world out right before our very eyes—and it's a beautiful thing to watch.

ABOUT COLIC

Colic is the incredibly common condition of uncontrollable crying with no known cause. The baby isn't hungry, wet, soiled, tired, in need of comfort, or ill—just cranky. It tends to get worse in the afternoon and can last for hours. Or days. Or weeks. Obviously, this can be tremendously stressful, if not devastating, for everyone, especially as there is no known cure, except for the baby growing out of it.

from → **DR. NANCY SNYDERMAN**

Colic can be no big deal, or it can be really horrendous. My first infant had colic, and the best way to soothe her was to let her take naps in her child carrier on top of the dryer. The heat, movement, and noise made her more comfortable.

Ask your friends and loved ones to come by when the baby's crying, to give you a little bit of a break. For some babies, being put in a safe carrier on top of a dryer or being driven around in the car will work wonders.

Addressing the Screaming
By RUTH PETERS, Ph.D.
TODAY Contributor and Clinical Psychologist

I was taking my daughter Lindsay, then three months old, to Sears to get her photo taken. I called her a wart, because she wanted to be held all the time and wouldn't leave me alone. She screamed and screamed until I picked her up.

Well, I'd had it by then, and I was determined to let that kid scream it out, which she did during the photo session. In between screams she'd suck on her arm, and then go back to screaming. I'll always notice that mark on her arm in the photo, and it kills me. I'll always keep it to remind myself that some things are not worth the battle.

Aside from that, I quit worrying so much about how my children would turn out. And I stopped trying to turn them into something I wanted, rather than who they really are.

PERSONALITY CHECK

Mary Ann: As one of nine children, I should have known better. I thought I could handle my baby just like I handle everything else in life—with will and determination. Instead, what I quickly learned is that your own will is no match for a baby's. Each baby enters the world with his or her personality firmly in place. Zurielle was a fighter from day one, yet when Arabella was born, peace came to the world (now, at eighteen months, it's a different story!).

Bottom line: A baby who likes to cry can't be forced to stop. A baby who's full of beans will not be happy lying still. We know how hard it is not to compare your baby with anyone else's—particularly if yours is easily upset and all the other babies in the Mommy and Me class never seem to make a peep—but this is one aspect of child-rearing that is totally out of your control.

Enjoy your baby's personality and quirks. They're what make your baby unique and wonderful.

SHOCKERS OF THE FIRST FEW WEEKS

There are some things about a newborn that can be a little *unexpected*.

> Sometimes babies look yellow from jaundice. Usually, a few minutes in the sun will do wonders.
> A baby boy's genitals are huge! This is totally normal and due to maternal hormones. In a few weeks those enormous testicles will shrink down to tiny baby size.
> A baby girl's vagina can also appear large. Some baby girls even bleed, as if they're getting a period. This might look a little bit freaky, but it, too, is due to the mother's hormones.
> Speaking of hormones, your own are going to be out of control for a while, so expect moodiness and hypersensitivity. You might burst into tears for absolutely no reason, or collapse in a fit of giggles. (This is not the same as postpartum depression, which we'll cover in Chapter 12.)

Alicia: Sometimes I'd be holding the baby and I'd hear certain words (which could have been anything from *love* to *Elmo* to *lullaby* to *Cheerios*) and just start crying, as if a Hallmark commercial were running on a constant loop in my head. A few minutes later I'd be totally fine again. Two days after having Jack I was still in the hospital and called my husband at three in the morning and just chewed him out. *"How dare you leave me here!"* I wailed. *"I'm here by myself not able to sleep a wink and the baby is crying! No one's here to take care of me. Okay, 'bye, see you later."*

Adjusting to the Baby

I have four siblings, so I always felt I was going to be a mom. Still, I was running so fast with my career that I'm awfully glad my husband reminded me to have a family, because I might have missed my chance otherwise!

Once you are a mom, there isn't a clear road map in terms of *how* to be and *who* to be anymore; and as with the creation of any new path, the obstacle you must surmount is the fear. Right off the bat, the fear knocks you

---

from → **DR. TANYA BENENSON**

While newborn jaundice is normal and occurs in half of full-term babies usually on day 2 or 3, it still needs to be monitored. If the jaundice gets worse and turns bright yellow, lasts more than 2 weeks, or is associated with poor weight gain or grogginess, then call your doctor.

from → **DR. NANCY SNYDERMAN**

After having two girls, I had forgotten about the importance of cleaning a baby boy's penis and clearing debris from under the foreskin. If it isn't gently cleaned when bathing, a baby boy can get inflammation or an infection.

off your feet and you can't function—you can barely express your breast milk—and you're just kind of *reeling*. What I needed most was help getting rid of the fear, which, of course, I soon realized would go away once I got knowledge.

Knowledge is power; fear is the enemy—and what I learned was that you are not a different person when you become a mother, you're just better, deeper, and more vulnerable to the heartbreak of loving someone more than yourself. There's no question in my mind that being a mother has made me a better journalist and a better human being. All of us are faced with the same problem of not having enough time, of feeling guilty while wondering whether we can still be good at work while being so physically knocked out that we're just sitting on our bottoms, wondering if we can get back up. What helped me was coming to the conclusion that if I do a good job at work and can provide for my children, they are going to grow up knowing that I made a difference—and that they can too.

I wish now that I had exercised more, but I never gave myself a chance; I wish I'd taken care of myself more, and taken care of my friendships—there are so many areas where I dropped the ball. Being a mother can make you forget who you are. Try to stay connected to yourself and your old life as much as possible, and remind yourself what a great job you're doing!

Having a baby will challenge you more than you thought possible. I don't see it as taking away your old life, but enhancing a new one. As I fell in love with my babies, that deep rush of bonding became the greatest roller-coaster ride of my life.

—**Ann Curry**

All new parents go through the initial phase of being overwhelmed—of not having the slightest idea whether they're doing the right or wrong things, no matter how much they prepare or how many baby books they read. I remember walking in the door with Josh and thinking, Now what? The answer: He starts to cry and pretty much tells me every two hours, "I'm hungry, I'm hungry again, now I have a poopy, okay, hungry again."

I was never more exhausted in my life than in those first two weeks. I remember thinking that this is what medical students must feel like when they pull all-nighters. You're not eating as much as you should, you're not doing what you should for yourself, and the baby is feeding around the clock. It's just really tough.

The first three months are wonderful and sweet and precious, but they're also a grueling, very trying time with no sleep and this all-consuming little human being who needs your every ounce of attention. I remember counting the hours till my husband would get home from work to at least give me an hour to shower and feel human again. That said, you quickly forget about the hard times and cherish all the kisses and snuggles and "I love you's" when your baby gets older!

—Natalie Morales

I read somewhere that having a baby can be described as having your heart live permanently outside of your body. That's the truth. You're immediately vulnerable and you see the world as a much different place. Plus this amazing sense of responsibility comes over you the moment you see that baby—you're the momma tiger and that baby is your cub, and you will kill anybody who threatens your child. And I think that's what you can't really anticipate until you feel it, as it's like animal instinct.

—Amy Robach

Let's be honest: In those first few weeks and months there is nothing the father can give that baby that he can't get from the mother. I can't breastfeed the baby, and I don't have that immediate maternal instinct.

Plus there was a sixth sense with Jack—as if he knew that, okay, this guy I'm looking up at right now doesn't seem supremely confident; he's not the guy to connect with right now. Mom seems very confident, so let's go to her instead!

—Matt Lauer

Special Delivery: My Adoption
By AL ROKER

My first daughter, Courtney, was adopted. At the last minute we got the call on a Friday and were told, "Oh, there's a baby and you need to be in western New York state by Monday."

I'll always remember driving to pick her up with an empty car seat, and then all of a sudden there's a baby in the back. You just look at her and she's looking at you and it's very odd. It was different when my second daughter, Leila, was born; there'd already been this whirlwind of emotion and nine months of buildup. And when Leila came out she was the most gorgeous alien you would ever want to see!

But from the instant I held Courtney, I knew she was mine.

The Things I've Learned

By CLAUDIA DAVID HEITLER

All those times my mother said, "You'll see when you have children of your own"—now I'm seeing! Every time I think they're out of some stage, a new one comes along. It recently dawned on me that this will proceed well into their adult lives. But I've still managed to learn a few things:

> If you think you're going to be knocking things off your to-do list, think again.
> If you get into the shower before 3 p.m. (if you get in at all), it's a good day.
> Internet shopping is your friend.
> One sure way to drive yourself insane is to read everything you can on taking care of your baby (except for this book, of course!). But you will anyway.
> If it ain't broke, don't fix it. As a friend says: "Don't try to make a happy baby happier."
> It's amazing what you can learn to do with one hand, and even your feet. It's all about slip-on shoes.
> "Sleeps like a baby" doesn't mean what you think it means.
> Baby poop stops being cute the day you start them on solid food.
> You won't remember the words to lullabies, and what you make up is pretty silly.
> Babies don't do weekends.
> Breasts aren't just decorations as I had previously thought. I nursed both my children (one for fifteen months, the other for over two years). During that time, my husband, Josh, used to refer to them as our kids' "restaurants . . . with two convenient locations." And now those two "convenient locations" are inconveniently located four inches below where they originally started. The impact childbirth has on a woman's body is well documented, while the impact nursing has on breasts somehow never came up. It wouldn't have changed my decision to nurse, but I might have had some kind of send-off party!
> For some inexplicable reason there always seems to be an uneven number of snaps on babies' outfits.
> Babies collect a lot of lint.

Baby Basics

> Milk that gets trapped under the baby's neck folds and armpits smells really, really bad.
> Playing and caring for your child is only a fraction of staying at home with your child. I had these idyllic visions of doing arts and crafts in a peaceful home and reading the newspaper occasionally with my obedient, well-groomed children. Ha! There is also an unreal amount of cooking, dishes, and cleaning that comes with the territory, not to mention negotiating. It's all great, but I wish I had known that!
> Babies are more resilient than we think. Probably even more so than adults. And they know what they're doing even if you don't, so relax.

What Freaked Me Out the Most
By RACHEL BURSTEIN

What freaked me out the most when my daughter was born was the tremendous sense of responsibility involved. Like all moms, I wanted to do everything *right* . . . after all, the stakes were the highest ones ever. Whatever I did or didn't do would affect my darling baby girl. It was as if I had this pristine, perfect child and all I could do was mess her up.

My mother gave me the best advice for handling this. She told me that the best thing about motherhood is that you get a chance to do it over again every single day. One day you might actually be the best mother in the world. And the next day, you might not be. And guess what—either way, you get up the next day and do it all over again.

On Becoming a Dad
By MATT LAUER

Yes, it's a major adjustment. I had my first child when I was forty-three. The good side is that you've been there, done that, and things don't freak you out as much. The bad side is that you're much more set in your ways, particularly in your lifestyle at home. All of a sudden here comes this little creature into the house who couldn't care less about order and routine and neatness or anything like that. It was a major shock for the system.

The first time I had to take the baby out by myself, I dealt with it as if I were transporting a ticking time bomb. Did I have enough diapers? What would happen if the baby got sick, or threw up? How could I prepare? When would I stop being intimidated? All those worries whirl through your head, but in the end you're pretty amazed that you can basically cope with everything.

DAILY DIARY SHEET

Alicia: My husband usually got home from work before I did, so he'd relieve the sitter. I noticed that there was always something missing in his details about the baby's day. "Did he poop today?" I'd ask.

"I dunno. I think so," he'd reply.

"Did he drink all the breast milk I left in the fridge?"

"Well, if it's not in the fridge anymore I'm sure it's gone."

If I wasn't going to be with him all day, at least I had to know how well he was eating, sleeping, and pooping. This chart put my mind at ease.

DATE:

TIME WOKE UP:

BOTTLES

Time	# of Ounces	Breast Milk	Formula

BABY FOOD

Time	Amount	What Food?

NAPS

Start	Finish

DIAPERS

Times	Pee	Poop

VITAMINS (one a day)

	Yes	No

ACTIVITIES

Time	What

CHAPTER TWO

The Boob and the Bottle: All About Food

BREASTFEEDING BASICS

Breastfeeding is nature's gift to babies, and seeing that liquid gold shoot out of your breast is beneficial in more ways than one. It not only gives babies the nutrition they need for their first months, but can be a wonderfully rewarding bonding experience between you and your baby. Not to mention, it's dirt cheap and totally portable.

That's the good news. The bad news is that a lot of people (including the lactation consultants you might meet in the hospital) won't tell you that breastfeeding can hurt, and can be incredibly frustrating. So we're not surprised that lots of moms have thrown in the towel earlier than they wanted to because they were erroneously told either that their bodies weren't "designed" for it or that they couldn't produce enough milk.

Think of breastfeeding as yet another job that only a woman can do. A really hard job—but one with a huge payoff. So belly up to the baby and get started.

BREASTFEEDING—HARD WORK BUT SO WORTH IT

Alicia: It's always been a running joke in my family that you could feed an army with my boobs—that's how large they are. So I assumed that I'd always have a distinct advantage once my baby was born. I'd have a nice, quick delivery, I'd take the baby in my arms, he'd latch on, out would flow the colostrum (that goopy yellow stuff that precedes milk production), and I'd just bathe in baby-feeding bliss.

Wrong fantasy. After Jack's birth, engorgement immediately set in. My mahoombahs (as my brother delicately named them) were filled to maximum capacity and were deemed too big by the hospital nurses. They were hard as rocks and incredibly painful.

The nurses and lactation consultants worked with me to get my latch correct. They told me that since my breasts were so large and my baby was "premature," they were going to have to look at other solutions. Say what? Jack was ten days early, not premature. Nevertheless, they recommended a nipple cap—a plastic cap about the size of a thimble that attaches to your nipple and acts as a feeding straw for the baby's mouth. I felt foolish using this while all the other moms had their babies right up to their breasts.

While this did work, and my baby began to suck, some of the other lactation consultants told me that using it was a big mistake. They were outraged that I was using the cap, because it wasn't the "natural" thing to do.

At feeding time, my mother, my husband, and I all looked at each other in dismay. Should I use the football hold, or the cradle, or had I forgotten another method? Why wasn't feeding getting any easier? How come the nipple cap wasn't working anymore? When would the bleeding and cracking go away? Sure, pumping did help reduce some of the engorgement, but the feeding itself was still a nightmare. It was hard to wake Jack up to feed and I didn't think he was getting enough milk.

So I did what any other woman in my situation would have done: I threw myself a pity party. I wanted to give up and run for that can of formula in my hospital bag. I wasn't enjoying this supposedly fabulous experience one bit. Not one bit at all.

Finally, my husband called one of the three lactation consultants recommended by the hospital. In walked Rose, who, within seconds of meeting me, asked me to strip from the waist up, then made these suggestions:

> No nipple cap. All moms need to know how to get the baby to latch on properly (and she showed me how).
> Pump at specific times to level off the engorgement.
> To keep the baby awake during feeding, unswaddle him completely down to his diapered little tush. Or splash a little water on his tootsies or tickle him on his ears and nose.

> Take vitamin D to help heal the bleeding, cracking nipples, and sit outside bra-less for thirty minutes a day. I sat on my apartment's tiny terrace. "Don't worry about your neighbors spying on you," she said. "The sun will heal you faster than any medication will."

> Don't worry about bottle feedings. It's okay to bottle-feed a baby your pumped breast milk if your feedings are unsuccessful. Neither of my children was ever confused about feeding, and they got used to the breast, bottle, and pacifiers from day one.

> Expect some pain, with a capital Yowza!!!! I remember curling my toes, biting my lip, and wiping the tears from my face at every feeding. But after six uncomfortable weeks, not only was the pain gone, but I started to like breastfeeding. Aside from Jack's 3 a.m. wake-up-and-feed-me cries, I grew to love providing the safety, comfort, warmth, and nutrition of the most natural kind to my son. I cherished our cozy time together and forgot all about the pain and stress. That was as much a miracle as giving birth.

tip: *Even if you are breastfeeding, save the free formula that you get from the hospital in case of an emergency. Stash it in a hard-to-get-to place like the cabinets above your fridge so you won't be tempted to use it if you're having trouble breastfeeding.*

from KATHIE LEE GIFFORD

My trick for engorgement is to freeze cabbage leaves, place them on your breasts, and wrap yourself up. It's an old wives' tale, but it helps soothe them a lot. You smell horrendous, but thankfully I was on television, not smell-o-vision, so it was fine!

On Breastfeeding
By KATHIE LEE GIFFORD

My breasts were the size of two Hindenburgs. My husband, Frank, used to say, "Don't aim those things at me!"

I had no idea how hard breastfeeding would be. After five weeks I stopped breastfeeding, and then for a week I pumped. Then I had to give up. I did the best I could. The week I did pump, Cody would be screaming in hunger and Frank would be in the bedroom snoring, all to the rhythm of the breast pump. We'd laugh ourselves sick over the noises—and that's what gets you through everything.

I must have had a million women over the years who told me we were pregnant together, and I'd say, "I thought you looked familiar!" That's the power of television: You can be their best friend, so if my nipples were sore and my stomach was stretching and I had gas and couldn't wait to get my control-top pantyhose off, misery loves company. Laughing about your misery also has a healing property.

MOMS NEED FLUIDS, TOO

All nursing moms need extra hydration, so when you go to feed the baby, get into the habit of drinking a big glass of water at the same time. We like bottled water enriched with vitamins (with no added sugar), but plain old tap water will do just fine.

Better yet, treat yourself to a very stylish carafe. Fill it with water in the morning and have it stationed on your nightstand or living room table for the whole day. If you want to get super fancy, www.williams-sonoma.com has a gorgeous monogrammed carafe. These would make great gifts for a new or second-time mom.

LEAKING AND SQUIRTING: BEEN THERE, DONE THAT

Alicia: One thing that I did *not* expect from my mahoombahs was how they were going to leak. Like an annoying faucet that doesn't turn off.

After trying every boobie pad ever patented, I finally settled on my personal saviors: the Lansinoh Disposable Nursing Pads. They're a bit more expensive than some other brands, yet worth their weight in gold. But they're not foolproof. Even the best breast pads will not always save you from embarrassment.

On more than one occasion I remember waking up after a few hours of sleep, thinking I'd wet my bed—but it was just my boobs leaking. The first time it happened, I freaked out. I'd step out of the shower and before I could even grab my towel, milk would shoot out in a horizontal spray across the room.

tip: *It's a good idea to have a waterproof mattress pad on your bed, or to use the baby's waterproof changing pads on your side of the bed. Also think about sleeping with your bra and breast pads on— because you might wake up wet.*

BURPING THE BABY

Mary Ann: Zurielle was a difficult burper, so I'd prop her so that her belly was flat on my shoulder bone and roll her over my shoulder as if I were rolling dough. I'd also put her on her back and push her legs toward her stomach. Yogis swear by this move during yoga sessions—they call it the passing gas pose!

My dad swears by this burping technique: Hold the baby in front of you with one hand on her stomach and the other arm under her bottom. The pressure on her little tummy helps relieve the gas.

Alicia: Don't be freaked out by the holds that you put on your baby, either. I visited Tiki and Ginny Barber in the hospital after they had their first son, AJ. We walked into the room and I gasped when I saw tiny six-pound AJ sitting in Tiki's lap. One of Tiki's huge hands was supporting his neck, and the other was calmly whacking AJ on the back. It didn't hurt AJ at all—as this method had been suggested by the hospital doctors.

After trying it a few times with AJ, I got the hang of it, and when I used it on my own babies, I was always guaranteed a hearty burp.

Mary Ann: If Zurielle was gassy, her pediatrician recommended a hefty dose of Milicon, an over-the-counter gas reducer. If this didn't work, I'd hand her over to my husband, who seemed to have more patience than I did.

NO, I'M NOT A FLASHER— BREASTFEEDING IN PUBLIC

Mary Ann: One of the greatest tricks I learned was how to breastfeed while I was carrying Zurielle in the BabyBjörn, starting when she was two months old. I'd put Zurielle in the carrier, facing me. Her head and neck were supported by the built-in neck rest. I'd loosen the straps on the side, allowing her body to relax into a position where her head was lined up with my breasts, even though she was still vertical. I'd latch her on, throw a blanket over us, and go. By the end of the feeding she'd usually be asleep, at which point I'd tighten the straps and do my errands, have lunch with friends, or take a stroll. I'd even feed her while I was cooking. One night, I was preparing dinner for eight guests, with three pans going on the stove and Zurielle sucking away. I couldn't help myself from singing, "I'm Every Woman!"

tip: *Don't worry about flashing anyone. You can find stylish covers designed to hide all, such as The Hooter Hider (yes, that's what they call it!). It's a stylish, fashionable little wrap, available at www.bebeaulait.com. There are also nursing bras, as well as garments designed to flip down easily for feeding. We like GlamourMom, Bravado!, and the Swedish company BOOB (they also make dresses).*

All I ever used, though, was a simple receiving blanket from my stash of shower presents. You can also try a burping cloth or cloth diaper. Be sure to have several stashed in your diaper bag, as you don't want to be out with a hungry baby and no way to feed without flashing!

tip: *It does get easier. One of our co-workers told us that she was so shy about breastfeeding at first that she'd hide herself in the bedroom. By the end, she was nursing in front of the construction workers re-siding her house—she didn't care anymore!*

Funny story: I was on assignment in Tulsa, to cover a story involving two families trading places. I had Zurielle with me, so when she got hungry I very discreetly started to feed her. "What the heck is *that*? What the heck are you *doing*?" the mom gasped at me.

"Um, I'm breastfeeding my child," I told her, perplexed.

"Oh my gosh, you crazy hippie New Yorker!" she said. It turns out she was so modest, she couldn't bear the idea of actually putting her babies to her breast. Instead, she pumped and fed her babies breast milk from a bottle—for a year! Some people still feel very uncomfortable when near a breastfeeding mom and baby. Even other moms!

Breastfeeding in Public

By ANN CURRY and RACHEL BURSTEIN

Ann Curry: Be aware that pumps can make a *lot* of noise in the women's bathroom, so brace yourself for some strange looks!

Rachel Burstein: I breastfed my daughter for nine months. I wasn't an "in-your-face" nursing mother, but I would take advantage of a bench on a nice sunny day in Central Park, cover myself with a blanket, and feed my daughter outside.

Well, for some reason, whenever I nursed in public, my bench became Grand Central Station. I must have had an invisible sign above my head advertising my alleged expertise about New York. Anyone and everyone came up to me to ask directions or for sightseeing advice; my favorite was the Indian couple who wanted to know where Central Park was. (Um . . . it's this large span of green we're standing in?)

HOW MUCH DO I NEED TO GIVE THE LITTLE SUCKER?

The numbers game is probably the hardest thing you'll deal with, as it's impossible to know how much your baby is actually eating at each feeding.

What saved our sanity was keeping a breastfeeding chart. Recording each feeding (breast or bottled breast milk) will help reassure you that the baby is getting a good supply of milk.

Mary Ann: My sister-in-law Darci kept her breastfeeding log by the rocking chair where she nursed her daughter, writing down the time and which side the baby started on. This was very helpful for pediatrician visits and for keeping track, especially when in a sleep-deprived state. She also put a paper clip on her bra strap on the side where she'd just nursed if she didn't have time to fill in her log.

For her second child I gave her a new device called "ITZBEEN" (as in "it's been" three hours since my last feeding), which keeps track of how much time has passed between sleep, diapers, and breastfeeding. There's a button for right side, another for left side, and a built-in flashlight so you don't have to turn on lights during late-night feedings.

SAMPLE BREASTFEEDING CHART

Date	Times	Minutes Fed
12/01	2:18–2:45	Left 9
		Right 8
	5:05–5:40	Right 11
		Left 6
	8:30–8:50	Left 10
		Right 4
	9:45–10:00	4.5 oz pumped milk
12/02	3:10–3:40	Right 7
		Left 7

AVOID THE SNACK ATTACKS

It's hard to tell the difference between a baby feeding to feed and just suckling to suckle because he likes it so much. After a few months, babies really begin to enjoy all the sensations that come with breastfeeding, and if you let them, you'll find a fifteen-pound appendage firmly clamped around your nipple. So then you either pry off the tentacles (oops, we mean *mouth*) and have an unhappy baby, or you can walk around for three hours with your baby glued to your boobs.

The best way to stop snack attacks is to make sure your baby gets a full feeding. Tickle him, run water on his feet, or sing loudly—just do not let your baby fall asleep on the breast if you can help it. At first, the feeding should take a while; perhaps thirty minutes on each breast. Once you get more efficient, you can feed on one breast for about ten minutes and then on the other for eight, and *voilà!*, everybody's done.

Alicia: My feeding schedule was every two and a half to three hours, and believe it or not, I didn't deviate from that once until my son was three and a half months old and could sleep through the night. If the baby got a little cranky, I'd look at my breastfeeding chart and realize that the last feeding had been over two hours before, so I needed to start the feeding in ten minutes. You need a will of iron to do this at first, because if your baby is fussy or crying it's very easy to give in.

Although some moms are fine with feeding on demand 24/7, we found it easier to stick to a schedule that the baby got used to.

from ▸ DR. NANCY SNYDERMAN

There is no magic to feeding a baby on demand. When my baby girl cried, I offered her the breast. I think crying is a normal way of communicating. Your baby is trying to tell you something.

Breastfeeding Your Baby

By JOAN ORTIZ, R.N., B.S.N., C.L.C.

President, Limerick Workplace Lactation Program

Your breast milk is the best source of nourishment for your baby, containing the perfect amount of fats, proteins, and carbohydrates for a newborn. It also contains antibodies that offer immediate protection from many serious, even life-threatening infections and illnesses. Plus human milk is more easily digested than any type of formula.

Because your milk is perfectly suited for your baby, breastfeeding will help your baby gain the proper amount of weight, at the right rate. Ultimately, this will lower the baby's risk for obesity and obesity-related diseases such as diabetes. But the benefits of breastfeeding go far beyond nutrition and growth, as breastfed babies also have reduced risks for asthma; cavities; childhood leukemia; digestive problems such as Crohn's disease, gastrointestinal infections, and ulcerative colitis; ear infections; lower respiratory tract diseases; and sudden infant death syndrome (SIDS).

Breastfeeding's Benefits for the Mother

Breastfeeding soon after delivery helps the uterus contract to its pre-pregnancy size and reduces the blood flow to the uterus; both are important for your immediate recovery. New research suggests that it provides long-term protection from certain health conditions, including some cancers. In addition, mothers who breastfeed are less likely to develop breast and ovarian cancer, and osteoporosis and heart disease are also less common. Breastfeeding also burns extra calories.

Giving Your Baby a Healthy and Secure Start to Life

As you nurse your newborn, your baby can feel and hear the familiar sound of your beating heart. This skin-to-skin contact while breastfeeding makes the mother feel relaxed and the baby feel secure. While breastfeeding, your baby will be exercising the muscles surrounding the mouth, which helps with proper jaw development.

Preparing for Breastfeeding

It is normal to have concerns about breastfeeding. Your ability to produce milk is not related to the size or shape of your breasts, and women with flat or inverted nipples, or who've had some kinds of breast surgery, can also successfully breastfeed.

Breastfeeding does not require any special preparations. Your breasts may be tender initially and increase in size as their milk-producing cells grow and multiply. The dark skin around your nipple (called the areola) will also get larger and darker as your pregnancy progresses; this is nature's way of making your breasts easy to find for your baby. The small bumps on the areola (called Montgomery glands) also play a role in breastfeeding. They produce a substance that softens the skin, may slow the growth of bacteria, and produces a familiar scent that will guide your baby to your breast.

Women used to believe that they needed to prepare their nipples (with nipple rolling or rubbing with towels to "toughen them up") for breastfeeding to reduce the likelihood of nipple soreness. But nipple soreness usually happens when the baby is not latched on correctly, so positioning your baby correctly on the areola, not the nipple, will help, although some adjustment soreness is to be expected.

Let-down Reflex

Once your baby has been vigorously sucking at the breast, or you have begun to express milk with a breast pump, you may notice a tingling sensation and a surge of milk. This is known as the milk ejection, or let-down, reflex. As the milk begins to flow, your baby's pattern of sucking and swallowing will become stronger, faster, and distinct. The milk ejected after the let-down is richer in fat than the milk taken at the start of the feeding. Several let-down reflexes may occur during a single feeding. Even if you do not feel the tingling sensation, there are other signs that the let-down has begun:

> Your other breast may start dripping milk.
> Mild uterine contractions may be felt during the first week after delivery.
> Your baby's sucking pattern will change. You will notice wide jaw movements and frequent swallowing, usually one to two sucks and then a swallow. You may even hear gulping.

At times, a strong let-down reflex can startle the baby and cause choking. Simply sit your baby up and let the baby rest before latching on again. As your baby gets older, he or she will learn to adapt to your strong let-down reflex.

Allowing your baby to nurse for as long as desired is a good way to be sure that the baby gets the richer milk. Your baby may fall asleep after nursing on one side and not be interested in the other breast. This is normal. Your baby does not need to nurse on each breast during each feeding. Simply offer the baby the other breast first for the next feeding. As long as your newborn is feeding eight to twelve times in twenty-four hours (you are nursing at least every three hours), you will be on your way to successful breastfeeding.

Many mothers experience the let-down reflex in response to a warm shower, thinking about or looking at a picture of their baby, or their baby's cry, touch, or even smell.

There may be instances when the let-down reflex is delayed. If your baby does not have a strong suck, or if you are expressing your milk, you may need to help out:

> Apply a warm washcloth or warm compress prior to nursing or pumping.
> Take a warm shower before nursing or pumping.
> Gently massage your breast. Start from the chest wall and stroke toward the nipple.

Deciding How Long to Breastfeed Your Baby

How long you breastfeed is a personal choice. Your baby will have a say in this too, as babies develop likes and dislikes at a very early age. The American Academy of Pediatrics recommends breast milk exclusively for the first six months of life, adding complementary foods until a year, then continuing to breastfeed for as long as mother and baby choose to. Some babies may start to wean once solids are introduced, while others can continue to breastfeed for years. Breastfeeding for any length of time is always good for your baby and you.

The Breastfeeding Learning Process

Prenatal education and support are vital to successful breastfeeding. Attending a prenatal breastfeeding class will help reassure you, show you different holds, and teach you what to expect as well as when you should be concerned and ask for help. You will have lots of questions and need reassurance, so establishing your support system before the baby is born is very helpful. Where to look for support:

> If you are working, check with your employer to see if they offer a workplace lactation program for their employees.
> Check with the hospital to see what type of lactation services are available.
> When choosing a pediatrician, look for one who supports and is experienced in counseling new moms about breastfeeding.
> Talk to family and friends to see who have successfully breastfed.

What Kind of Help to Request

1. Talk to your health care team. Let everyone caring for your baby know that you want only breast milk for your baby. Ask your baby's pediatrician to write an order to provide breast milk only, preventing your baby from inadvertently receiving a bottle.

2. Breastfeed right away. Your baby is alert and ready to feed immediately after delivery. When placed on your chest, the baby will instinctively crawl to the breast and get latched on within an hour. Feeding early and often and providing lots of skin-to-skin time is the best way to get a good start with breastfeeding.

3. Room in with your baby. Ask to have your baby with you twenty-four hours a day while in the hospital. The baby's baths, diaper changes, and checkups can be done at your bedside. This will allow you to get to know your baby's feeding cues so when you take your newborn home, you will be confident and relaxed. Observing for feeding cues from your baby will allow you to breastfeed early and often. Feeding cues include coughing, fussiness, hand-to-mouth movements, rapid eye movement, soft cooing or sighing sounds, squirming, or sucking movements and yawning. Crying is a late sign of hunger.

4. Allow for unrestricted breastfeeding. Offer your breast to your baby at the earliest sign of hunger and allow your baby to nurse for as long as desired. Your newborn needs to be breastfed at least eight to twelve times in

twenty-four hours. Providing many opportunities for the baby to lie naked (with only a diaper) on your bare chest will encourage breastfeeding.

5. Breastfeed exclusively. Hospitals often offer free formula for all mothers, even when there is no medical reason to supplement a baby's diet. Avoid giving your baby any formula unless medically necessary. Your early milk (colostrum) is all your baby needs. Giving formula will make your baby too full to breastfeed and may interfere with your ability to make more milk.

6. Avoid pacifiers or artificial nipples. Breastfeeding infants should not be given anything other than the breasts until both mother and baby are adjusted to breastfeeding. By delaying the introduction of pacifiers and bottles, your body will make more milk. Having a good milk supply will make breastfeeding easier for you and your baby.

7. Ask for a lactation consultant. Before leaving the hospital, ask a specialist to watch you and your baby during a feeding (bring the nursing pillow you will be using at home to the hospital). The lactation consultant should teach you how to know your newborn is getting enough milk and what to do if not. Ask whether the hospital has an outpatient clinic for new moms so you can bring your baby in for a weight check and have the lactation consultant observe another feeding in the next couple of days. Make sure you leave with a phone number you can call with any breastfeeding questions.

How to Keep Breastfeeding Going at Home

Although nothing could be more natural, breastfeeding will require some patience, practice, and persistence. In the first few days of life, babies learn how to coordinate their sucking, swallowing, and breathing in a rhythmic way. The thick, nutrient-dense colostrum you produce is the perfect starter food. Your newborn's stomach capacity is very small: a small marble on day one, a large shooter marble by day three, and a Ping-Pong ball by day seven. As long as you are feeding your baby a minimum of eight to twelve times in twenty-four hours, the baby will get the necessary nutrition.

Some babies will breastfeed every one to three hours around the clock while others will feed every hour for three to five hours and then sleep for three to four hours. Each baby is different. To get the eight to twelve feedings in during the twenty-four hours, you may need to wake your sleeping baby (especially during the first two weeks until baby gains back birth weight).

Watch for feeding cues, as babies may not always cry for a feed during the first few weeks.

Time your feedings from the start of a feed. The total time it takes to feed your newborn will be about an hour, which includes latching your baby on the breast, burping, changing a diaper, and the actual feeding. If you start a feed at 6 a.m. and are done at 7 a.m., your next feed will be at 8 or 9 a.m. This can be very tiring on new parents and does not allow much time for anything else. Talking to your family and friends ahead of time and coming up with a plan will help make this time easier and more enjoyable for you.

It does get easier after the first month. When your baby was in utero, it was fed and held 24/7. You are weaning your baby from this routine during the first month.

Breastfeeding mothers often worry about whether their babies are getting enough milk because they cannot see how many ounces are taken at each feeding. The most important measure is weight gain. It's normal for a baby to lose weight after birth, so make sure you know your baby's weight at hospital discharge. As long as babies weigh more than their discharge weight at day four and are back to birth weight by day fourteen, they are getting enough. Breastfed babies grow at different rates than formula-fed babies, so ask your pediatrician for a special chart developed for breastfed babies to track your baby's growth patterns.

Good Indicators Your Baby Is Getting Enough Milk

1. Your baby has exceeded its hospital discharge weight by day four.
2. By day four, your baby has at least six wet diapers per twenty-four hours.
3. By day four, your baby has at least two to three loose, yellowish stools per twenty-four hours.
4. By two weeks, your baby is back to its birth weight.
5. Your baby is gaining one-half ounce to one ounce per day after the first week.
6. Your baby is breastfeeding at least eight times in a twenty-four-hour period.
7. There's no fussiness or feeding cues from the baby after a full feeding.

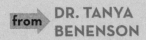
Signs of an Incorrect Latch

If you have any of these signs, seek help from a lactation consultant or physician.

> You feel pain throughout the feeding, rather than just at the start.
> You hear clicking or sucking noises.
> Your baby detaches easily from the breast.
> Your baby swallows little or not at all.
> The baby's lips are tucked in instead of turned out (flanged).
> Your nipple is flattened or creased after feeding.
> Your nipples are cracked and bleeding.
> The baby does not have enough wet or dirty diapers.
> Be sure to call the pediatrician if your baby is not meeting the minimum feedings and stool and urine output, or is still passing meconium (black, tarry stool) by day five

Call your doctor immediately if your baby has signs of dehydration. (See sidebar at left.)

Engorgement

Between two and six days following your delivery, your breasts may appear extremely full, or engorged. Engorgement in the early days of breastfeeding happens when breast milk changes from colostrum to mature milk; blood flow increases and the surrounding tissues swell. The best remedy for engorgement is frequent nursing, at least every two to three hours.

If the engorgement causes the nipples to flatten, latching on may be difficult. You may need to hand-express some milk to reduce the fullness before offering your breast to your baby. Many women find they get relief from a warm shower, warm compresses, or gentle breast massage before feedings. Applying cold cabbage leaves, ice packs, or bags of frozen peas in between feedings can also help.

Mastitis

Some women experience something beyond the normal feeling of fullness as the mature milk comes in. If this happens, try to nurse your baby frequently, and you may gently compress the breast as you nurse to help with milk ejection. Call your health-care provider if you notice any of these warning signs of mastitis: breasts that are hard, red, painful, and warm to the touch; fever greater than 101°F; and/or flu-like symptoms such as soreness, headache, nausea, weakness, and chills.

Breastfeeding Products

There's an overwhelming amount of products on the market for new babies—the best advice is to keep it simple.

You'll want a breastfeeding bra. Your breasts will change size during the breastfeeding months, so find a bra that you can easily adjust in both cup size and width. A cotton bra that fits comfortably and does not leave indentation marks on your skin is best. A bra that's too tight can prevent proper drainage of the breast. You may want to ask your lactation consultant to help fit you properly for a bra.

Your breast and nipples require little care. There is no need to clean your breast before a feed. Washing your breast once a day with clear water and a mild soap (optional) in the shower or bath will keep your nipples clean. Applying expressed breast milk after a feed will help them feel comfortable. If your skin gets dry you may use a modified lanolin cream, unless you're allergic to wool or lipstick. Consult your pediatrician or lactation consultant before applying anything to your nipples.

You may find you need to wear nursing pads to protect your clothes from getting wet when your milk lets down. Remember to change your nursing pads often. Do not use pads with plastic lining, as this will trap the moisture and may cause damage to your nipples. Pads that are made of soft layers of cotton are recommended. As your body adjusts to your baby's nutritional needs and you are feeding or pumping regularly, this becomes less of an issue.

There are many types of breast pumps, and the Food and Drug Administration has developed guidelines to define these types as either hospital-grade (multiple-user) or single-user pumps. A hospital-grade pump has been cleared by the FDA as safe to be used by more than one person, as it can prevent cross-contamination caused by milk back-flowing into the motor. A single-user pump means the breast pump should be used by only one woman because there is no way to clean and disinfect the pump if milk back-flows into the motor. (A single-user pump reused by different mothers can carry infectious diseases like HIV or hepatitis.)

When choosing a pump, consider how often you'll be pumping; why you need the breast pump (for occasional pumping, for returning to work, or to establish or increase your milk supply); and cost, ease of use and cleaning, and whether it's light and comfortable.

PUMP IT UP

Mary Ann: I liked breastfeeding. I *hated* pumping. With pumps there's the unscrewing and the fixing and the cleaning and the putting away and the mess. And you'd better invest in some industrial-strength nose plugs if you forget to clean that thing out!

But breast pumps are, of course, a lifesaver for busy moms, as you can pump whenever you need to and stash the milk in the freezer, where it'll still be good to go several months later. I learned that the hard way. When I went back to work I had a terrible sinus infection and hadn't stockpiled, so when I first started pumping I could barely get a few ounces. In a panic I called Joan Ortiz, NBC's lactation consultant, crying because I was sure my daughter was going to starve!

"Mary Ann," she told me, "you're sick, you're on antibiotics, give yourself a break. As soon as you get your rhythm down you'll be fine." And I was.

I used three pumps: the Avent hand pump when I traveled; the Medela electric pump; and the PJ Comfort, which I loved, because the suction cups that attach to your boobs aren't hard like the Medela's.

A hand pump is a suction system that works by you pumping on a lever; it gets tiring fast. But hand pumps are good when electricity isn't available, such as in an airplane bathroom. An electric pump is great if you want to do hands-free pumping; you can strap on a specially designed bra (think *Barbarella*, with your nipples exposed; you tuck the plastic suction cups into the bra), pump away, and knit a scarf at the same time.

Make sure you have someone who is experienced with your pump model show you how to use it, because if you have one

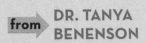

from **DR. TANYA BENENSON**

Ideally, no medications are given to a breastfeeding mother. But the general rule on taking medications during nursing is if it's safe enough to give directly to your infant, then it's safe enough to use during breastfeeding. Before taking any medication, talk to your doctor. Discuss with him or her if the benefits of taking medication outweigh the risks.

little gizmo out of place it won't work. The first time I pumped I felt like Elsie the cow, sitting there with wires and bottles and plugged into the wall, and I was so embarrassed that I locked myself into the room and wouldn't let my husband watch (that didn't last long!). As soon as I started this machine I heard a roaring sound like an F-14.

But I have to admit that despite my embarrassment, the noise, and the whole idea of it, I was secretly relieved because I knew that every ounce meant FREEDOM!

Alicia: My first pumping experience happened in the hospital. It was late at night, my boobs were killing me, and I had to relieve them. I wasn't having any luck getting Jack to breastfeed, so I decided to pump. How difficult could it be? Of course I remembered to pack my hair dryer, my makeup, and my cute pajamas and robe for my hospital stay, but didn't pack my practical pump. (I guess there wasn't room.)

I ended up borrowing the hospital pump. Man, that thing looked like a shiny new carburetor on wheels, except this monstrosity wasn't getting put into a car, but latched onto my chest. After a ten-minute tutorial from a kind nurse, and a request that I not keep it long because other moms needed to use it, I sat back, pumping away to the blast of this motor, watching, of all things, *The Nanny* on TV.

My number-one suggestion is to get your pump and pack it immediately into your overnight bag. There's no place better than a hospital to learn how to use it.

tip: *Pumps are expensive, so it's okay to buy a gently used hospital-grade pump and then pass it on when you're done. We both gave our pumps to friends when we finished using them. You can replace all the plastic parts that transport the milk into the bottle.*

CLEANING THE PUMP

A great device is the Medela Steam Bag. It's perfect for sterilizing breast pump gear and it's faster than boiling, more effective than dishwashing, and super-easy. Just throw what you want sanitized into the steam bag with a little water. After about three minutes in the microwave, everything is steamed and sterilized, with 99.9 percent of all harmful bacteria and germs removed. This also works on pacifiers, nipples, and bottles.

BREAST PUMP COMPARISON CHART

Type of Pump	Purpose	Rental Price	Purchase Price
Hospital Grade Pump (prevents cross contamination)	Initiate, establish and maintain milk supply	$50-90 /month plus deposit & one time kit cost $40-$65	$525-$2000
Retail Pumps (do not prevent cross contamination)			
Double electric pump	Pumps both breasts at same time		$220-$350
Single electric pump	Pumps only one breast at a time		$65-$199
Manual Pump	Hand pumps only one breast at a time		$35-$50

For more information, go to www.limerickinc.com

STORING BREAST MILK

Alicia: Oh, how I loved my freezer full of breast milk. I loved the challenge of seeing how many more bags could I cram into my stockpile. Too bad if there was no room for food—every new bag was one less to worry about down the road. Pumping was turning into a drag at times, but I was so happy counting those stacks of frozen bags.

That is, until I was in California with Jack in 2003, and on a broiling hot August day in New York City there was a total blackout. My husband called to tell me he was okay, but that he didn't know when our power would come back on. I just kept thinking how lucky I was that Jack and I weren't there.

Twenty-four hours later, with me still in California and with the power still out in our apartment, my own light bulb went on: My beloved stash of breast milk was STILL in the power-deprived freezer. All those bags I'd so happily counted every night were melting!

I called my pediatrician and asked all my breastfeeding friends for advice. According to the American Dietetic Association, breast milk can be stored at room temperature for two hours; the American Academy of Pediatrics says one to four hours. But all my friends said, "The breast milk is *probably* fine, but would you risk making your baby sick with spoiled milk?"

Grr. Once back in New York, I counted each bag as I dumped them into the trash. I was so sad to seem them go; they were like really good friends to me. Then I sat down with that trusty pump, snarled, sniffed, and started all over again.

tip: *We have a friend who used breast milk in her pancake mix when she ran out of the cow's stuff. She said it made them extra fluffy. While we never tried this at home, it is a good idea to know what your breast milk tastes like; that way you'll know when it's gone bad.*

Breastfeeding and Alcohol
By JOAN ORTIZ, R.N., B.S.N., C.L.C.
President, Limerick Workplace Lactation Program

An occasional alcoholic drink is acceptable, but caution should be used according to the American Academy of Pediatrics. Alcohol does get to your baby through breast milk, so the amount you drink determines the effect on your breastfeeding baby.

Alcohol levels peak in your breast milk 30 to 90 minutes after drinking, so if you have one drink, the American Academy of Pediatrics recommends waiting two hours to breastfeed. One way to check to see if there's any alcohol in the breast milk is to do a milk-screen test with a dipstick. (These are available at www.milkscreen-moms.com.) If you're worried about the alcohol in your system, then it's time for the pump 'n' dump. Make sure you have a few bottles of breast milk already stashed in the fridge in case your baby wakes up for a feeding.

ON THE JOYS OF A LACTATION EXPERT

Leila had trouble latching on. I loved it that we could call in a lactation expert. I joked that if the IRS ever audited her, she'd have to explain that her job was teaching babies how to latch on to boobs. Wow!

—Al Roker

Business Trips and Breastfeeding

By JOAN ORTIZ, R.N., B.S.N, C.L.C.

Planning ahead will make it possible for you to provide breast milk for your infant when you're traveling without the baby. You will need to express and store milk for several weeks prior to your trip, and this may involve pumping after you feed your baby at the breast or pumping an extra five to ten minutes longer when you express your milk at work.

When making your hotel arrangements, request a refrigerator in your room to store your milk. You will need to pump at the times you would normally feed your baby in the morning, in the evening, and at night.

When flying, review the Transportation Security Guidelines for traveling with breast milk at www.tsa.gov/travelers/airtravel/children/formula.shtm. Currently, breast milk can be brought on board an airplane as long as you declare it before you go through the screening process and keep the bottles in a ziplock bag separate from other aerosols and liquids you may be bringing on board.

from MEREDITH VIEIRA

I had to get up early to go to California. Preparing for a trip, I put the breast pump parts into a pot of water on the stove to sterilize them, but I was so tired that I fell asleep. When I woke up, the house was full of smoke. We got everybody out, thank God. The fireman said, "What's in this pot? It's black melted rubber." I told him it was my breast stuff, and he burst out laughing. That story soon made the rounds in our small town.

Then, after my second child, Gabe, was born, I got into cleaning mode. I was vacuuming some stairs using a canister vacuum cleaner. The canister was on the top landing (there were five steps) and I was down at the bottom vacuuming the last stair. I must have pulled too hard on the vacuum hose because the canister came flying down the staircase and bonked me on the head. I ended the day with a visit to the hospital. Moral of the story: Don't do anything involving the stove or heavy equipment when you're sleep-deprived.

TRAVELING AS A BREASTFEEDING MOM

Mary Ann: I made a big mistake on my first long trip with Zurielle, when she was only three weeks old. We were both strapped into the taxi when she got hungry, and it was a hellacious ride. Needless to say, the cabbie got a little more full frontal then he was expecting as I precariously perched over my baby to breastfeed her.

Travel with at least two milk bottles for your baby, one empty and one already full. If you can't get to an area where you can breastfeed, you can still feed the baby.

WHEN TO STOP BREASTFEEDING

Deciding to stop breastfeeding is a personal decision, and you shouldn't feel guilty if your schedule, commitments, or fatigue make it necessary to stop earlier than you'd originally planned. Bear in mind that while you may be heaving a sigh of relief when you stop, it's hard not to feel many bitter-sweet twinges that your tiny baby is growing up.

Alicia: I breastfed Jack for nearly a year, but then I got sick and needed antibiotics, so my pediatrician suggested I use this time to wean. Jack so desperately wanted to be breastfed—not just for the milk but for the cozy time with me—and I felt the same. A few days later, when I was healthy again, I tried to get him back on board but he wanted nothing to do with me. He was pissed!

I needed to go back to work earlier with Lucy, so I stopped breastfeeding at six months but continued to pump. She was totally fine with it, as she liked our cozy time together much more than the breast, which made weaning more relaxing for me. There were only a few days of discomfort when I stopped.

from ▶ DR. TANYA BENENSON

Not all antibiotics are the same. Some are safer to use in nursing than others. If they are necessary, your doctor will choose the safest one that is appropriate for your condition.

Mary Ann: I set a goal of one year, and although there were plenty of times when I asked myself what the heck I was doing (such as when I was stuck on a layover in a dingy airport, crying as I was pumping because it was another thing added to my very full plate). Now that it's over, I'm really glad I persevered as long as I did.

For me, breastfeeding was easy. Zurielle latched on right away, and my only problem was that I waited too long (seven weeks) to introduce a bottle of breast milk so my husband could help with the feedings. She fought us off for two weeks until we were traveling in the car and there was no other option—it was basically either take this bottle, or go hungry! I should have followed Alicia's technique and introduced the bottle from week one. This is especially important for working moms who know they'll be going back to their jobs, so try to get your baby used to bottle feeding sooner rather than later.

At the year mark, I timed Zurielle's weaning around a business trip. She was already used to drinking from bottles, and on the recommendation of my pediatrician I'd introduced her to four bottles of kefir, liquid yogurt filled with beneficial bacteria, each day. At first, Zurielle was cranky and would paw at me, so I was really glad I could go on my trip. When I came home four days later, the worst was over.

I had to go on a business trip when my second daughter, Arabella, was ten months old. My mom was babysitting; naturally, Arabella got sick, and all she wanted was breast milk. She plowed through that stash in a hurry—but luckily, Zurielle had a toddler's tendency to leave her half-full sippy cups of kefir all over the house, so Arabella started drinking them. (My pediatrician said it was okay.) She certainly wasn't going hungry—she was getting two bottles of kefir and two bottles of breast milk every day.

When I got home, she refused to breastfeed and I was crushed. There went my one-year goal. So I kept pumping for another two months, and then gradually tapered off and switched to all kefir.

Man Boobs

By AL ROKER

When Leila was a baby I was on-air at 5 p.m., 6 p.m., and 11 p.m., and just about an hour after I got home she'd wake up for a feeding. My wife was breastfeeding but Leila would also drink from a bottle; I could have given her a beer mug and she'd drink from it! Anyway, a couple of times I stumbled down into her bedroom without my shirt when I was heavier, and she just saw a breast and went for it. I'd tell her, "You're not getting anything out of there, sweetie. Come on, unlatch!"

ABOUT BOTTLE FEEDING

Some moms breastfeed for a very short time, if at all, and there's nothing wrong with that. Funny how the social pendulum swung from all breastfeeding to no breastfeeding starting after World War II, then back to the Boob Is Best mantra. Yes, breastfeeding is the "ultimate" in feeding for its health benefits, but if you can't do it, you can't. Don't let anyone guilt-trip you into feeling you're less of a mother because you give formula to your baby. Formula is safe, it's nutritious, you know exactly how much your baby is drinking, and it's easy to take with you wherever you go.

One of the huge pluses of bottle-feeding is that anyone (dad, friends, or caregivers) can give the baby a bottle and enjoy watching the big guzzle.

tip: *Ask your pediatrician for advice about which formula will be best for your baby. You might have to go through several different brands or types (cow's milk, soy milk, or goat's milk) to find one that your baby tolerates easily.*

Alicia: With Lucy I was a lot more relaxed about feeding and didn't stress about subbing some feedings with formula. It was the best of both worlds because I didn't feel like a slave to my pump, which at this point was seriously getting on my nerves.

When You Want to Breastfeed but Can't
By LESLYE FAGIN and AMY ROBACH

Leslye Fagin: I was going to be Mom of the Year, and my boobs got so big I could have breastfed the whole hospital floor. I'd get drenched just walking from my bed to the bathroom. But when Jenna would latch on, I could not produce enough milk. I nursed her all day at home, and by the time I burped her it was time to eat again. So I bought every pump known to woman, and sometimes used the manual pump on one breast and the electric on the other, but that didn't work either.

At that point, my doctor told me to switch to formula, which filled up Jenna's little tummy and helped her sleep through the night. It was very disappointing, but it was reassuring to know that my baby was finally getting enough food.

Amy Robach: After being in the hospital for three weeks, my emotions were wild—I gave birth, got a massive blood infection, then had appendicitis. Plus it took my doctors several months to realize I had thyroid disease, which explained my mood swings. Then I had to go back to work, and I just couldn't see myself on assignment, asking for the pump room. I had to be realistic and admit that breastfeeding wasn't going to be feasible (to be honest, I wasn't that crazy about the idea anyway).

Still, I saw the looks. But I explained my circumstances very matter-of-factly, which made people less likely to offer their opinions and criticism. If you decide not to breastfeed, be firm; you give people less ammunition if they know you're not budging.

THE MILKING MACHINE

It starts with the brutal "milking machine," as I called it. I would sit at the kitchen table with my electric pump, feeling like a human cow. Breastfeeding was not easy, and my milk only really came in on one side . . . making me pretty lopsided. One boob grew bigger and bigger by the hour, while the other remained pretty small. When I first started pumping, I remember sitting with that machine attached to me for a full hour to get only one ounce of milk—talk about painful!

I went back to work when Josh was four months old, and it was very hard to continue breastfeeding. I tried pumping at work for a day, but that didn't last. Fortunately I had been supplementing throughout and he didn't seem to mind the bottle, so the weaning was not as difficult as I expected.

—Natalie Morales

INTRODUCING SOLIDS

If you're like us, you'll be counting the days till the six-month mark when you can start introducing solids. You'll have the box of rice cereal and the cute little spoon and bowl all ready, while hovering with the camcorder to record baby's first bite, and you'll be so thrilled and excited with this latest milestone . . . until a few hours later, when the result ends up in the diaper. You've never smelled anything so rank in your life!

The American Academy of Pediatrics (AAP) suggests, "Give baby one new food at a time and wait at least two to three days before starting another. After each new food, watch for any allergic reactions such as diarrhea, rash, or vomiting. If any of these occur, stop using these foods immediately and consult with your child's doctor."

Alicia and I fed our first-born babies with the "introduce-a-new-food-

and-wait-a-week-to-see-if-there's-an-allergic-reaction" method that both our pediatricians recommended. But once our second babies were born, out went these rules. We justified a more lenient eating schedule because neither of us has a family history of allergies. Here are some other solid food suggestions:

> Our babies loved the rice cereal, so we started them on other cereals like barley, oatmeal, and mixed grains. We then added fruits and veggies to the mix to cut down on constipation.

> Making your own baby food is economical, but it sure is a pain and is time-consuming. Alicia's sister, Kathryn, was incredibly organized about making her own baby food. She bought several extra ice-cube trays and dedicated one day to filling them with foods such as sweet potatoes, applesauce, peas, and peaches—buying fruit and vegetables in season.

> If you don't have much time on your hands, it's very easy to mash up a banana with a little bit of breast milk or formula, or mush up some avocado, and let your baby merrily spread it all over his face, hair, tray table, and bib (anywhere but in his mouth!).

> Start using a bib from day one. If you wait, you might find yourself with a baby who hates the feel of anything around her neck, and you'll have an even bigger mess to clean up after each meal. If your baby absolutely will not tolerate a bib, try taking off the onesie or shirt prior to feeding. It's a lot easier to clean up the baby's skin than to do five extra loads of laundry to get the stains out. Or try the plastic bibs with the catch area.

tip: Luckily, healthy prepared foods for babies are readily available at local health food stores or online. In addition to Earth's Best Organic, sites such as www.homemadebaby.com and www.happybaby food.com provide nutritious alternatives to regular jar foods.

> If you use a spoon to transfer food from the baby-food jar into your baby's mouth, you can unwittingly infest the jar with bacteria from the baby's saliva. Since baby food isn't cheap, always pour out what you think you'll need into a bowl prior to feeding. Always throw the leftovers away, store the unused baby-food jar in the refrigerator, and use it within 2–3 days.

> Some babies are picky eaters, and some love prunes and other foods you might not care for. Let your baby be an adventurous eater, but never force food. Unlike grownups, babies are self-regulating eaters, stopping when they've had enough.

GOING ORGANIC

If you do choose to go organic, it's reassuring to know that you aren't unwittingly giving your baby an unwanted dose of antibiotics, pesticides, or hormones each time the baby eats. But in many areas organic food is much more expensive than non-organic food. Look for specials, as many supermarkets have them regularly, and then stock up.

tip: Read labels. The fewer ingredients, the better. It's much better to have "peas and water" (even if not organic) than "peas, water, and high-fructose corn syrup," which is an unhealthy form of sugar that may lead to obesity.

from ▶ JEAN CHATZKY

When my kids learned to eat solid food, I remember stressing about having the green and the orange and the cereal at every meal. My mother finally said, "It's not what your kids eat at any particular meal or on any particular day—if they get good nutrition in a week then you did a good job. You're not going to be able to accomplish this at every meal." That was really great advice.

CHAPTER THREE

Everything You Never Wanted to Know About Pee and Poop

There's nothing like having a baby to cure any squeamishness about bodily functions—because there's simply no avoiding the fact that babies are eating, peeing, and pooping machines. And guess what? Mommy's in charge of cleanup!

Lots of your experienced mommy friends might not be in the mood to get blunt about poop (even after cleaning up 2,359 dirty diapers), so we're happy to do it for you.

THE POOP COLOR CHART

We're sure you never dreamed that one day you'd be reading about how your baby's poop is going to appear in nearly all the colors of the rainbow. Yep, it's true.

Alicia: One of the pamphlets I got while leaving the hospital explained how a newborn's poop was going to change during its first few weeks. I thought, you've got to be kidding. I'm sure you're already ten steps ahead of me, because when Jack's poop turned colors, I dug out that little pamphlet faster than you can say Pampers. It received a prominent place of display on the refrigerator. Where we used to have recipes and menus, I now had the world's most descriptive poop color chart.

This chart came in very handy when the poop went from mud brown to

Dijon mustard yellow to bright green, which scared me half to death because I was sure it meant my baby had some kind of horrible disease.

But don't worry if you baby's poop changes color on a daily basis, or goes from smooth and consistent to tiny little rabbit pellets. Even the bright green was within the normal range.

> tip: *If you're ever worried about any aspect of your child's poop, place a tiny bit of evidence in a clean small jar and take it in to the doctor. Or take in your baby's dirty diaper in a ziplock bag.*

Then there's regularity. Every single time I fed the baby, the baby pooped. This is often the case for breastfed babies.

> tip: *Once your baby is a few months old, the second you hear that gas come out, stand guard with the wipes, because that poop can leak up the back of the diaper before you can say changing table. When putting on the baby's diaper, make sure you pull out the fringe on all sides, as this will help prevent leaking. Also, buy diapers one size larger than he needs.*

> tip: *Cashmere (or dry-clean-only baby clothes) feels nice and soft, and some non-moms might think they're great shower presents, but no baby should ever be clad in a garment that can't easily be thrown in super-hot water (and a gallon of stain remover). Still, never say no to a onesie, as you'll go through more of them than you'll ever think possible.*

from ▶ DR. TANYA BENENSON

WORRISOME STOOLS

There are other colors of stool that are of concern and may require immediate medical attention: black tarry stool after the first few days of life (after the dark meconium has already passed), red bloody stool, light-colored mucous stools, and "currant jelly" stool, a combination of blood and mucous. Talk to your doctor about what to look out for and when.

DIAPER DAZE

Choosing the best diaper for your baby is a matter of personal preference—and physiology. Some babies do fine in the cheapest brands from discount stores. Others are leakers and need the more expensive, heavily cushioned diapers. One brand might work best on skinny babies with teeny butts, while other brands might suit bigger tummies.

Unfortunately for the onesie wardrobe and your sanity, the only way to find out what diapers best suit your baby is to try a whole bunch. For newborns, Alicia and I like Pampers Swaddlers. They wrap quite snugly so there are fewer accidents, and have a quilted fabric-like feel. It's a sad day when your baby outgrows the quilted goodness of these tushie tamers, which are good until the baby weighs fifteen to twenty-two pounds.

tip: If your baby is a sound sleeper yet pees a lot, try Diaper Doublers—they're absorbent pads you insert in the diaper, and they hold a ton of moisture.

When shopping for diapers, be sure to check out different delivery options, as diaper packages are heavy and hard to schlep around with baby in tow. There are many diaper delivery services available. Check out the options at Babies 'R' Us, at www.amazon.com, or from companies like Tushies. Do an Internet search for the best options in your area, or ask other local moms for tips. Superstores also have frequent sales, and you wouldn't want to miss them. Otherwise, nothing beats a trip to Costco or Sam's Club for stocking up on diapers and a few cartons of wipes.

THE DIAPER DEBATE—WASHABLE VERSUS DISPOSABLE

Babies go through a whopping seven to nine thousand diapers before being toilet trained, so this is a hot-button topic.

Most people who live in New York City do not have washers and dryers in their apartments, so for us, washable diapers were not a practical consideration. That said, the ecological impact of disposable diapers is a huge worry—but so are the energy needs of power-sucking washers and dryers. A compromise we're comfortable with is to use Seventh Generation diapers, which are chlorine-free. Or you can try using cloth diapers when home and save the disposables for outside trips. If you choose washables, companies will get you started with a beginner's kit that includes all the cloth diapers you need as well as diaper bags and covers. Bummis, for example, includes a dozen diapers and two covers that close with either Velcro or snaps. Or look for G Diapers—eco-friendly, flushable inserts with washable diaper covers. You might want to try a starter kit and see how well they work for you.

DIAPER DISPOSAL

Speaking of the environment, never forget to dump the poop in the toilet before you throw away the diaper. It's easier to remember to do this when you're not using disposable diapers. Human waste does not belong in landfill, which is where it goes if you dump it in the trash.

The Diaper Genie wraps each diaper in a plastic bag and keeps it in a large container until it's full. Lots of moms love it because it makes disposing diapers less of a chore, but it's not the most earth-friendly system. However, our *TODAY* tech expert, Paul Hochman, recommends the Diaper Champ, since it can take any plastic bag, including the ones you get from the grocery store, so at least you are reusing a bag you already have.

KEEP A P. LIST

Brace yourself: One of the first things you'll be asked on your initial pediatrician visits is how many times your baby has pooped in the last twenty-four hours. Excuse me? You're in such a stupor of exhaustion and emotion yet you're supposed to keep track of the pee and poop?

This is where the checklist on page 25 in Chapter 1 will come in handy. (Those who are scatologically minded can call it the S**t List.) Whoever's looking after the baby on a given day simply has to fill in the chart to keep track of how many times the baby soiled diapers, especially once the baby gets older and starts eating solids.

This chart will save some tears, especially if you have mommy brain like us. We'd go to the doctor and be asked, "When did she last poop?" We weren't sure. The next question was, "When did you feed her last?" Uh, sorry, no clue.

When that happens, you can feel terribly guilty. In fact, you can feel as though you're failing the test when you didn't even know what the questions were going to be.

Keeping a P. Chart will not only give you the answers you need, but it is a good way to keep track of your baby's regularity.

The Saga of One Baby and His Poop
By CECILIA FANG WU

How come all the "What To Expect" books never tell you how much poop your baby will produce on any given day? How was I to know as a brand-new mom that I should keep a pee and poop diary for the first month of the baby's life?

What I eventually learned was that for the first month, a baby poops with almost every diaper change—just a little bit, and that's okay. If you're breastfeeding it's yellowish and very, very watery. My husband and I would dread the sound of bubbles coming from our newborn son, Christian, which was almost always followed by a big smile. We thought, how sweet, he was a happy baby after doody time! Well, that was until we found out babies smile because they're gassy—and not because they are happy.

When Christian was five months old he was weaned off the breast, and the world of poop became an entirely different story. Gone were the days when he pooped all the time; it became once every three days. Gone were the days when the poop didn't smell that bad; that was replaced by a stench that the entire neighborhood knew intimately. Gone was light-yellow poop; it became dark and green.

But, hey, like the pediatrician taught me, as long as there are things going in him (i.e., formula) and things coming out of him, that means he's growing A-okay. And now that he's learned to smile for real, he flashes me a big ol' smile after a dump. I think it's his way of saying, "Thank goodness, I don't have to clean that up!"

TIME FOR A CHANGE

Alicia: Wherever you change the baby, the trick is to use a contoured changing pad, which has slightly raised sides. Babies snuggle in it as if it's a little cocoon. This pad is easily portable and can be laid on any flat surface: a large table, a desk, even the floor.

I used a tabletop, put a contoured changing pad on top, and organized my diapers, lotions, and potions in a cute little basket. Some of our friends were aghast, wondering how we'd keep the baby from rolling off the pad. But think about it: If your hands are on your baby while you're changing him, he's going to be safe.

If that argument doesn't work, try this one: My nephew, Logan, was a wiggle worm who hated getting changed, so his smart mom always changed him on the floor. She kept all the supplies in the bottom dresser drawer, and she never worried about his wriggling so much as to put himself in danger.

Place waterproof pads on the changing table and under the sheets in the baby's bed, as well. This will protect all areas from pee and poop damage. Buy them in multiples, so they're cheaper and you can throw them in the wash.

CHANGING BABY ON THE GO

> What do you do when your baby chooses the most inopportune moment to do number two? Stay in line and apologize for the stink. If the poop is leaking and is a gooey mess, don't be surprised if people invite you to go ahead of them in line. Smile and thank everyone for their understanding

> Be considerate of others. We're both guilty of doing the super-quick change in the airplane seat (for pee only) if nobody's sitting next to us or can see what we're doing. On a positive note, what comes out of breastfed babies is usually pretty stink-free.

> When on a plane or train, don't take anything into the bathroom except baby, a changing pad, a diaper, a travel packet of wipes, and a bottle of hand sanitizer. Always use a wipe on the area before you put your baby down.

> A travel lifesaver is the Munchkin Diaper Duck Travel Buddy Dispenser. It's basically a little roll of plastic bags.

THAT RASH IS NASTY!

With all the peeing and pooping going on, it's not surprising that babies often get diaper rash. Some babies are more sensitive than others.

For babies who don't often get rashes, plain old zinc oxide or Vaseline provides a good and cheap barrier against wetness and irritation. For babies whose skin reacts more easily, we like a combination of Triple Paste and Aquafor cream.

Another way to help cure a rash is to keep your baby's butt exposed to the air. Keep the baby on a waterproof mat in case of accidents. Nothing's cuter than a little naked baby butt rolling around the house.

Any persistent rash must be examined by your pediatrician.

OUR FAVORITE BUTT CREAMS

Eco-friendly/Organic Products

Avalon Organics Baby Soothing Zinc Diaper Balm
Baby Cakes Rear Repair and Over There Ointment by Zen Momma
Earth Tribe—Tribe Kids Baby Balm
Healing Anthropology Nurturing Baby Bottom Cream
Terressentials 100% Organic Terrific Tush Treatment

Regular Products

Balmex Extra Protective Clear Ointment
Boudreaux's Butt Paste
Flanders Buttocks Ointment
Fougera Zinc Oxide Rash Ointment
Rite Aid Zinc Oxide
Triple Paste Medicated Ointment for Diaper Rash
Vaseline Baby

WIPES WE LIKE

Eco-friendly/Organic Products

Avalon Organics
Seventh Generation
Tushies

Regular Products

EO Sanitizing Hand Wipes
Huggies Natural Care
Kirkland Premium Unscented Baby Wipes

Stain Guide

By ELIZABETH MAYHEW

TODAY Contributing Editor and Lifestyle Expert

Having kids is messy, no doubt about it. But I wouldn't trade the pleasure I've had in watching my son devour a chocolate ice-cream cone as it drips all over his white T-shirt for all the tea in China (wait, does that stain, too?). The truth is your babies are going to get dirty, and dirt means stains on their pretty Peter Pan collars.

Stains should be treated as soon as possible—not that I'm advocating that you run around following your baby with a Clorox pen, but the sooner you pre-treat a stain with a stain remover such as Shout or Oxi-Clean, the better chance you have of removing it.

Never rub a stain; blot or dab it instead. Rubbing a stain will only rub the dirt deeper into the fibers.

Always wash a stained item in the hottest water that the fabric will allow (with the exception of protein-based stains—see below). Hot water will help to loosen and remove dirt. However, always check to see if a stain has disappeared before you put it in the drier. Dry heat (unlike the moist heat of the washer) will "bake" in the stain. If you have a stubborn stain that does not come out after one washing, treat it again with a stain remover and rewash.

Protein-based Stains: Blood, Diaper Accidents, Formula/Milk

Treat protein-based stains first by soaking the item in cold water for about twenty minutes to loosen the stain (if you pre-soak it in hot water, you will "cook" the stain). Remove the item from the water and treat the stain with a dab of an enzyme-based detergent like Biz, Era Plus, Wisk, or Axion and let it sit for thirty minutes.

If the stain persists, dab it with some diluted white vinegar or diluted ammonia to bleach the remaining color. Finish with a regular rinse cycle.

Urine

Rinse the item in cold water, then wash. For mattresses, first sponge the area with a solution of detergent and water, then rinse by wiping it with a solution of one part white vinegar to two parts water. Allow the area to air dry.

Colorful Stains: Baby Foods (such as Sweet Potatoes), Berries, Fruit Juice, Grass

Most of the above stains are removed by pre-treating the item with a pre-wash stain remover, then washing the item with detergent in hot water. After washing, if the stain persists, dab it with some diluted white vinegar or diluted ammonia to bleach the remaining color. Finish with a regular rinse cycle.

Out, Damned Spot!

Unusual stains will be a new and permanent part of your life. An easy solution to stains is at your local pet store. Pet stain and odor removal products are industrial-strength stink and mess removers. Obviously you want to go as organic as possible, because these are products you'll likely be using a lot once you start toilet training. We like Nature's Miracle Stain and Odor Remover, Omega Zapp Skunk Odor Pet Shampoo (use as laundry detergent), and Simple Solutions Stain and Odor Remover (use as a pre-soak as well as on carpets).

Alicia: One of the best stain-removal products I've used is Folex, a water-based carpet cleaner that gets out the worst of kiddie stains, too. It's non-toxic, odor-free, nonflammable, CFC- and petroleum-free. It's been a lifesaver in my home.

THE DIAPER BAG

There are countless adorable (and expensive) diaper bags, but you don't need to buy any of them. Sure, you might like to tote a super-cute one around, but we're of the Practical Poop School—which means it's much more important for our diaper bags to be super-lightweight and easy to clean, with room for all the junk and without any gimmicks that get in the way of your grabbing a diaper and wipes when you need them most.

Mary Ann: I bought an expensive diaper bag because I thought I needed one, yet the one I've used most is the one they gave me at the hospital. It's plain and black and hides the stains. When I travel, a large bag with lots of zippered compartments and different-size pockets has always worked better than a diaper bag.

Alicia: I loved my super-simple black Eddie Bauer backpack, with bottle holders on each side. It even came with a foldable changing pad, which made it perfect. I never had to worry about it slipping off my shoulders, either.

I recommend the Dakine Girls Mission Pack, a cool-looking snowboarding backpack (www.dakine.com/snowboard/packs/snow/girls-mission). It won't hurt your back, has tons of compartments, is washable, and is tough enough to defend against the elements and an impromptu hurl. It comes with a contoured harness that fits a woman's back; it also has a water-bottle packet, a fleece-lined pouch (great for keys, glasses, cell phone, and a quick-access snack), and a padded back.
—Paul Hochman, *TODAY* Gear and Technology Editor

PACKING THE DIAPER BAG— AND YOU THOUGHT YOU WERE JUST GOING TO THE SUPERMARKET!

Once your baby arrives, you won't be leaving the house with just your favorite purse slung over your shoulder for a *very* long time. But you can minimize the heft of the diaper bag by packing it smartly.

tip: *Try to replenish the diaper bag at the end of each day, no matter how tired you are. Nothing's worse than discovering you're out of diapers when your baby's just had a sudden explosion. It's very easy to forget something when you're rushing out of the house in the morning, or when the baby's crying. Some moms like to make checklists and keep them by the door as a reminder until restocking the diaper bag becomes second nature.*

tip: *Always pack at least twice as many diapers, wipes, and changes of clothing as you think you're going to need. Trust us, you're going to need them. If your baby gets diarrhea when you're on the move, life as you know it will be temporarily over.*

tip: If you're like us, you've received more than one diaper bag. Whether it was a present, a gift from the hospital, or a hand-me-down, turn the smallest one into a "go" bag that's ready for quick trips out the door with baby. This is all you'll need if you're hurrying to the supermarket or the dry cleaner. Keep your favorite bag stocked with everything else and make this your "primary" diaper bag.

tip: To eliminate mommy bulk, try to dedicate one pocket of the diaper bag for your stuff only: keys, cell phone with doctor's numbers pre-programmed, wallet, sunglasses, "to do" list, lipstick, concealer to hide the bags of exhaustion under your eyes—you know, the essentials!

DIAPER BAG BASICS

> Diapers
> Diaper cream
> Hand sanitizer
> Wipes
> Waterproof changing pad, either disposable or reusable.
> Blanket or baby sweater. Temperatures rise and fall as you move from the car to the store to the restaurant to the doctor's office.
> A few onesies and a pair of simple elastic pants. No fancy outfits. Pack colors that are interchangeable with other items that the baby is already wearing.
> Bibs and/or burp cloths—at least two.
> Plastic bags for soiled diapers and/or wet clothes.
> Baby's portable medical kit, if you plan on being out for more than a day. This should include an instant-read thermometer, baby nail clippers, aspirator, Milicon, and your choice of fever reducer (non aspirin).
> Pacifiers or your baby's soothing vice of choice.
> At least two baby bottles and milk, whether breast or formula.
> For older babies, little snack bags of Cheerios or jarred food, with spoons.

PACKING THE DIAPER BAG WHEN YOU TRAVEL

> Your daily diaper bag might not be suitable as your travel diaper bag. You'll probably need something bigger. Look for a bag that's wide open at the top (such as a duffel or backpack), so you can just dive in to grab whatever you need.

> Ziplock everything: bottles, a change of clothes, snacks, and toys— you never know when something is going to leak or break.

> Always pack several changes of clothes in your diaper bag, because you'll want them when your baby poops more than usual. You can't pack enough onesies.

> Put babies in their pajamas, with a sweat suit on top. Traveling is not the time to show off their cutest outfits, because whatever they wear is going to get filthy.

> Bring an extra pacifier or two. They're usually the first items to get lost, and you don't want to be on a long plane ride with a binky-less baby.

> Bring extra blankets to keep your baby well wrapped if the plane or train gets cold.

> Don't forget your breast pump. A hand pump will work wherever you go.

> For older babies, take favorite toys. It's also a good time to introduce a brand-new toy that might engage your baby for a few minutes more than usual.

> Use travel-size products to minimize weight.

CHAPTER FOUR

Getting Babies to Sleep

Large dark circles under the eyes. Lank hair. Incoherent babbling. Laughing and crying hysterically (often at the same time) for no reason. Fingers too heavy to push the remote buttons (if you can find it). Zombie shuffle: Yep, we know the look. You're a new mom!

Sleep and babies can be tough.

LET NEWBORNS SLEEP!

Caring for a newborn whose tiny tummy needs refilling round the clock means comfy hours snuggled under the blankets will soon seem like a distant memory. And the less sleep you have, the more you need it.

Let new babies sleep! After you know your baby is gaining weight, resist the temptation to wake him or her because baby is so delicious, or you're worried something's wrong. Trust us, pretty soon you'll get used to having your baby around and realize that the baby is going to be fine. When your baby starts waking at all hours, you will be fervently wishing the baby was still asleep.

Once your baby is several months old, it's time to choose some kind of sleep training so the baby (and you) can get uninterrupted sleep. If you take a stroll through the child care section of your local bookstore, you'll be amazed at how many books there are on this topic—each promising results (and many contradicting each other).

But these books can only help so much. Only you can figure out your

comfort zone of sleep deprivation, or whether you're going to be able to tolerate any crying. While you may have been attracted to one kind of sleep philosophy before the baby was born, you might find it doesn't suit either your personality (some moms thrive on rigid schedules; others balk at the mere suggestion of anything but feeding-on-demand 24/7) or your baby's (easygoing and easy-to-conk-out, or a crier who resists comfort and doesn't like to sleep). So then what do you do?

Mary Ann: I kept trying to force Zurielle into the *Baby Wise* (by Gary Izzo) three-hour pattern—half-hour feed, half-hour play, put baby down for two—that my friend with triplets swore by. Well, Zurielle didn't take too kindly to this method, but the *Baby Wise* advice that helped the most was to make sure your baby gets a good feeding and is not a snack attacker. I'd tickle Zurielle's toes or run a wet washcloth over her to keep her up long enough to chow down.

Alicia: When they were about six months old, I was able to sleep train my babies using a version of the Ferber Method that my girlfriends told me about (*Solve Your Child's Sleep Problems*, by Richard Ferber), where baby learns to fall asleep on his own after a few nights of crying it out. It's considered controversial because not all experts believe it's okay to leave a baby alone to cry, even for a small window of time. Be warned. It's painfully difficult the first few days, when 10 minutes *feels like* 10 hours, but there's a full night's sleep—for all—by the third or fourth night. The toughest part about sleep training was between my husband and me. He'd want to get Jack out of the crib and cradle him to sleep before the waiting time was up, while I insisted we leave him in there and let him cry it out.

At times like this, I'd suggest you pour yourself a glass of wine and stick it out. This is the best time to use those portable baby monitors, because it's easier to cope from a distance when you're in another room or hiding in the basement.

SWADDLE THAT LITTLE BURRITO

Babies love being swaddled. It might look like a piece of cake, but it's a bit more difficult to pull off on a squirming newborn than you might think.

As maternity nurses are pros at the swift swaddle, ask for instructions and practice time while you're still in the hospital.

Then practice on your own, either when your baby's in a placid mood and doesn't mind being a "dummy" or on a doll of similar weight. If the swaddle isn't a nice, tight bundle, it won't be effective.

Depending on their size, most babies can stay swaddled up to the age of about three months. Once they can worm their way out of the swaddling, put them in blanket sleepers instead.

from **DR. NANCY SNYDERMAN**

Put a fan in the nursery. Keeping the air circulated around the room seems to dramatically reduce the risk of SIDS (Sudden Infant Death Syndrome). One study found it was reduced by 72 percent.

THE ARM'S-REACH CO-SLEEPER

Mary Ann: For any new mom who's worried about crushing the baby, the Arm's Reach Co-Sleeper (www.armsreach.com) is the greatest. It's a three-sided bassinet that attaches to the side of any size mattress, and it allows you to sleep with your baby next to you but protected so you don't have to worry about rolling over on top of the baby. There's room for storage underneath, it can convert to a play yard and changing table, and it's portable. It's one of the most practical items you can buy.

After each feeding, I would swaddle my baby, place her in the co-sleeper, and she'd instantly go back to sleep. Be aware that the co-sleeper is not a crib, so once babies are able to pull themselves up or crawl into your bed, stop using it. Zurielle was able to stay in it until she was about seven months old.

THE CO-SLEEPING DEBATE

We know lots of moms who used the co-sleeper, or even put their baby in the bed with them, and didn't mind being woken up, poked, or prodded for more nighttime feedings. Co-sleeping is, in fact, often recommended for preemies, or for newly adopted babies who may have come from orphanages. It is also an integral part of cultures where the family bed is considered normal.

We're not fans of co-sleeping, but if it works for you, then you don't need to justify your decision to anyone. Bear in mind, though, that you may have a very tough time getting your baby out of the family bed.

I am really firm on this issue. I have never let our girls sleep with us.
                                                        —Amy Robach

Josh is four and still sleeping with us. You have been warned!
                                                        — Natalie Morales

HUSH, LITTLE BABY—GETTING YOUR BABY TO SLEEP THROUGH THE NIGHT

Mary Ann: I put Zurielle down at 8:30 p.m., then always gave her a midnight feed, right before I went to sleep. Every single night, between 2:30 and 3 a.m.—just when I was in the deepest of desperately needed sleep—she'd wake up for a snack attack and holler and scream. So I'd feed her, which took less than five minutes, and then down she'd go. She hadn't been hungry, of course; it was a habit.

This was driving me crazy, so my husband and I had to do one of the hardest thing we've ever done: train her to sleep through the night by cold-turkey crying it out.

We weren't looking forward to it, as we were living in a small one-bedroom apartment in a large building, where for some reason other families might not be overjoyed by the dulcet tones of a howler monkey at three in the morning. But we steeled ourselves for the inevitable and moved Zurielle into the kitchen, as I thought the farther from the usual smells of the bedroom and mommy's milk, the better. Sure enough, at 2:48 a.m. Zurielle was up and screaming. And then she cried and cried for forty-five horrendous minutes while I lay in bed and cried, too, feeling like the world's worst mommy who was deliberately torturing her child, and willing myself not to go to her because I knew we had to break this habit or it would only get worse. As my pediatrician had said, "If you think it's hard now at six months, just think of how hard it's going to be in a year when she's *really* vocal. Let her cry it out now."

Then it stopped. Forty-five minutes of pure hell, and it was over.

The next night, we did the same thing. Zurielle screamed and hollered for twenty-five minutes. Next night: twenty-five minutes again. Fourth night: ten minutes. Fifth night: blissful, sweet, deliriously wonderful silence. It was absolutely worth it.

This sleep training helped in other ways, as I realized that I didn't have to run to her every single time she cried (unless she'd injured herself). She became better at self-soothing, and we both got the sleep we needed.

After I went back to work, Alicia told me Zurielle didn't need the midnight feed anymore. Bingo! Zurielle slept from about 7:30 p.m. to 7:30 a.m. Instead of feeding, I pumped at around 11 p.m. and put the milk in the fridge, which meant I had one fewer pumping to worry about at work the next day. I just wish I'd given it up sooner!

Some moms think it's better if they go in and pat the baby. I tried this and it would whip Zurielle up even more. So while the sweet pats might make you feel less guilty, in the end it will probably make it worse for the baby.

Alicia: I couldn't go in during the night and pat my children on the back. If either of my kids saw me, they'd only see the milk machine attached to my chest. So it was usually Daddy's responsibility to go in while we were sleep training our babies.

> **tip**: *Decide beforehand how much crying you can stand, and then set a timer. A minute or two is not enough. Try to last for at least ten minutes (which will be the longest ten minutes of your life), as in most cases the baby will fall asleep before then.*

Try to have the baby as far from your bed as possible. Or put the baby down, close the door, turn down the monitor, and force yourself to resist going in before the timer rings. Some moms just can't do this, and if you can't, you can't. It'll all work out eventually.

When I'd braced myself for Jack's coming ordeal, I delivered cookies to all the apartments on my floor with a note saying, "Sorry, we're doing a little sleep training, please forgive us if this disturbs you. It should only take a few nights, and will end up making nights a lot less noisy for all of us." I think the neighbors were so thankful to get something homemade that they totally forgot about the crying.

> **tip**: *Start sleep training only after your pediatrician gives you the go-ahead. Most doctors recommend waiting until your baby weighs at least twelve pounds.*

Peace at Last

I am married to a pediatrician and he believed in a regimented sleep routine. Nonetheless, my first two children did wake up every three to four hours as infants. Funny how even the pediatrician in the house never heard them crying. He would tell you his babies were great sleepers. Hmm.

By the time the third child came around, I was exhausted. She turned out to be my best sleeper because I just couldn't get up! She cried the first night for fifteen minutes . . . the second night for five . . . and then she gave up. She figured if no one's coming, might as well not bother, and by four months, she slept through the night.

—**Debbie Kosofsky**

We tried to sleep-train both of our kids according to Dr. Marc Weissbluth's book *Healthy Sleep Habits, Happy Child*. Listening to our first one cry was excruciating, but being consistent really worked. I also spent a lot of time charting his natural sleepy-times so that I could somewhat scientifically see a pattern emerge. I did this for eleven weeks before I really let him belt it out. Once we did it, it worked great.

The problem is that we did the same thing with our daughter, Lois, with different results. When she was about five months old and our pediatrician gave us the go-ahead, I told our son, Arlo, that he'd have to endure listening to Lois cry for a few days because we were teaching her how to sleep on her own. Well, she cried for weeks and weeks, and would wake Arlo up. After a while it just made sense to keep her as quiet as possible so that at least two out of four people could get some sleep.

One funny story about the sleep training is that prior to bedtime, I would try to calm our house. We invested in not just lullaby CDs but a CD set from a scientist who makes music that's supposed to tap into alpha, theta, delta, and some other brainwaves that foster sleep. While these CDs were playing, my husband and I were practically losing consciousness, while our kids were still ready to party.

—**Claudia David Heitler**

No Bedtime for Mom
By TIKI BARBER

Sleep issues are obviously more of a challenge for mothers, mainly because of the breastfeeding responsibility. My wife, Ginny, is a light sleeper and every time there was a peep, she would wake up, so she didn't sleep much. It didn't help that Ginny doesn't like to nap. People always ask how long it takes until you get used to sleeplessness, and the answer is that you don't! The adjustment period ends when your baby sleeps through the night.

I had a completely different sleep experience. For the first month of AJ's life, I was in football training camp with the New York Giants. That obviously had its pros and cons—I got full nights of sleep, but I was away from my precious newborn son. My wife knew that I had to be up early for long days of football practice and meetings and that my performance was directly tied to how much sleep I was getting, so she handled all the night feedings, woke up when the kids cried, and sacrificed her sleep for me.

My Secret for Getting Baby to Sleep
By MATT LAUER

Jack was a tough one to get to sleep. I got really good at holding him in a certain position, rocking him, swaying my body back and forth, and knowing which songs would work. And if we were in real crisis mode I'd put him in the car seat, get in the car, and drive around for twenty minutes. I spent a *lot* of time driving that baby around!

SNOOZE OR LOSE—MOMMIES NEED SLEEP TOO

Sleep deprivation can lead to a lot of things (and in Mary Ann's case definitely added to her postpartum depression). When you aren't rested, the smallest events can become magnified out of proportion, and you can feel as though you're trapped. That leads to hopeless feelings that you can't get anything done because the baby never sleeps . . . so you're a mess and the house is a mess and you're snapping at loved ones and can't remember the last time you took a shower.

If you're having a tough time steeling yourself for sleep training, remember that your own needs are important too. You can't take the best care of your baby if you don't take the best care of yourself.

Well-rested babies eat better and cry less. In the end you are giving your little one a valuable tool—the ability to self-soothe.

MAKE SURE EVERYONE KNOWS
THE SLEEP RULES IN YOUR HOUSE

Mary Ann: One of my babysitters is a real softie, and I had to be very stern with her. I warned her that Zurielle actually liked to cry herself to sleep, as it was a ten-minute vent of her daily pent-up stuff, and then she'd conk out and not wake up again till morning. I was quite adamant that this sitter (and all other sitters) follow my sleep rules and let my baby cry. Sometimes it takes only one night to undo six months of training.

Don't worry that you might not know the difference between a settling-down-for-the-night cry or a truly needy cry. Most moms become adept at deciphering the difference between the "I'm sick, Mommy" cry (which warrants immediate attention) and the "I feel like kvetching tonight, Mommy" cry (which warrants benign neglect).

> tip: *Moms worry they won't hear their baby cry at night. Trust us, if your baby really needs you, she'll make herself heard.*

A LITTLE NOISE IS A LOT OF HELP

> Don't have a silent house. Babies are used to noise; they grew inside a womb where they were accustomed to the sound of their mommy's heartbeat, tummy gurgles, and all sorts of bizarre noises.
> Take your baby out as much as possible to learn to sleep in the car seat or stroller while surrounded by noise.
> Keep a low-level light on or the curtains open so your baby doesn't need total darkness in order to sleep.
> White noise is a good idea. If you don't want to purchase a white noise machine, either place a fan in the corner or have your radio or CD player on low, playing soothing music.

MIX IT UP TO HELP YOUR BABY SLEEP

A baby who gets used to sleeping only one way, in one bed, in one room, is a baby who's going to have a lot of trouble adjusting to any new environment. So many moms fall into the trap of thinking that their baby must be in the bed in a darkened and silent room (or in a car seat) for all naps, and that if something shifts in the routine, the baby is going to be very unhappy.

Even if you have a predictable schedule, mix things up for your baby every once in a while. Let the baby figure out how to sleep at naptime.

We have a friend who knew she'd be traveling a lot with her kids, so she bought several similar wind-up music boxes (in case one broke). No matter where her family was, she wound up the music box before sleep time, and that was the comforting signal to her kids to nod off. Her routine became an integral part of mixing it up.

HELP! MY BABY'S A BELLY SLEEPER!

Mary Ann: At about one month, Zurielle would kick off the swaddle no matter how tightly I'd wrap it, and push it away. She had amazingly well-developed neck muscles for such a tiny baby and could already move back and forth. I put her on her back or her side, as directed by my pediatrician, and guess what, the only way she would ever get to sleep was on her belly.

So I have a horrible confession to make. I let her sleep that way.

Naturally, I guiltily told my pediatrician, and he basically said that was contrary to all medical recommendations and I was endangering my child. Next, I confessed to my mom, and she told me that all nine of her children slept on their bellies, but now she's hesitant to recommend it because sudden infant death syndrome has decreased dramatically since pediatricians started recommending that all babies be put down on their backs. Still, no one cause of SIDS has definitely been pinpointed yet; it may be genetically determined, or caused by babies being overheated or lacking sufficient oxygen during sleep.

Be aware that some babies have a great deal of difficulty sleeping in any position but face-down. (It might be a self-soothing thing, where the pressure on their little bellies helps them relax into sleep.) Talk to your pediatrician, and don't drive yourself crazy with guilt if yours is one of them. Be sure your crib mattress is super-firm, that the crib sheet fits tightly, and that there are no items in the crib. Use a crib monitor, and no bumper pads.

When Arabella was born, I figured she'd sleep on her back and I could stop worrying. Guess what? Once she was old enough to kick off the swaddling, she would only go to sleep on her belly. Except this time, I wasn't quite so freaked out.

from ➤ DR. NANCY SNYDERMAN

Although most of us slept on our stomachs, I can't agree with Mary Ann. You should *not* let your baby sleep that way. When the American Academy of Pediatrics changed their rules on this issue, it greatly reduced the number of babies who died from SIDS. For additional information, please refer to the AAP website at www.aap.org.

PACIFYING BABIES

We want our children, even as infants, to look clean, perfect, and beautiful even if reality more closely resembles baby-food peas smeared all over the beige carpet. But nothing's going to be perfect, except perhaps your love for your baby.

Start with the pacifier. Pacifiers don't fit on a perfect, beautiful face.

But who cares? Shove that thing right in there. For most babies, a pacifier is the handy-dandy soothing tool of choice. Or your baby might have a hallelujah moment when she finds her thumb and the endless hours of enjoyment it can bring.

If your baby does love the pacifier, always have a whole bunch of duplicates stashed away, as they get lost before you've even had a chance to blink. You don't want to be making drugstore runs in the middle of the night because the binky disappeared.

Even if your child is not a pacifier-lover, keep some in a drawer just in case. They're helpful for self-soothing if you have to travel. Also, you might have to try a few to see which one your baby likes—and once you find that one, buy in bulk!

After about eight months or so, think about cutting down on pacifier use. Avoid giving it easily during the day, and try to limit its use to nighttime.

Alicia: This fail-safe bit of advice was actually given to me by one of my husband's former college buddies. (I know what you're thinking, but you can often be surprised by who's got some splendid ideas for babies.) Simply cut the off the nipple part of the pacifier and give it to your baby like that. When I gave the "cut" pacifier to my babies at bedtime, they were excited to get it but frustrated that the pacifier didn't stay in their mouths. (Other moms do something similar by poking pinholes in the nipple, so it's not satisfyingly chewy for the baby to suck on.)

I'm sure you're wondering why I put them through this horrible hazing-type ritual—well, it was so they'd be mad at the "malfunctioning" pacifier and not at me. Fast forward a few nights, and the pacifier habit was broken.

NATURAL DISRUPTIONS IN THE SLEEP CYCLE

So there you are, pleased as punch with yourself that you've finally gotten your baby on a nice, predictable sleep routine, when wham! In comes the first tooth, along with many nights of inconsolable screaming.

All of us have endured nights when we're sure our baby will never again sleep solidly and all our heartbreaking sleep training was for naught. But when babies are sick, growing, or teething—and if you're really lucky, all three at the same time—their sleep gets disrupted. This is totally normal. In fact, it's very common right before a big milestone, such as sitting up or crawling.

If you've already established good sleep habits, your baby should click right back into them once the current situation has resolved itself. There are times, of course, when the baby wakes up in the middle of the night and nothing you do works, and you find yourself pacing around the house with a wailing baby squirming on your shoulder while you silently beg and plead for him to just cut it out. You can't beat yourself up too much when that happens—because it happens to everyone.

CHAPTER FIVE

Skin Like a Baby's

Giving a bath to a newborn takes getting used to. You're terrified you might drop the baby, or get water up the baby's nose, or startle the baby into wails of terror.

Alicia: What worked for me was to bathe Jack in the kitchen sink, which was the perfect size for a newborn. My mom showed me how to cradle him with one arm while wiping him down with a washcloth with the other. Sure, he was a slippery little bugger, but because I was standing up I had more control so I was less worried about him sliding out of my reach. Both my kids had sink baths till they were too big to fit in it.

tip: *Change the faucet on your bathtub to a scald-free unit. This will keep the temperature at comfortable levels unless an adult manually adjusts it and will help prevent accidentally scalding your baby. Also, place a hand towel or washcloth over the bathtub faucet, as it can get very hot when water's coming out of it. The One Step Ahead catalog (www.onestepahead.com) sells faucet covers shaped like cute animals.*

Is there anything more delicious than the scent of a baby? Follow our tips and your baby's skin will be soft, sweet, and protected from the elements.

BATH-TIME BASICS

> As babies are too small for a regular tub, use a baby-sized tub placed in your bathtub and put something under your knees for traction and comfort, such as a yoga mat, nonskid bath rug, or gardener's mat.

> Think about changing your fixed showerhead to a hand-held unit. Babies usually love to get squirted, and this makes it easier to direct spray when you're washing hair. With a hand-held unit you don't even have to fill the little tub—you can squirt babies, soap them up, and then squirt them down again. This technique is also useful after a diaper accident.

> Never leave your baby unattended for even the few seconds it takes to get a towel or answer the phone. Place all towels on the floor near you prior to running the bath, and if you need to answer the phone, bring a cordless handset into the room. Babies can drown in a mere inch or two of water, after being submerged for only a few seconds. If you need to leave the room, take the baby out of the bath first.

> It may be a lovely part of your daily routine, but it's not a medical necessity to give your baby a bath every day. This is especially true if your baby has eczema or a tendency toward dry skin.

GET YOUR BABY USED TO WATER

Sometimes babies who love to splash happily for hours in the bath suddenly become very afraid of water, especially if it's gushing noisily out of the faucet or trickling down near their eyes. This can turn into an epic nighttime battle, especially when your baby really is dirty and in need of a good scrubbing.

You can resort to heavy-duty sponge baths or, better yet, sometimes it helps to take the baby over to a friend's house at bath time. Seeing another baby splashing merrily in the tub might do the trick.

Alicia: For my kids, bath time is pure joy. I realize for us busy moms that sometimes it just seems like one more thing to do before bedtime, but why not make it entertaining for you, too? Sure it's messy, and nine times out of ten there's probably more water on the floor or on me than on my baby. But I've never heard more giggles than in the tub. This is one of those times when you need to relax and have as much fun as your baby. My daughter Lucy even goes crazy over lotion time after the bath—she just loves a massage, and I love giving her one.

Another solution is to get babies used to the feel of water on their faces from day one, and we like the time-honored technique of dumping a bucket of warm water on their heads. Once babies know that water-on-the-face is part of a regular bath-time routine, it becomes just another fun thing to play with Mommy.

tip: *In addition to all the whatchamawhozits you use as tub toys, put a few small beach buckets in the bath. They're fun for babies to grab and put their small toys into, fill with water, and dump over their heads. They're also good for rinsing out hair.*

tip: *You can bathe yourself along with the baby as long as the water is shallow, you have slip protection and towels placed on the floor near the tub, and the water temperature is not as hot as you may usually like it.*

ARE THE FANCY SHAMPOOS AND CREAMS WORTH IT?

Many babies have little to no hair, so their scalps can be washed with the same tear-free baby wash used on their bodies. You don't need to pay a lot for a fancy baby shampoo. The fewer ingredients you put on your baby's tender skin, the better.

tip: *Since all four of our babies have dry, sensitive skin, we try to avoid any bath or hair products that contain dyes, synthetic foaming agents (such as sodium lauryl or laureth sulfate, or ammonium lauryl or laureth sulfate), parabens, fragrance, and petrochemicals. These are all potential allergens. Bubble baths are seldom recommended for infants, as sitting in them can cause bladder infections.*

tip: *Alicia followed her mother's advice and used only water for cleansing.*

BATH PRODUCTS WE LIKE

Aveeno Soothing Baby Bath Treatment
Burt's Bees Baby Bee Shampoo and Wash
California Baby Shampoo and Body Wash Super Sensitive
Little Twig Shampoo and Baby Wash
Method Baby Squeaky Green Hair and Body Wash
Nature's Baby Organics Shampoo
Tom's of Maine Baby Shampoo and Body Wash
Zoo on You Spunky Monkey 2-in-1 Shampoo and Pampered Polar
     Bear Body Wash

LESS-THAN-PERFECT SKIN: RASHES, CRADLE CAP, ECZEMA, AND (GASP!) BABY ZITS

Babies are great at getting rashes. Sometimes the rash means they're getting sick with a virus like roseola, but often the rash is nothing more dangerous than a mere skin irritation. Of course, it's hard not to panic when you see a rash blooming where nothing had been a few hours before.

Mary Ann: When Zurielle was a few weeks old, I took her in the BabyBjörn to a checkup at the pediatrician's. That day was unbelievably hot, and when we got home and I took her sweet little sweating body out of the carrier, I noticed she had a vivid pattern of red dots all over her. I totally freaked out, thinking she had measles, but it was only heat rash.

tip: *If a sudden rash is accompanied by a fever or unusual behavior, such as lethargy, call your pediatrician immediately.*

In addition to rashes, babies are prone to cradle cap (which is not dandruff, but seborrheic dermatitis) and zits. Baby acne might look unsightly, but it's due to a transference of maternal hormones and nearly always clears up on its own within a few weeks. Nothing can be done to treat it, so leave it alone.

I thought Zurielle had cradle cap, but it turned out to be nothing more than a buildup of lotion that I had put on her bald head. That was a good reminder that too much of any product is not a great idea for tender baby skin.

She also had eczema, which is dermatitis, or inflamed skin. It is a very common condition, ranging from mild and intermittent to severe. There is no known cause, and it tends to be hereditary, particularly if there are already allergies and/or asthma in the family. To deal with it, I took Zurielle to a chiropractor who specialized in allergies. He tested Zurielle by putting her on my lap, then placing different test tubes next to her skin. He also did muscle testing on me. I expect this sounds like quackery, but this chiropractor told me Zurielle was allergic to processed cheese and oatmeal; as soon as we removed them from her diet, the eczema disappeared. There are many pediatricians who specialize in allergies as well.

SKIN CARE PRODUCTS WE LIKE

Eco-friendly/Organic Products

Burt's Bees Baby Bee Apricot Kernel Oil

Earth Mama Angel Baby—Angel Baby Oil

Earth Tribe—Tribe Kids Body Balm

Munchskins Skin Care Cradle Me Scalp Rub

Pure Baby Cradle Cap Care Sensitive Skin Formula

Regular Products

Aquaphor cream or lotion

Aveeno Eczema Care cream

Eucerin cream or lotion

Jo Malone Vitamin E Gel (fancy stuff, but we love it)

Lubriderm for Sensitive Skin

HOMEGROWN TREATMENTS THAT WORK

You don't need to shell out for expensive creams and lotions to treat simple rashes or dry skin when some of the best are cheap and easy to find. One of these is Vaseline. Some pediatricians discourage the use of petroleum-based products, but it works in a pinch.

Mary Ann and Alicia's favorite creams for dry skin and eczema are Lubriderm, Eucerin, and Aquafor. Babies with eczema often respond to pure shea butter—it's a common ingredient in emollient skin creams and is safe for use on tender skin. Be sure to get organic shea butter at a health food store, and warm it up between your fingers for a few seconds before applying to your baby's skin. Also, Weleda Baby Calendula Lotion is great for delicate skin and can be found in your local health food store.

Always check with your pediatrician before using any cream on your baby if eczema has been diagnosed.

tip: *If you're determined to stay organic, you can use any organic plant-derived oil as a moisturizing skin cream. We like jojoba oil, sweet almond oil, coconut oil, and even olive oil. They smell yummy and are easily absorbed, but be aware that nut oils can cause a reaction if baby is allergic to nuts.*

tip: *"Fragrance" in any cosmetic is one of those ingredients that can cause irritation or allergic reactions. If you're using an oil and aren't crazy about the smell, try adding a few drops of a soothing, organic essential oil like rosemary or chamomile. Only a few drops are needed, and as essential oils are highly concentrated, never apply them directly to any skin.*

SUN PROTECTION FOR BABIES

It is a fallacy that babies need a lot of sunshine to be healthy. Yes, all babies need a minimal amount of sun exposure each week to stimulate vitamin D production, but we're only talking about ten or fifteen minutes of an ankle exposed to the sky. Nearly all children get much more than this during incidental exposure—walking out to the car, sitting in the car, or being pushed in a stroller to the playground. Sun exposure ages the skin and causes cancer, and as melanoma rates are rising at an alarming rate, particularly in young adults, get in the habit of daily sun protection as soon as you start taking the baby outside.

Many sunscreens formulated for babies contain chemicals (and other potential irritants). Most pediatricians recommend not using them on babies under the age of six months.

Babies over the age of six months should use sunscreen every day, just like Mommy does. Yes, Mom, this means you, too! Use a daily sunscreen with an SPF of at least 30, as we do. There's no such thing as a "safe tan" from the sun.

> The best and easiest form of sunscreen is clothing. Babies should always wear opaque sun hats with a shielding brim in warm months and hats in the winter, too. Try to walk on the shady side of the street, and if you're having a picnic, sit under a shady tree.

> Always use a large shade when pushing your baby in the stroller. If you spend a lot of time in the car, put a shade in the backseat window near the car seat, too.

> Strollers' shade covers usually don't offer enough sun protection. Add a stroller sun-shade over your stroller—it's huge, is light-weight, and should fit any size or shape stroller. It is easily removable and offers a tremendous amount of ultraviolet protection.

> Use sun hats with ties or Velcro on the bottom. Even if you've been given lots of adorable hats, if your baby can figure out how to pull the hat off, the baby will go right ahead and yank—Babies who get used to wearing a hat from day one will be much less likely to fight wearing it once they hit the toddler years.

> Pump-spray or continuous-spray sunscreens are the easiest to apply, especially for babies without a lot of hair. Look for no-tear formulas, as babies can rub themselves and then put their fingers near the eyes. Regular sunscreens can sting a lot.

> If you have baldies, don't forget to apply sunscreen to their scalps.

SUNSCREENS WE LIKE

Eco-friendly/Organic Products

Aubrey Organics Natural Sun SPF 25 Green Tea Protective Sunscreen
Avalon Organics Natural Mineral Sunscreen SPF 18
California Baby No Fragrance SPF 30+ Sunscreen Lotion
UV Natural Baby SPF 30+

Regular Brands

Banana Boat Tear-Free Sunblock Spray Lotion SPF 50
Eucerin Extra Protection Lotion for Face SPF 30
Hawaiian Tropic Baby Faces Sunblock

The Eyes Have It

While it is true that sunglasses can help little Jimmy look cool ("Please, no pictures, Mom!"), the best-designed kids' sunglasses are really about safety. Studies show that the sun's rays are getting more and more intense every year (more than twice as intense as fifty years ago), and the American Cancer Society says that keeping skin and eye damage to a minimum before a child turns eighteen helps lower a child's risk of getting disease by about 50 percent.

Which means that babies need sunglasses too. However, getting them to wear sunglasses is easier said than done, as many babies hate the feeling of anything on their faces. If you can get your baby to wear sunglasses without a fuss, I recommend Julbo sunglasses, as they're designed to fit an infant- or toddler-width head. The Looping 1 and Looping 2 ($30 from www.julbousa. com) also have little elastic straps that keep the darn things on when your baby is lolling off to sleep. They offer 100 percent UVA and UVB protection and look great. The sooner you can start your little one on the sunglass habit, the easier it is to keep it going.

— **Paul Hochman**

CHAPTER SIX

Baby Gets Sick

Babies eat, pee, poop, cry, smile, roll over, fill your heart with love . . . and then get sick. Nothing is more heart-stopping—and it can be completely terrifying the first time your darling little dumpling gets more than a tiny sniffle. Especially if the baby zooms from totally fine to really sick in what seems like a nanosecond.

Of course it's easy to say not to panic when it's not your baby. We've been there. We've panicked. Big time.

FINDING THE PERFECT PEDIATRICIAN

In an ideal world, you should interview pediatricians and be all set with one you love—and who will be great to your baby—before the baby is born.

You know what? We interviewed pediatricians, and we didn't know what the heck to ask. After some nice conversations, we walked out not knowing what their bedside manner would be like with an actual baby, or how well they'd respond to panicked midnight phone calls, or if their staff was responsive, or if we'd spend three hours twirling our thumbs with a screaming sick baby in the waiting room.

For us, the best way to find a pediatrician is through someone you trust.

Alicia: We ultimately picked a doctor that we didn't pre-interview. Instead, right before Jack's due date, we asked our good friends the Zolands, who had preemie twins, for advice. We chose our pediatrician because the

Zolands gushed about how attentive and loving he was with their boys, plus he'd made extra hospital visits to see the twins. He was on board with this family before they even set foot in his office. Here are our tips so you can find the best pediatrician for your baby:

> Trust your gut. The doctor might have great credentials and years of experience, but if you just don't click, find someone else. Remember, you'll be spending years in a relationship with this person, and you have to at least like being in his or her company.

> Don't be intimidated by the fact that the pediatrician has an M.D. and you don't. Sure, doctors are experts, but you're paying for their expertise, and you are worthy of respect, too. It's not a crime to speak up and be assertive when you are with a medical professional. A lot of moms we know (okay, count us in that number) don't want to seem pushy or picky. They want the doctor to like them, so they are always nice even when they feel dismissed or like screaming.

> You want to ensure that there's plenty of staff to answer the phones promptly and courteously.

> How quickly the doctor or nurse calls you back is extremely important. This rule is not so much for your baby's survival as it is for yours.

> *Who* calls you back is important, too. You want your primary physician—someone who's familiar with you and your baby—to call you, but in some large practices, the doctors might rotate who's on call at night. This can be a headache when you love your own doctor but not the other partners in the practice, but it goes with the territory.

> Mary Ann's new pediatrician even makes next-day follow-up calls. Talk about service.

> Make sure there's a separate section for vulnerable newborns or babies who have a rash or other communicable condition. One of your biggest fears will be that your healthy baby will catch something from the sick babies in the waiting room— and guess what, it happens more than you'll want to believe. Don't expect anything fancy. Our doctors let sick infants and their caregivers sit in their own offices to wait.

from ▶ **DR. NANCY SNYDERMAN**

Try to find a pediatrician while you are still pregnant— because that way, if there are philosophical differences, you can make sure you and your doctor are on the same page. If you're a fairly flexible person, a doctor with a rigid ideology might not be a great fit. If you believe in a certain method of raising your child, as a vegetarian for instance, find someone who understands you and is willing to work with you. You don't want to go to every visit feeling a need to defend your beliefs. Instead, think of your relationship with your pediatrician as a partnership.

- In case of emergency, or if your baby needs surgery, you want your doctor to be affiliated with a good nearby hospital, preferably one with a pediatric emergency room.
- It might not seem important at first, but having a doctor close to your home is a huge asset, especially if your baby gets sick a lot. Having to schlep to the doctor's with a sick, screaming infant in the middle of a snowstorm is not our idea of a fun few hours.
- Make sure there are flexible hours. This means weekend hours, early hours (pre-work), and late hours (after 5 or 6 p.m.) at least one or two days a week.

Alicia: Many pediatricians have drop-in hours; mine is from 8 to 9 a.m., mainly so working parents can zoom their kids in for a quick appointment. I can't tell you how many times I've used this service. It's a real lifesaver.

- When you're scheduling an appointment, try to always be either the first appointment of the day or the last one. If the baby's not sick, wait another week or so to get these prime spots. When you're first the wait is shorter, and when you're last, the waiting room has already cleared out. Before any appointment, unless you're the first, call before you leave the house or work to see if they're running late. And if they admit to running late, ask for a realistic estimate. Lots of times you'll hear "fifteen minutes" when they know it's more like an hour and fifteen minutes.
- Make sure they have a clearly understandable payment policy. If your baby is very sick and you just want to get home, or is screaming after getting shots, the last thing you want to do is to have to wait in a line for ten minutes to hand over your co-pay. Some offices send a bill later. Others let you take care of the co-pay or fee prior to seeing the doctor if it's for a routine appointment. This may sound silly—until you have a squirming, miserable baby and you're just desperate to get out of the office.
- Ideally, you want to find a pediatrician who takes care of the mom as much as the baby. After waiting in the office, and having the doctor pay attention to your baby and do a thorough examination, it means so much if the doctor looks at you too and asks, "How are you doing, Mommy? Do you have any questions?"

YOUR BABY'S FIRST VISIT
TO THE PEDIATRICIAN

Your baby's first appointment is a great milestone. Your baby will be fine. You, on the other hand, might be surprised to find yourself a nervous wreck. First you'll be terrified someone will crash into your car, or that the car seat isn't latched properly, or that you put too many layers on the baby, or not enough layers, and did you bring enough clothes and blankets? Did you remember to stash extra diapers in the diaper bag? What diaper bag? Right, you forgot the whole thing.

And just wait till the baby gets his or her first shots. Knowing your baby is going to feel pain, even a momentary pinch, can leave you as upset as your child.

Alicia's pediatrician wanted to see her newborns three times during the first month, but your own doctor might not ask to see them that often (and it usually isn't a medical necessity). During these appointments, it's very reassuring to know your baby is growing and thriving—that is, until the doctor says, "Great, we'll see you once a month now," and you're thinking, What? You don't want me anymore?

tip: When required doctor visits diminish from once a month to every three months, then every six months, keep a running list of questions you may have. Otherwise it's extremely easy to forget them. Get a notepad or file specific to baby questions, or keep a medical diary (which will be fun for the baby to look at when he or she is older). Be sure to have a pen and this notepad handy when you go into the doctor's office so you can take notes about medication dosage or other information. If you keep these notes in chronological order, they'll become a helpful diary of your baby's medical treatments and progress.

GETTING MEDICAL INFO AFTER-HOURS

The doctor may explain what illness your baby has, and with your nerves already frazzled, by the time you get home and feed the baby you may realize you have more questions. Not emergency questions that warrant a call to the service, but questions nonetheless. If you're like us, naturally the doctor's office will already be closed for the night by the time you want more information.

It can be helpful to have a human Google—a more experienced parent whose kids have already survived every known illness. A human Google is no substitute for a medical professional, but is not meant to be. She (or he) is meant to be there for you when you need someone to reassure you that your child is going to be okay.

If you don't have a human Google, going online can often help. Communities like Urban Baby will always have someone online to answer your questions at two in the morning.

Baby reference books written by M.D.s can also be very reassuring. They're well indexed, so you can find what you're looking for even if your hands are shaking. We like the AAP book *Symptoms from Birth to Five*. It has clear photographs, which is handy if you're looking up a rash or something topical, as well as checklists to go through for symptoms. We also like *Your Newborn Head to Toe*, by Dr. Cara Natterson.

If you're ever worried about anything, always call your pediatrician, day or night. Don't worry about waking somebody up. Doctors expect these calls. No book, website, or friend can replace medical advice from the doctor who knows your baby.

HEALTH CARE COSTS

Heath care costs are skyrocketing out of control, and in some cities you may find that your pediatrician of choice doesn't accept your insurance (or *any* insurance). Yet because babies must have regular checkups, paying out of pocket is not only horribly expensive, but downright scary in case of a catastrophic illness or injury.

If your employer does not pay for health care, go to this website for more information about how to insure your child: www.insurekidsnow.gov.

tip: *No hospital can turn away a sick or injured baby, even if you are uninsured. If you go for a non-emergency situation, however, be prepared for a very long wait.*

from DR. NANCY SNYDERMAN

Search online at the American Academy of Pediatrics (www.aap.org), the Centers for Disease Control (www.cdc.gov), the Mayo Clinic (www.mayoclinic.com), and other websites affiliated with major hospitals or professional medical associations before driving yourself into panic mode.

IT'S TIME TO GET A NEW PEDIATRICIAN WHEN...

> The doctor is consistently and chronically late.

> The staff is rude or unhelpful.

> You don't feel as if your concerns are being taken seriously.

> You're rushed through appointments.

> The doctor's bedside manner when doing something unpleasant (such as giving shots) is not kind and sympathetic.

> It takes too long to get called back when you need to speak to someone after office hours.

> It takes too long to get an appointment. One practice we know has a message on their answering machine saying, "Sorry, but we're having trouble with our telephone system. If you don't get a call within an hour, please call back." New parents might not know that they've had that message on their machine for years.

> You don't think the toys in the office have been cleaned since your last appointment.

tip: You are entitled to copies of your baby's medical records. You do not need to give your old doctor an explanation if you decide to leave.

Mary Ann: I kept putting off finding a new pediatrician because my girls were pretty healthy. But my pediatrician and staff kept me waiting forever, and made me feel like a criminal for delaying the start of my daughter's immunization. Finally, after a visit when Arabella was covered with a horrible red rash, the nurse practitioner told me, "If the rash goes away, great. If it turns purple and starts to blister, rush her to the hospital because it's an emergency!"

Well, the rash went away but my rage at this ridiculous advice did not. When the rash returned with a vengeance a month later, I took Arabella to a new pediatrician, who had office hours on a Sunday. He told me she had hives, was basically allergic to being sick, and would respond to antihistamines. After one day on Benadryl she was rash-free. Even more amazing—this wonderful doctor called me back numerous times to check on the baby. Now that is what a pediatrician should do.

DOCTOR'S WAITING ROOM

One doctor came highly recommended, so we checked her out—and were shocked to find a cramped, unappealing waiting room, with a scruffy carpet and dingy paintings. Worse: There were no toys or amusing things to look at (like a fish tank). What kind of pediatrician doesn't care about making the (long) wait more fun for kids and less stressful for parents? The kind of pediatrician you won't be seeing.

MANAGING THE WAIT

> Even if your pediatrician's office is loaded with toys and playhouses, always bring a nice assortment of your own toys and books. This will give your baby something to play with in the exam room (and you won't have to worry about other babies' germs).
> Always wash your baby's hands as well as yours before and after seeing the doctor. Use a hand sanitizer if it's hard to get to a sink. And if you're like us, make sure not to put your baby down anywhere in the doctor's office, hospital, or emergency room. Wipe everything down first or don't touch it at all. Let your baby see what you're doing so it becomes a habit for all as your kids get older.
> If your child's sick, coughing a lot, or has a rash, or you fear your child has a communicable illness, be a responsible parent and tell the receptionist right away. Keep the baby as isolated from the other patients as possible. This might mean you need to check in, then go back outside and sit in the car until you're alerted that a room is available.

CHOOSING AND USING THERMOMETERS

Rectal thermometers are the most accurate, but try convincing most squeamish moms to use one on a squirming, fussy baby and you'll be greeted with either a blank stare or wicked laughter. Most moms we know are happy with ear thermometers, although they can be slightly inaccurate—bring yours to the pediatrician's office and ask the doctor to show you how to use it correctly.

We love temporal thermometers. Test one on yourself first, and you'll see how easy it is to use. Slide the thermometer in a reasonably straight line across your forehead, midway between the eyebrows and the upper hairline, and the reading takes only seconds. It's a brilliant invention, and a wonderful shower gift.

USE TECHNOLOGY TO HELP YOUR BABY GET BETTER

Alicia: How many times have we been to the doctor and said, "Well, I called because last night his cough wouldn't stop," or "His face was so red and blotchy an hour ago" . . . and then of course the baby didn't cough and his face wasn't red anymore?

Technology can be wonderful when you're trying to explain a number of conditions to your doctor that the doctor can't see or hear when you come in. Try using a digital camera, a cell phone, or a tape recorder if it's just a cough, to capture that rash, cough, or allergic reaction and bring it to the doctor. It's especially useful for comparisons.

TEETHING PAINS

Teething pains are often mistaken for illness, but bear in mind that cutting teeth really does hurt, often causing disrupted nights and misery for both baby and mommy. Drooling and wanting to chew on wood or any old electrical cord lying around is usually a pretty good indication that teeth are about to erupt, so brace yourself for the fun to come.

> Frozen mini-bagels are good for gumming, but take them away once they get soft enough to swallow.
> Many parents swear by Hyland's Teething Tablets (homeopathic).
> You can give appropriate doses of baby Tylenol.
> Freeze a wet washcloth and let the baby chew on that.
> For babies old enough to sit in high chairs, try baby frozen peas and small wild blueberries.
> Get colorful teethers that have liquid in them and come in designs like butterflies or fish. We kept several in the fridge so there was always a cool one ready when needed. You may want to stash a few at the homes you regularly visit, like Grandma and Grandpa's.
> As for brushing, your pediatrician will no doubt tell you to start wiping off the gums and teeth with a damp cloth once they start

to come in. Do we know one mom on this planet who would ever do that? No. But it is a good idea to get a very soft baby toothbrush and at least pretend to use it once in a while, to get your baby used to the sensation. Let the baby watch you brush your own teeth, too, and make it sound like it's lots of fun.

> Once there are enough teeth to start brushing regularly, never use fluoridated toothpaste on any baby under the age of two. It can discolor teeth, and fluoride is not meant to be swallowed.

ABOUT VACCINATIONS

Vaccinations are controversial; actually, Alicia and I disagree about vaccine schedules, so we usually avoid talking about them. There are those convinced that certain shots, namely the MMR (Measles-Mumps-Rubella), have a clear link to autism, with mostly anecdotal evidence; and there are those who dispute this, backed up by controlled studies that are often difficult for the layperson to understand. It's up to you to speak candidly about this with your pediatrician, talk to other moms, weigh the pros and cons, and do some research. Be sure to go only to reputable websites for your information, as there is a lot of quack medical advice floating around out there, and some of it can be dangerous. And even if the autism/vaccine theory is someday proven to be legitimate (for now, there is no scientific proof), there is no disputing that vaccinations have saved countless children from early death due to diseases.

Whatever you believe, be aware that many school districts mandate proof of vaccines before your child can be enrolled, save for medical reasons (such as an egg allergy, as most vaccines are cultured in eggs) or philosophical or religious reasons (which some school districts will not accept), so this is an issue that can't be avoided.

Even if you wholeheartedly endorse vaccinations, as most medical professionals do, it's a nightmare to have to hold your baby down and know the baby is going to be screaming a minute later. (We can always tell who's getting a shot when we're waiting in the pediatrician's office, as there's a moment of silence followed by hysterical screaming.)

Some pediatricians will recommended, if the baby's old enough, to predose with Tylenol before the appointment or wait two hours after the shot. You should also ask what kind of side effects to expect. Some babies have no problems, while others may get flu-like symptoms or fevers. In very rare cases there can be serious complications from some vaccines. Because babies' responses to vaccines are unpredictable, you might want to schedule the shots for a Friday, in case your baby doesn't feel well the next day. This way, you know you'll be home to soothe your cranky baby.

Mary Ann: One of the reasons I switched pediatricians was because I was tired of having to defend my decision to wait to vaccinate. When Zuri-elle was two and I started her vaccinations, she got each shot individually. She had to endure more shots, but if she had a reaction I'd know the cause. This was a compromise that worked for me.

About Vaccinations
By DR. NANCY SNYDERMAN

I'm a big believer in childhood vaccines, which I think are one of the greatest scientific breakthroughs ever. It's easy to forget what it was like to watch children die of polio, measles, and whooping cough. There is no science to support a link between vaccines and autism. Not vaccinating your children puts them at risk. It is imperative to know that vaccinations are one of the best and most effective tools you have to keep your children safe. Contrary to some popular opinions, vaccines are actually intelligently thought-out, based on research by physicians and scientists who know what happens to a child's developing immune system. The amount of actual protein in a shot is smaller than a flake of dust. This knowledge has led to the specific schedules for all the shots. I know it concerns some parents that there are so many required shots now, but there are simply more vaccines available to fight childhood illnesses. Some of these vaccines require multiple doses in order to become fully effective.

The Centers for Disease Control have an excellent website with detailed information about vaccinations at www.cdc.gov.

> **from DR. TANYA BENENSON**
>
> I strongly believe in immunizations. They work by "herd immunity," so we are protected by those immunized around us. If people don't get immunized, we lose that protection.

YOUR BABY'S FIRST COLD

Having a cold is no fun, and we panicked when the sneezes started flying. Was it our fault? Did we take our baby for a walk and stand next to someone who sneezed all over her? Did we forget to wash our hands? Did the baby get a chill? Believe us when we say that if your baby is fussy and miserable, you're going to be miserable, too.

Don't beat yourself up if you're on a plane and the only person coughing and sneezing is sitting right behind you, and then, naturally, your baby gets a runny nose or a cough. There's really nothing you can do about it. Babies get colds—and become fussy when their sweet little noses are stuffed up. Using a baby-sized bulb syringe (not the kind that point straight out, but the flatter ones with a stop line) to suck out mucus from their noses works like a charm, but your baby is unlikely to find it a charming experience.

COPING WITH THE COMMON COLD

> Germs are everywhere, and it's usually not a catastrophe to expose your child to the great outdoors, to city life, and to other people. With our first babies, we made sure that the pacifier was always sterilized properly if it fell out. Now, our cleaning method is more like running water or a little spit.

> You can minimize exposure to colds by washing your hands frequently. Have tissues handy. Know that colds come and go, but they never go soon enough.

> Avoid dry air in your home. Use a humidifier at night if your little one is stuffed up. If they need some extra TLC, we like to put the baby in the bathroom (on a bouncy seat or in daddy's arms) while we're in the shower. The steam will help loosen baby's mucus.

> Use saline drops or a spray like Baby Simply Saline, available at local drugstores. It helps to add moisture in those cute little noses before sucking out the not-so-cute buckets of snot.

> Babies scream, cry, and thrash around when their noses are getting sucked out, so it helps to have another pair of hands.

> Keep a bottle of hand sanitizer near the door, and make a point of using it when visitors arrive. They might want to use it, too. Moisturizing Hand Sanitizer by Susan Brown's Baby (susanbrownsbaby.com) is great. It doesn't dry out your hands, plus the packaging is adorable.

from ▶ **DR. NANCY SNYDERMAN**

Cold and flu medications are not safe in children under the age of six and are ineffective anyway. Stick to ibuprofen and acetaminophen to bring down a fever (never aspirin). A steamy shower and mild percussion on a baby's back can also help.

COLD ALERT

It sounds simple, but many moms forget to do this: If you've scheduled a playdate and your baby wakes up with a cold, call the other mom right away. Some moms will be okay about keeping the date; others will freak if you show up with a baby who has a runny nose. Nothing's worse than fearing your own baby will get sick because your friend forgot to tell you about Junior's sneezing fits. By the time the babies are near each other, it's usually too late.

AN UNUSUAL USE FOR BREAST MILK, A.K.A. STUFFY NOSES AND EYE GOOP— THE BREAST REMEDY

Mary Ann: I am one of nine children, and after my mom had her third baby (me), she became a breastfeeding addict. She insists—and my pediatrician agreed—that goopy eyes will clear up right away if you put a few drops of breast milk in them, and first colds will go away too if you put a bit of breast milk in the baby's nose. Let me tell you, I laughed at first, but these techniques worked wonders on my girls. Although my husband did look at me a little strangely when he walked in and I had my nipple dripping milk into Zurielle's eye!

GETTING THOSE MEDS INTO YOUR BABY

It's tricky giving babies medicine, but sometimes it has to be done. Ask your pediatrician to show you how. We use a dispensing syringe, held in one hand while your other hand props open the baby's mouth, to gently dribble the medicine along the side of the baby's cheek.

tip: A nifty trick is to dribble the medicine in, and then gently blow on your baby's face. It causes babies to swallow. Try doing this before a feeding, when babies are hungry and more likely to open their mouths. Or you can give them a pacifier and then slowly squirt the medication in right as they're sucking away.

If your baby is bottle fed, and always drinks a certain amount of formula at feedings, ask your pediatrician if it's okay to put the medication directly into the bottle. This can backfire, though, if your baby suddenly decides not to drink it all up and you have no idea how much of the meds have been ingested. It's better to put the medication in a small amount of formula or breast milk to ensure it's swallowed.

tip: *One great new invention is the Medibottle. It has a built-in medicine dropper so sick kids can sip their medicine along with the breast milk or formula, and voilà! Medicine's gone! It's only $15 and can be found at www.savibaby.com.*

If your baby hates medicine and spits it out or throws it up, speak to your pediatrician about suitable techniques for administering medicine. Some pain medication comes in suppositories, which work extremely fast. (Be prepared for some screaming when you insert them, but at least you know the baby is getting an accurate dose.)

tip: *Ask your pharmacist for nonstaining medications, if available. Some medicines come in lurid colors that will stain your clothes and bedding. Or put your baby in the sink or baby bathtub when you brace yourself for the ordeal.*

SICK AND HURT BABIES: WHEN TO PANIC— AND WHEN NOT TO

Mary Ann: I'll never forget Zurielle's first Christmas as we flew from Tulsa to Montreal. She looked so cute in her little pink dress. But as I was leaving the plane I slipped in my bulky snow boots, and Zurielle, who was snuggled in the BabyBjörn, fell forward with me. She let out a terrifying wail as blood gushed from her forehead. I burst into hysterical tears—which, not surprisingly, made my daughter even more upset.

An ambulance and firefighters quickly arrived to take us to the emergency room. At that point, I knew that Zurielle just had a bad cut and this was not a life-threatening emergency—but it sure felt like it was!

Inside the ER, the doctor cleaned Zurielle's wound, squeezed it together, poured on super-glue (not stitches), placed a butterfly bandage on top, and said good-bye. And I learned a very important lesson: If your baby gets injured, you must do everything you can to remain calm. My panic made my daughter panic. Luckily, I was still breastfeeding, and that calmed her down quite quickly once I stopped sobbing. But if I had not gotten so upset, this incident would have been much less traumatic for both of us.

Before hitting the panic button, our rule is that if you're worried, call the doctor. Otherwise, you won't stop worrying. If something strikes you as unusual—your baby just doesn't look right, or act right—trust your instincts and get help.

That rule served me well one horrible day when both my girls came down with the same virus. They were puking, had diarrhea, and were just miserable. Arabella was only a few months old and soon became limp, unresponsive, and so pale she looked green. I rushed her to the ER. After treatment for dehydration, she was fine.

This scare happened at night, and I didn't want to wait till morning. Good thing that I trusted my gut, as dehydration is a huge killer in countries where intravenous fluids are not available. Tiny infants can become seriously dehydrated very quickly.

> **tip**: *If your baby is better by the time you get to the emergency room, don't turn around and go home. Have the baby checked out anyway. It's worth the waiting and the co-pay. No mom is ever sorry she took her sick baby to the ER. Mothers are sorry only if they don't go.*

> **tip**: *When you're packing to go to the ER, take your stocked diaper bag, toys, something for you to read or do when the baby sleeps, a cell phone to call for backup as any ER experience is extremely difficult to endure alone, and something for both of you to eat (if you aren't breastfeeding, bring several bottles). If the baby is in what seems to be critical condition, call 911 and let the paramedics handle it. They can triage the baby in the ambulance and begin treatment.*

If your diaper bag isn't stocked and ready to go, call a friend as you're running out the door—someone who can meet you at the hospital and bring the things you need. You're going to need a friend or family member to help you get through the ordeal anyway. In the ER, a shoulder to cry on is as important as a stocked diaper bag (and chocolate for Mommy—she's earned it).

from → DR. NANCY SNYDERMAN

A good indicator for dehydration is the number of wet diapers. A newborn should have 8 to 12 a day.

Another indicator for dehydration in a baby is the pinch test. If you pinch the baby's skin and the skin stays up and doesn't go back right away, that is a positive sign that your baby needs fluid fast—and that warrants a call to your pediatrician or a visit to the emergency room.

Surviving a Medical Scare

If your baby needs surgery, it's hard not to panic. My son needed a hernia operation when he was barely two months old. I had to watch my tiny little love being taken into the operating room, surrounded by huge metal equipment, and the anesthesia being administered with that plastic cup going over his face. I watched him cry and fight it and then go limp. And then I was asked to leave the room.

Bottom line: Arlo came out of it amazingly well; babies recover from surgery incredibly fast. Arlo was back to himself by the end of the day, and his hernia was completely repaired. But it took *me* a lot longer to recuperate!

—Claudia David Heitler

When my daughter Maya was six months old, she started tilting her head to one side. She had torticollis, which basically means "head tilt." Silly me went on the Internet, only to find tons of scary information—including a walkathon for torticollis kids. I was beside myself.

We took Maya to all sorts of specialists, none of whom had an answer—she was perfectly fine otherwise. Finally, our team of doctors advised us to have an MRI done, so when Maya was ten months old, I had to watch doctors strap her to a gurney and put her to sleep. There is nothing worse than watching your child immobile like that.

In the end, Maya outgrew the tilting and received a clean bill of health. No one could figure out why it happened.

Bottom line: Sometimes what you think is a major medical disaster . . . isn't. Panicking and obsessively Googling are not going to help you—they'll only make you more anxious than you are already.

—Rachel Burstein

My son had seizures when he had fevers; his first came when we were in a mall. One minute he was sitting on a bench; the next, he had fallen off and passed out, eyes rolled back and foam coming out of his mouth. The ambulance took too long to arrive, so we drove him to the nearest hospital. He was taken care of and released that evening and tested for any lasting effects on his brain. All was well.

Bottom line: When you suspect a fever in a very young infant, call your pediatrician for advice. I use tepid wet cloths as a cool-down. Remain calm so you can concentrate—you can cry afterward, when the baby is sleeping soundly.

—Melissa Lonner

When I was pregnant with Jake, I remember my doctor saying, "Boy, he has a really strong heartbeat." In fact what he had was a murmur that was rushing the blood through more strongly. It turned out he was born with a congenital heart defect and needed heart surgery at three weeks, at one year, and at five years old.

Bottom line: You learn very quickly that you're willing to do things for your kids that you would never do for yourself. I fought the health insurance system. I fought doctors. One good thing I learned, and that Jake learned, is to let go of the fear. I believed he would be okay. Once he got through that, I knew he could get through anything.

—Jean Chatzky

One day, I put five-month-old Cody on one of those little cloth rockers on the kitchen counter, turned to feed our puppies, and heard the sound no parent ever wants to hear—the thud. I thought I'd killed my baby. We spent all day long at the hospital, as he had a major concussion. I was devastated, and told myself, I do not deserve this child. The next day he was fine, thank God, and I told Regis about it on the air. After work, I stopped in the fish market to pick up dinner, and this woman walked over to tell me she'd dropped hers on his head the day she brought him home, and he was fine. But I still felt terrible.

—Kathie Lee Gifford

I remember feeling terrible the first time Ben rolled off the couch. It was nerve-racking, but that wasn't the only time he bumped his head as an infant. Our country house had a kitchen island that had pots hanging overhead. My husband, Richard, was playing a little game with Ben and threw him up in the air, and he hit the pots . . . boink! We were so upset, but then when there was no lasting damage (Ben is now a college student), we realized babies are pretty resilient.

—Meredith Vieira

CHAPTER SEVEN

Gearing Up: What You'll Need

A friend of ours likes to joke that the must-haves for baby gear are very simple: a Phillips screwdriver to open the battery compartments of all the toys that will soon be driving you crazy; rechargeable batteries plus their charger; a drawerful of regular batteries, as you'll be too tired to remember to charge up the rechargeable batteries; and a sharp pair of scissors to cut the plastic off the clamshell packaging on all the toys that will also be driving you crazy when you can't find the batteries.

Seriously, though, babies have simple needs. You might *want* the super-chic stroller or the designer label diaper bag, but your baby won't. When it comes to gear, all the baby wants do to is puke, pee, or poop all over the new object the second it's delivered to your doorstep.

The way to manage what can quickly become unmanageable is to make two lists. Itemize what you really need on one list, and then make a wish list on the other (and give this to the grandparents). Just don't go crazy. Babies managed to thrive for thousands of years without off-road-capable strollers, 400-thread-count crib sheets, and a closet full of adorable clothes they'll outgrow before you cut the tags off.

SETTING UP THE NURSERY

Cribs

Alicia: For the first three months of your baby's life, the only furniture you need is a bassinet or Pack 'n Play for sleeping. In fact, you'll probably never use the baby's room except to host all the visiting company. My girl-friend Ginny bought me a Moses basket that never left my bedside those first four months. I'd even tote it from room to room so that Jack was sleeping nearby as I folded laundry, made dinner, or showered. Once Jack grew too long to sleep in it, we moved him to the crib.

While wide-eyed, pregnant, and in full nesting mode, I bought a beautiful Italian crib because I thought Jack needed "the best" crib around. Sure, that $600 was a good investment that ended up lasting without a scratch through two kids, but in hindsight, that kind of expense was totally unnecessary.

> tip: *Don't worry about buying a crib with a drawer that fits underneath, because you'll never use it, and it will most likely fall off the crib.*

Changing Tables

Because of space and money, Mary Ann and I never had changing tables. If you do have the room and budget for a changing table, look at one that's multipurpose, such as a hutch with storage. Otherwise any old bureau will do, as long as the surface area is large enough to hold your baby and the necessary items (diapers, wipes, cream, et cetera) safely, and is a good height for you so you don't have to bend over too much to clean up the mess.

Diaper Pails

See the section on Diaper Disposal in Chapter 3 for more information.

Rocking Chair/Glider

These are great for breastfeeding your baby, but rocking chairs and gliders aren't small. If space is tight, be sure to measure your room before making the investment.

Room to Grow

By ELIZABETH MAYHEW

TODAY Contributing Editor and Lifestyle Expert

Reach for the sky.

When decorating their rooms, most people don't maximize wall space—especially vertical wall space. The nursery is no exception. As little as babies are, they have a lot of paraphernalia, and as they grow, so does their stuff.

Look for furniture that reaches as high—and as wide—as possible to provide you with maximum storage space. Modular shelving like the Elfa system (available at the Container Store; www.containerstore.com) allows you to rearrange and reconfigure your shelving as your child grows. Fill shelves with bins or baskets to keep items organized.

Put your toys away.

Knowing where things go and how to put them away is an important lesson for kids and parents. You need to invest in a closet or shelving system to help get—and stay—organized. (Remember, it's about finding what you need when you need it.) With toys, I like to group like items together—stuffed animals in one bin, Legos in another, and so on. I also like to label the bins (just as teachers do in their classrooms). You can draw a picture of the items in the bin as well as the name of the toy. Make sure you store items that you don't want your children to get their hands on up high and, conversely, items they have free rein over down low. You will see that as a child grows, so does his or her collection of toys. I like to periodically go through the toys and encourage my children to part with the ones they no longer play with. Learning to edit is a good lesson for them, especially if their toys are being passed on to those less fortunate.

Realize it's just a stage you are going through.

When purchasing baby furniture, look for items that convert, such as a crib that converts into a toddler bed, a changing table that converts into a dresser, or a play table that converts into a desk. Your investment will be rewarded twofold.

Rock the night away.

Make sure you have a comfortable chair in your nursery for those late-night feedings. Instead of a glider, I chose an upholstered club chair that would work in my daughter's room well after she passed the rocking stage. Look for chairs with easy-to-clean slipcovers—once the baby arrives, they will need to be washed periodically.

Don't pick sides yet.

Whether you are having a boy or a girl, I suggest painting your walls a neutral shade, giving you the flexibility to easily change accessories and bedding. Some of my favorite neutral wall colors are Benjamin Moore's Bird's Egg (a light blue, #2051-60), Potpourri Green (#2029-50), Hawthorne Yellow (#HC-4), and Early Morning Mist #1528 (a great basic gray-tinted beige). Use paint with a Satin finish—it will be easier to wipe away crayon streaks! Also look for Benjamin Moore's Eco Spec line of "green" paints that are less harmful to the environment.

Rug-a-buy baby.

Whether you have wall-to-wall carpet or hardwood floors, it's a good idea to have an area rug in your child's bedroom. Not only do area rugs provide a soft, cushioned place on the floor to play, but they are easy to clean and replace if need be. I particularly like the inexpensive cotton-striped rugs from www.dashandalbert.com, and, because they have no pile, they do not absorb dust and dirt. Also check out the modular floor tiles from www.flor.com; you can customize the color and size of your rug and if one tile gets stained, you can easily replace it.

Don't forget Captain Hook.

Hang hooks low so that, in the future, toddlers can reach them. It's an easy way for them to hang up costumes, hats, backpacks, towels, and coats. Look to hang hooks on empty wall spaces and backs of doors.

Favorite Sources

www.potterybarnkids.com
www.containerstore.com
www.moderntots.com
www.stacksandstacks.com
www.target.com
www.giggle.com
www.store.babycenter.com
www.landofnod.com
www.babygizmo.com

GETTING ORGANIZED

I had *no* idea what a big mess a baby can make. My son has unzipped (and actually been inside) every couch cushion. He has taken the pieces of paper out that identify the contents of our filing cabinets. So, after a lot of time at the Container Store, my new system is this:

> Every single thing has a place in our house (hence the containers).
> If we haven't used it for a while, it's gone.
> If I can't put every single thing in its place in one day, then we have too much stuff. Then other things need to go.
> Not all toys need to be out at once. I rotate toys in and out of other containers in the garage, and keep some in a closet that only I can access (mostly because they have a lot of pieces).

It's still a work in progress, but it seems to be working.

—Claudia David Heitler

SENSATIONAL SHOWER GIFTS

While that size-newborn punk rocker T-shirt might look awfully cute (until it's covered in spit-up), we're firm believers in letting the other shower guests go for cute—we go for the kind of practical gifts moms will truly appreciate and, most of all, *use*.

Great Baby Gifts to Give

> A few months of diaper deliveries. One of our co-workers was expecting twins, and Mary Ann's gift was a case of her favorite swaddler diapers.
> A fully stocked first-aid kit.
> Save the seriously cute stuff for when the baby's older than six months. Don't think you need to stick with newborn or three-to-six–month sizes, either. One of our all-time favorite shower gifts was a set of baby pajamas in six different sizes.
> A bassinet (for moms with space). Once the baby outgrows it, it makes an ideal doll bed.

> If you or the mom-to-be has a weakness for monogrammed items, be sure you know exactly what the child will be called (which is not necessarily his or her first name). Monogrammed items are not returnable.

> Handmade coupons offering services you provide when mommy needs them most (a few hours of babysitting, cleaning, errand-running—you name it).

> Your favorite (or your husband's favorite) childhood books.

> A sexy (but comfortable) robe or kimono for mommy.

> A vibrating bouncy chair.

> A digital camera or a video camera. Alicia's favorite is the Flip Video Camcorder that doesn't require tapes or DVDs. All you have to do is aim, shoot, and upload.

> A sling or front carrier. It not only keeps mommy's hands free, but helps soothe the baby as he or she is carried close to the mother's heart.

> A Mommy Survival Kit.

Alicia: The Mommy Survival Kit might not be a very sexy gift, but it's *very* necessary once new moms leave the hospital. Most moms never talk about all the things you'll really need to survive those first few weeks post-partum, such as pain relievers and hemorrhoid creams (extra strength), sanitary napkins (with wings), nipple cream and nursing pads (Lansinoh), and a nursing pillow (My Breast Friend). Camouflaged with a little cellophane, colorful tissue paper, and some curly ribbon, this gift will leave guests in gales of laughter and you'll be the hit of the party. Just think of the conversations it'll spark!

Baby Gifts Not to Give

> New mothers are going to get enough really nice blankets to swaddle their babies from here to the moon. And the more they get, the guiltier they'll feel for not using them.

> Stuffed animals are a smothering hazard and can't be used in a crib. Though they're adorable, they aren't practical for babies. Wait till the baby's older.

> Anything that requires assembly more difficult than opening the box.

> Anything that needs batteries, unless it makes music.

THE "WELCOME TO THE MOMMY CLUB" UNMENTIONABLES PACK

When the baby arrives, you deserve only the best—a quick jaunt to Kmart or Target for granny pants, a.k.a. disposable briefs. These are cotton underpants you wouldn't be caught dead in on date night with your husband, but you're sure going to need them post-birth. The trick is to buy one size larger than your pre-maternity size, and have them be as tight as possible without causing discomfort—the better to hold you in, my dear. There's no guilt (just a huge sigh of relief) throwing those suckers out once your six weeks of recovery are over (and your belly is no longer looking quite so large).

POST-PARTUM ESSENTIALS

> Try to keep as much of the mesh hospital underwear (and maxi pads) as you can.
> If you really want to live like a queen, buy disposable skivvies from www.wearonce.com. They help keep everything tucked in and will start you thinking that maybe one day you'll get your figure back.
> Lansinoh ointment (for applying to the nipples after breastfeeding).
> Lansinoh disposable breast/nursing pads. (Alicia bought them in bulk.)
> At least three breastfeeding bras. Buy more when you figure out which ones you like and that function best.
> "Soothies" Gel Pads (these should always be stored in the refrigerator).
> A good lip gloss and hair clips. Your hair will always be up and your face devoid of makeup in those first weeks, so these things will keep you looking fresh.

THE FIRST THREE MONTHS—GEAR YOU NEED

> A Moses basket or some sort of portable, movable sleeping bassinet for your baby.
> The Arm's Reach Co-Sleeper.
> A diaper bag. Shop around to find one you really like.
> A breast pump.

- The My Breast Friend Strap-On Breastfeeding Pillow, which is great for the on-the-go mom. The Boppy also works well.
- A portable medical kit: nose aspirator, thermometer, nail clippers, Milicon gas relief, and fever reducer (non aspirin).
- A snap-and-go stroller, where the car seat snaps right into this frame of a stroller.
- A bottle and baby food warmer—faster than boiling water to heat frozen breast milk or (gasp!) sticking it in the microwave. Just stick frozen bagged breast milk into this warmer and minutes later it's ready to go.
- Various shapes and sizes of pacifiers. (You will not know which one your little one favors, so you might have to go through a few.)
- Various shapes and sizes of bottles. We both used the Playtex drop-in system/nurser for a while, until Mary Ann switched to BornFree bottles. There are also plenty of BPA-free plastic bottles on the market, and some of our mommy friends even switched to glass. Everything old is new again.
- A bouncy seat. They're basically all the same, so pick the one with the songs that won't drive *you* crazy.

AGE THREE TO SIX MONTHS—GEAR YOU NEED

- A front carrier, like the BabyBjörn (Mary Ann's favorite).
- The Crib Mobile—Symphony in Motion.
- Colorful shakers and squeeze toys (for the stroller, and to stick in the diaper bag).
- The Bumbo baby seat. It goes wherever you go in the house—but must only be used on a floor.
- A play mat.
- A crib, as the baby will have outgrown the Moses basket or bassinet if you used one.
- You can never have enough onesies.
- Stroller straps or clips.

AGE SIX MONTHS TO ONE YEAR—GEAR YOU NEED

- A high chair. Pick one that's easy to wipe down.
- If space is tight, buy a lightweight portable high-chair seat

with a high back and a tray. These easily tie on to a grown-up chair.

> Teethers. Put them in the fridge and keep them on hand for those difficult days.
> An all-weather picnic blanket—especially if it has a built-in handle, so you can tote it around easily.
> Klean Kanteen makes a great reusable sippy cup that is BPA-free and eco-friendly.

MONITORING THE MONITORS

We live in small apartments, so monitors aren't neecessary, but if you have bedrooms on different floors they're very useful. They're also handy when visiting friends, if you want to enjoy some time outside in the yard while the baby is sleeping.

Paul Hochman's Monitor Pick: The Philips Baby Monitor with DECT Technology

Many parents have had this exciting moment: the gurgle of their baby's voice over the baby monitor replaced by somebody else entirely. Wireless baby monitors are a great way to keep tabs on your sleeping sweetie, but thanks to the proliferation of these devices in densely settled neighborhoods, sometimes you pick up your neighbors' noises, too.

The Philips baby monitor has "guaranteed zero interference," thanks to DECT (Digital Enhanced Cordless Telecommunication). You get a clear, un-interrupted connection, with zero interference between the baby's monitor and the parent's receiver. The technology even switches to one of sixty unused channels without interruption if it detects another device using the same channel. And for those who absolutely must know everything, the Philips baby monitor also remotely monitors your child's room temperature, plays five lullabies, and constantly confirms your continuing link to the baby's unit.

WALKING WITH YOUR BABY—STROLLERS AND CARRIERS

The stroller is one of the most important pieces of equipment you'll use, so take your time trying them out. You might be able to find them less expensively online, but you do need to push a few around in a baby store to get a feel for them. Some brands are highly touted, yet you might not like them or may find them hard to collapse or reopen.

> Ask your mom friends close to your height for recommendations. Those who are very tall or very short can have real problems pushing a stroller that's not adjustable.
> Think about everyone who'll be pushing the stroller. If your husband is much taller than you are, or your babysitter much smaller, the stroller that's easy for you to push will leave them with a permanent backache.
> If you travel a lot in a city like we do, portability is huge. Look for a stroller that's lightweight and, most of all, folds easily.
> If your baby likes to sleep in a stroller, look for one that fully reclines.
> Don't succumb to hype. Some strollers will make you faint from sticker shock. Your baby is not going to be endangered because you haven't spent four times the price of the durable yet inexpensive stroller on a designer name your snobby acquaintances insist is a must.

Alicia: The only exception to the Hype Factor rule is the Husband Vanity Factor. Strolling outside to show off our baby became one of my husband's favorite activities. He even used to clean the stroller's tires when he got home so he'd be stylish on the next stroll. I think he even Armor-Alled the tires for a while! He loved the attention, and I loved to get some time to myself when he was out strutting.

Paul Hochman's Stroller Picks

The BOB Revolution Stroller: The BOB is a smooth-riding, beautifully engineered running and hiking stroller that doesn't have the high price of some of the fashionable brands but is, frankly, much better built. The "revolution" in the BOB is in its 360-degree swiveling front-wheel design, which allows the parent pushing it to make quick turns without tipping the front of the stroller upward. The result is a stable, three-point ride for the baby. The BOB also made its name with its incredibly smooth feel in off-road or trail environments—hydraulic shocks and widely spread pneumatic (air-filled) wheels keep babies and toddlers insulated from bumps—and its ingenious fold-up design allows quick stowage in trunks, closets, and mud rooms. (www.bobgear.com)

Phil and Ted's Kiwi Explorer–for Two Kids: Phil and Ted's excellent adventure in product design has resulted in a stroller that has the narrow footprint of a single stroller (perfect for proper sidewalk and supermarket-aisle etiquette) but also has a cool double-decker design that turns it instantly into a double—for two toddlers, one toddler plus one infant, or, God help you, twins. It's also brilliant because it reclines flat, which is ideal for the baby. A ratcheting handlebar adjusts for parents of different heights, the wheels release with one touch (great for quick storage in the trunk), and a dual rear break keeps the thing under control. It handles up to eighty-eight pounds of smiling, burbling, mewling kidlets. (www.philandteds.com)

ABOUT CAR SEATS

When we left the hospital, we were so clueless that we struggled for ages, with the meter running, to attach the car seat base in a taxi and strap the belt around it, only to learn later that this is totally unsafe.

Car seats are not only required, but they can save your baby's life. Before you start shopping, check for ratings in *Consumer Reports*. Also, the American Academy of Pediatrics has a useful guide on its website: www.aap.org/family/carseatguide.htm. "The best seat is the one that fits your child's age and size, is correctly installed, fits well in your vehicle, and can be used properly every time you drive," they explain. "Don't decide by price alone. A higher price does not mean the seat is safer or easier to use."

In addition, they advise you to avoid used seats, especially if they have any cracks or missing parts, or if you don't know the seat's history; you can check the label for the date of manufacture or ask the manufacturer to find out how long they recommend using the seat. Do not use a seat without a label or one that's expired.

Car seat recalls can be scary. To find out about your model, call the manufacturer or contact either the Auto Safety Hotline at 888/DASH-2-DOT (888/327-4236) or the Consumer Product Safety Commission (www.cpsc.gov).

You must have a car seat in your car in order to leave the hospital, so I did a lot of research. At first I got a Graco infant car seat, and then the Britax Marathon, which is great as it can hold around sixty pounds. So far it's held up for four years.

The installation freaked me out, though, as I had no idea how to do it, so I went to my local fire department and they looked at it and said, "You know what, the guy who's really good at this is at the police department," so off I went. They installed it, explained how the three-point harness system worked, and showed me where you're supposed to put everything. That lesson was incredibly helpful, as I can now take the car seat in and out of the car myself.

—Natalie Morales

tip: Make a friend; save your sanity. Like Natalie, ask someone at the local police precinct or fire station to help install the car seat. In many states, these public servants have been trained to do these installations.

More About Car Seats

By PAUL HOCHMAN

TODAY Gear and Technology Editor

Child seat regulations vary from state to state (check those laws on your state's DMV website), but there is no dispute among experts at the National Highway Transportation Safety Administration or at the American Academy of Pediatrics: The safest place for any child under the age of twelve is in the backseat, in the center. In fact, the NHTSA says *all* kids should be in some kind of car seat or booster through eight years of age, eighty pounds, or up to four-feet-nine inches tall, whichever comes later. But remember: backseat, center, far away from all air bags.

For all children under one year or under twenty pounds (whichever comes later), a rear-facing infant seat/carrier is a must. The reason: If your little baby is facing forward in a crash, she does not have the neck strength to protect herself from whiplash, or worse. Facing backward means her head and neck are anchored and supported. Some of the more conservative folks in this world believe your child should be rear-facing until they're two, so when in doubt, play it safe.

My favorite car seats are "convertible." They make the list because, in addition to overall quality, they also convert; when your baby is old/large enough to turn forward, the car seat can be turned forward, too. In my view, they're worth the money.

Britax Marathon Convertible Car Seat

No, it's not cheap. But this American-made car seat is amazingly useful—it rear-faces for kids from five to thirty-five pounds and forward-faces until your child is sixty-five pounds. And, unlike most car seats, it has side-impact pads that adjust to the height of your child. No other manufacturer that I know of has that kind of arrangement. Plus, the straps and latches on this one are incredibly wide (so they don't twist) and easy to use. This is a big deal. I know: You're thinking, "Wait, don't lots of car seat makers make it easy for sleep-deprived parents to use their buckle systems?" Sadly, they don't. And here's another fun feature: a variety of seat cover choices. My favorite: Cowmoo-flage. (www.britaxusa.com)

Sunshine Kids Radian Convertible Car Seat

While the Radian is highly regarded by tons of reviewers (including this one), what I like about it is perhaps its simplest feature: It actually reclines, and it folds flat for storage or to fit in the overhead compartment of an airplane. This is another big deal, as many babies have an understandably difficult time falling asleep when they're sitting straight up. The Radian both rear-faces and forward-faces for kids from five to sixty-five pounds. (www.sunshinekidsbaby.com)

Evenflo Triumph Advance

For those who want to spend a little less but get top quality, this may be the best value out there—yes, there are fewer features, but there is a lot to recommend. First, it's both rear- and front-facing, so it will last from infancy until your child weighs fifty pounds. Plus, the impact-absorbing EPS foam that surrounds the interior is great (and mostly seen in more expensive models), and it's incredibly easy to adjust the harnesses for your child's growing height. Finally, a nice little head cradle keeps that bob-bob-bobbing of your kidlet's head to a nice minimum. (www.evenflo.com)

GEAR-SWAPPING

If other moms ask if you want their old stuff, *say yes!* Since babies grow so fast, they usually grow out of their clothing before they've had a chance to wear it out (or even wear it at all). The only exception, of course, are those garments that are stained beyond all recognition.

A great way to stock up on new or gently used baby gear is to have a Gear Swap Day. This way you can hang out with your mommy friends, relax in their company, and get rid of the super-cute outfit that's so super-cute you're super-sick of it, in exchange for something more practical, like booties or a sweater.

Alicia: Gear-swapping goes a long way toward shaving expenses and being green by recycling items that won't end up in landfills—plus it's fun to be part of something bigger. Tiki and Ginny Barber had their son AJ a year before I had Jack, and when AJ grew out of his stroller and car seat, Jack came along and Ginny loaned me those two items when I needed them most. When Jack outgrew them, I cleaned them up (my husband cleaned the tires), and we gave them back to Ginny, who'd just had Chason. When Chason outgrew them, along came Lucy!

That stroller and car seat took a licking by four kids yet they're still going strong. Right now, they're in storage waiting for one of us to have another kid. Did I just write that?

Hand-Me-Down Clothing
By CECILIA FANG WU

There's a famous Chinese legend that in certain Chinese villages, a long time ago, every time a baby was born the village women would sew together a patchwork quilt of one hundred pieces of old clothing (cut into squares or other shapes) to make a blanket for the new baby. They called it the 100 Wishes and 100 Years of Life quilt, and it would bring the baby luck.

There's also a lovely old Chinese saying that loosely translates as "A child who wears clothes handed down will grow up good." This really touched my heart, because it doesn't just mean "good" as in well behaved. The actual phrase means good in everything, and that the baby will grow up with all the prosperity, luck, health, wisdom, and morality of all the previous children who have worn the clothes. That means extra blessings for my newborn.

So I definitely take all hand-me-downs and used clothing from friends and family. No, it's not because I'm too cheap to buy my own child new clothes—he has a lot of those too—but because of what my mother taught me as I was learning to be a mother myself. And I call old clothes "wearable gifts of luck" for my little one.

CHILDPROOFING THE HOUSE

We know quite a few people who spent thousands of dollars to have their homes childproofed, but you don't have to go that far. All you have to do is get down on your hands and knees, and look at the world from the same position as a crawling baby.

> *tip: Childproofing is needed only when your baby is ready to crawl, although we recommend you do it long before then so you don't have to worry about it.*

> Get covers for all electrical outlets.
> Stash electrical cords out of sight.
> Put stoppers on doors.
> Put anything breakable away or on a high shelf.
> Make sure your television (or anything heavy) can't be pulled down.
> Place foam around sharp table corners.
> Put childproof fasteners or a lock high up on all doors in your

kitchen and/or bathroom where the cleaning or other toxic products are stashed.

> Hide all pills (including vitamins), medications, and boxes of matches in high, inaccessible-to-babies places.

> Get into the habit of cooking on the back burners, and always keep pot handles angled away from the floor.

> Attach a safety cover to all toilets. Just be sure you know how to use it, because they're tricky. Sometimes you'll be desperate to pee, and just can't get the dang thing open. The goal is to avoid using the baby wipes on yourself.

> If you have a staircase, get a good gate installed and figure out how to use it before your baby starts crawling.

> It's never too early to start teaching boundaries to babies. This doesn't mean you should keep your favorite crystal figurine on the coffee table and expect your baby to understand "Hands off!", but babies can begin to understand when you say, "Hot! Don't touch!" and mime blowing on the hot item.

Our kids quickly learned that when Mommy was cooking in the kitchen, they were not allowed to come in. Then we didn't have to worry about knives slipping or food falling or soup boiling over. When we weren't cooking, our babies could crawl in and open the lower cabinets, banging on the pots and pans to their hearts' content.

tip: *If you're about to have your second child, check every single toy you have, as your older child may already have progressed to toys that are choking hazards for babies. If you don't want to throw the toys away (or give them away to a charity or to friends), hide them in a closet until your baby is past the choking-hazard stage.*

And remember, babies are going to fall even if you have your entire house covered with foam.

YOU CAN'T GET RID OF GERMS, BUT YOU CAN DETOX YOUR ENVIRONMENT

One easy way to ensure your baby stays as healthy as possible is to have a chemical-free (and, of course, a smoke-free) home. Make sure your environment is as detoxified as it can be—which is easy enough to do with the new generation of nontoxic cleaners that are good for the environment and a lot better for your kids. If any cleansing product makes your eyes water, what do you think it will do to your baby?

Baby Tech for New Parents
By PAUL HOCHMAN
TODAY Gear and Technology Editor

> **Griffin Evolve iPod Wireless Speaker System:** The insidious enemy of any sleepy parent is the creaking floor, which inevitably squeaks when the parent is inches from the nursery door—one peep and the baby's wide awake (and howling). Griffin's Evolve iPod wireless speaker system allows you to put soothing music into your nearly dozing infant's nursery without entering the room. The connection between your iPod and the speakers is wireless and works up to 150 feet away. So you can sit in the living room while the speakers receive the tunes in the nursery and gradually turn the tunes down as your child drifts off to sleep.

> **Apple iMac Personal Computer:** Other than on Halloween, more people make home movies around the birth of their child than at any other time in their lives. The iMac makes that moviemaking incredibly simple, even for people who've never made movies before. Press "play". Can you say "Spielberg"?

> As a video bonus, the iMac has a built-in camera, which lets you introduce your new baby to the grandparents, no matter where they are in the world, for free, live. Just hold your new kidlet up in front of the computer's built-in video camera and say "oochie-koochie." The software is called iChat (included with all Macs), and in a matter of seconds, it lets you have live video conferences for free with any other Mac user.

> **Non-Mac Solution: The Logitech QuickCam Fusion Webcam:** If you don't have a Mac, you can share live pictures and videos of your baby with the Logitech QuickCam Fusion Webcam. It has an image sensor compensating for low light (avoiding that grainy look); and the way it clips to the computer, it can be situated at eye level, making you look more personal and natural—which is key when you're being streamed through the Internet.

Baby Basics

› **Pure Digital Portable Camcorder:** Your child has arrived, and so have the bills. The thought of shelling out $500 for a good camcorder is too much. Instead, the best deal on a good-quality video camera is the Pure Digital portable camcorder. To use it, press the red "record" button and point at the subject. That's it. When you're done shooting (it holds up to one hour of video on its built-in flash memory), press a button on the side of the camera and a spring-loaded USB connector pops out, allowing you to download the video directly to your computer by just plugging it in. No cables, no experience necessary. I recommend you spend the extra money on the 1- or 2-gig versions. The camcorder outputs decent quality, too—roughly that of a DVD—and even has an autofocus and 2x zoom. Simple, smart, easy.

› **Olympus SP-560 UZ Digital Still Camera:** There's a brand-new type of digital camera: the Ultrazoom. Ultrazooms are compact, but they have simple controls that let you manage your picture taking, and their fantastic zoom lenses let you get as close as two centimeters away (to focus on baby's eyes). The Olympus SP-560 UZ is the best of the bunch; it has easy controls, is light and compact, and has an amazing zoom lens that goes from 43mm to 480mm.

› **Asus Eee PC:** Slightly smaller than a notebook, this PC weighs less and is loaded with features. It's perfect for parents on the go who want to stay in touch with family without breaking the bank, as it has voice and video so you can join www.skype.com and communicate with other Skype users for free.

CHAPTER EIGHT

A Box Is Better than the Toy Inside: Playtime and Travel Time

As Mary Poppins said, "In every job that must be done, there is an element of fun!" You can turn anything into a game, which is why playtime with your baby should be fun and easy, and take place all day long. You don't need anything special—just you and your imagination.

Baby playtime doesn't have to be any more complicated than "games" like peek-a-boo, grab a mirror or rattle, pick up and drop the blocks, bang the pots and pans, push the button, chew on the book (chew on anything, actually), tickle the toesies, "Where Is Thumbkin" (or any body part), Mommy's off-key sing-along, and any other silly little thing you like to do. What's important about all these activities is that you're engaged with your baby, and you're both having fun. This is the best way for babies to learn.

One of our favorite games is called "Go Outside and Take a Walk." There's something about fresh air and looking at the sky that stimulates babies and holds their interest. This game is especially good for very small infants who are still facing you in the stroller. Keep a nice monologue going with your baby, even if you're just grabbing Cheerios off the shelf while grocery shopping.

Alicia: It's also quite therapeutic to constantly chatter about what's racing through your mind with your baby. Somehow I knew there was a deep understanding even though all I'd get in return was a very wet raspberry at the end of my confessionals. I'm sure I solved many of life's problems just by strolling and chatting with my baby.

tip: *One of the sweetest things about babies is how responsive they are to attention, and once they're able to grasp objects, they love examining them, mouthing them, dropping them, and then starting all over again. Constant repetition is how they learn, so while it may drive you a little batty to play peek-a-boo for an hour straight, just tell yourself that this is how your baby is learning about object permanence.*

BABY TALK IS GOOD TALK

We did a segment once about how babies learn, and discovered that those silly, repetitive sounds you make when talking to your baby actually stimulate brain development. That doesn't mean you should only speak baby talk, but try to mix the higher-pitched singsongs with complete sentences.

ESSENTIAL TOYS FOR BABIES

Babies don't need toys until they can pick up and grasp them. Don't push toys or stuffed animals near babies until they're ready to hold them. They can inadvertently become choking or smothering hazards. Here are some of the toys and objects our babies loved:

> A rattle.
> A plastic key chain they can manipulate into their mouth.
> A soft book or two they can chew on and you can throw in the washing machine.
> A sturdy mirror at eye level.
> A colorful play mat with different activities. They're great, as you can put them down anywhere that's flat and hard.
> Swinging chairs or bouncy chairs (with vibration).
> Firm cushions to crawl on.
> Small wooden blocks.
> Plastic containers and plastic cups—a huge hit for in and out of the bath.
> Empty coffee cans with the plastic lid firmly on top.
> Small pots and pans.

> Musical instruments like small maracas and shakers.
> Flashlights. We used to shine a light on the walls or ceiling and watch as our babies tried to catch the light. Kids don't tire of this for years.
> A stationary play center, which supports babies in an upright position in the middle and has a variety of tactile activities. They take up a lot of space and are costly, but moms love them because they keep babies occupied and safe so you can actually take a super-quick shower.

GOOD TOYS, BAD TOYS, AND TOTALLY RIDICULOUS TOYS

A good toy is something your baby can contentedly teethe on and play with over and over again without breaking.

A bad toy needs eight batteries and breaks after you step on it in the middle of the night. Babies do not need toys that run on batteries. (The only exception would be any toy that plays music.)

A totally ridiculous toy is hugely expensive, is never played with, can't be cleaned in the dishwasher or washing machine, and never lives up to claims that it'll make your little darling an instant genius.

"Educational games" certainly fall into that category. Babies do not need flash cards. They do not need drills. The only educational game they need is an attentive parent or caregiver who speaks to them all day long, sings songs, and laughs.

Alicia: I think it's just a mental game we parents play on ourselves. As long as the toy or video says "educational," somehow we think we're accomplishing two things at once—having fun and learning. But fun is already learning. If a toy brings a little smile, peace, or happiness to my child, where do I get more?

tip: *www.babyplays.com is an online toy rental program, like a Netflix for baby toys. Renting toys is an inexpensive way to see if your baby even likes them.*

Playtime is almost hands-down the most important contribution to your child's sense of nurturing, memories, and development.

I love toys. I love researching toys and buying toys. I feel like I know almost every toy on the market. My guides are the principles from the organization Campaign for a Commercial Free Childhood (www.commercialexploitation .org) and the book *Einstein Never Used Flashcards*.

I've also learned from watching my children that nature is the greatest toy—a fallen log, a big rock, a piles of leaves. I love open-ended toys, household items, and our imaginations. My favorite toys to buy are wooden toys from Plan Toys and Woody Click. My son also loves trains (the wooden tracks are great because the combinations are endless). I justify any purchases based on this criterion. I don't buy electronic toys or many plastic toys. So far, so good.

—Claudia David Heitler

DANGEROUS TOYS CAN KILL

The only good thing we can think of that has come out of the recent, worrying scares about toys contaminated with lead and other toxic ingredients is that parents are now more vigilant about what toys they're buying, and how and where they're manufactured.

Buy toys from reputable toymakers. Never buy cheap toys from vending machines or dollar stores, as they often do not meet U.S. safety standards.

tip: *All toys manufactured for the U.S. market must be clearly labeled on the front with the intended age of the child meant to play with them. Even if you know your baby has advanced motor skills, an eleven-month-old should never be playing with a toy labeled "Not Intended for Children Under 3," as it could be a choking hazard. The general rule is that no baby should have any toy or object to play with that can fit inside a toilet paper roll. Never give any toys with magnets to babies, as these are easy to swallow and can be lethal.*

Finding the Safest Toys and Products

By JANICE LIEBERMAN

TODAY Consumer Correspondent

We hear about these horrible "freak" accidents that occur from unsafe baby products. We worry about SIDS—sudden infant death syndrome. And we were all worried about the toys we let our kids put in their mouths after the recent lead scare. So how do you know what you are buying is safe?

Research. Before you purchase any new product, check with the Consumer Product Safety Commission to see if there have been any recalls. They also offer advice on items such as cribs. They advise against using crib bumpers or bedding because of the risk of suffocation. The distance between the slats in cribs is also regulated. Retailers sell safe cribs, so if you are accepting a hand-me-down you might want to check with the CPSC to see whether it meets their recommendations.

Consumer Reports also publishes their ranking of baby products, from cribs to strollers to high chairs.

Consult your mommy friends. They are a good resource when it comes to what works and what doesn't, and what does and doesn't seem safe. Share your insight and they will share theirs. Every mom loves to be an "expert" and will happily share her advice if asked, and sometimes if not!

TOY CLEANUP

Since babies tend to mouth everything they get their adorable little mitts on, everything also needs to be washable. Simply put all the plastic toys in the top rack of the dishwasher and anything cloth in the washer (and use hot water) on a regular basis.

Board books are great for reading time, but as babies like to chew on the corners, toss them if they start to fray. And wipe them down with a non-toxic, organic cleanser.

Stuffed animals should be thrown in the washer, too, as they are magnets for dust.

BABIES NEED DOWNTIME

As much fun as it is to play with babies, remember that they need downtime, too. Overstimulation can be as much of a problem as understimulation. Leave babies alone to amuse themselves. That doesn't mean you have to leave the room if you don't want to, but babies happily engaged on their play mat do not need you hovering. Babies are perfectly content to watch shadows dancing on the ceiling—if you let them.

Try to be realistic about who your baby is and what he or she is capable of as an infant. Your baby is not going to be guaranteed a spot at Harvard if you play Mozart all day long, or be the next Tiki Barber if you play roll-the-ball back and forth for hours on end. During the first year all you want is a healthy, growing, stimulated, engaged baby.

Pack 'n Play playards are a must for babies' downtime. (Back when our parents were growing up, these were called playpens.) Put your baby inside with some blocks or other safe objects, and then go do what you need to do. You can put the baby near you in the Pack 'n Play while you're in the kitchen or doing laundry.

BABY GENIUSES? BABY DVDS AND TV

The American Academy of Pediatrics is blunt about baby DVDs and TV shows. "Don't do it!" says their website, at www.aap.org/sections/media/ToddlersTV.htm. "These early years are crucial in a child's development. The Academy is concerned about the impact of television programming intended for children younger than age two and how it could affect your child's development. . . . Any positive effect of television on infants and toddlers is still open to question, but the benefits of parent-child interactions are proven. Under age two, talking, singing, reading, listening to music or playing are far more important to a child's development than any TV show."

This assessment merely fuels the controversy between those who think it's okay to pop in a baby DVD for twenty minutes to divert your cranky-due-to-teething ten-month-old (that's us) and those who claim the real genius behind the Baby Einstein series of DVDs for babies is the person who came up with the name.

Alicia: Baby DVDs were a lifesaver for me, especially when I was home during my maternity leave and wanted to cook a hot dinner every night. I'd put in a short DVD, and Jack amused himself while I made dinner in peace. Or sometimes I'd pop one in if Jack or Lucy got fussy or frustrated. I never used the DVDs as a babysitter, plonking the kids down in front of them for hours. And baby DVDs tend to be short (as babies have a short attention span). They're likely to tire of them before ever seeing the end.

Mary Ann: A happy compromise for me was to have my girls watch only DVDs in French or Spanish. *Comprende?*

READING TO YOUR BABY—IT'S NEVER TOO EARLY

We started reading to our babies as soon as they could sit up. It's one of the most important habits to get into as a new mom. Sitting with the baby on your lap and an open book—even if only for a few minutes to start with—will not only acclimate your baby to one of life's greatest pleasures, but make reading an important part of your daily routine.

tip: Ask your baby-shower guests to bring a book and inscribe it to the baby. Baby board books cost little more than greeting cards, and this is a wonderfully meaningful way to not only encourage reading but create a lovely library from friends.

MUSIC FOR BABIES THAT WE LOVE

Babies are captive audiences, and it's never too soon to introduce them to the music you love. Putomayo has great compilation CDs of music geared to children, from all over the world. We also like Laurie Berkner, The Wiggles, Dan Zanes, Justin Roberts, and the Dirty Sock Funtime Band.

Don't feel that you have to shell out for music compilations just for babies or small children, though. Whether you love the Beatles, Beastie Boys, or Beethoven, make music an integral part of your life.

MOMMY AND ME—CLASSES FOR BABIES

There's no shortage of mommy and baby classes, and they can be a great way to meet new moms. Check out your local YMCA or other community groups to see what's available in your area. Libraries and bookstores often have story time, and these are always free.

Babies often do well at music classes, as they love anything with rhythm. Older babies can hold on to and "play" instruments like maracas, tambourines, and bell sticks. Many classes can be expensive, though, and a total waste of money if your baby gets several colds and you have to miss a few weeks, or if the teacher turns out to be a dud, or if logistics get in the way (translation: You're too exhausted to leave the house and besides, it's sleeting outside).

Alicia: I started taking Jack to a music class called Little Maestros when he was four months old. The first few semesters were more for Mom (who are we fooling). But when Jack was about seven months he really started to enjoy it, and then we really had fun going. I wanted to instill a love for music in him, and we ending up going for four solid years. Jack still talks fondly about it.

Mary Ann: My babysitter took Zurielle to a baby massage class at our prenatal yoga center, and it was wonderful bonding experience for them both. As Zurielle had a bad belly, my babysitter was taught soothing techniques. The techniques also worked to calm Zurielle whenever she was having a bad day.

Baby yoga is also a wonderful experience for mommy and baby.

HAPPY BIRTHDAY TO YOU!
BABY'S FIRST BIRTHDAY PARTY

For many babies, their first birthday is a welcome introduction to the wonderful world of conspicuous consumption. For parents, of course, it's an unwelcome introduction to the wonderful world of dreadfully overpriced and overrated toys, toys, and more toys!

At twelve months, babies are still much more interested in putting the ribbons from the presents in their mouths than in opening the boxes. Nor will they remember the festivities. But a first birthday is still an important milestone, and photos and movies of your baby's first birthday will provide years of enjoyment and happy memories.

Our recommendation is to save your money for the later years when kids need more in the form of entertainment at their parties. Get or make a nice cake with lots of luridly colored frosting for baby to smear all over the face, invite family members and a handful of close friends over, take loads of photos and make a DVD, and shed a few sentimental tears.

If you want to get extravagant, feel free (and don't feel guilty about it). But don't go into debt—you'll have the next seventeen or so years of birthdays to do that.

Alicia: Jack's first birthday party was in a private room in a bar. It was clean, big, and had beer for those who wanted. To save a few bucks and to put a personal twist on the event, I made the invites, the cupcakes, and the decorations myself. I catered the food (a simple lunch that could be enjoyed by kids *and* adults), and put things like Cheerios and Goldfish in large colorful buckets for the kids. I called in a musician to sing songs, do the parachute, and hand out musical toys. Simple as that. I saved the picture-taking/cake-in-the-face moment for just the immediate family—it's best to bore only family with those kinds of details.

> tip: *A simple solution to the not-wanting-piles-of-toys-that-will-get-played-with-once-and-then-forgotten problem is to ask guests not to bring a present. Instead, they can make a donation to specific charities that are meaningful to your family.*
> *And there's always regifting!*

PLAYING ON THE ROAD WITH YOUR BABY

As seasoned travelers, we know that traveling with babies is nothing to dread. It just takes a bit of organization (some of it mental), which will make life with your baby easier, anyway.

Top Travel Tips
By PETER GREENBERG
TODAY Travel Editor

Airlines and airports are not day care centers. In fact, almost all of them seem to go out of their way to discriminate against mothers traveling with babies. As a result, you have to anticipate almost everything that can happen on a trip before you set foot in an airport.

> - Invest in a second seat where you can place a hard-backed CRM (child restraint system) that is Federal Aviation Administration approved. Even though this isn't required by the FAA, it's crucial when it comes to your child's safety in case of turbulence.
> - Ask for a bulkhead seat. Some international airlines have hooks for an onboard bassinet on the bulkhead. This is a great help, especially on long-haul flights.
> - Despite ongoing liquid restrictions, moms can bring breast milk, formula, baby food, and juice, and they don't need to be in ziplock bags. However, you do need to declare them at the security checkpoint. And, no, they won't ask you to taste any of the items at the checkpoint.

- Your hotel room most likely won't be childproofed the way that your house is. A few years ago, the U.S. Consumer Product Safety Commission did spot checks on hotels across the country, and what they found was disturbing: woefully inadequate situations with cribs. If the crib mattress isn't supported properly, it could fall through and suffocate a child; and then there were pillows, loose hardware, and jagged edges.

- Many hotel chains, such as Loews, Four Seasons, Westin, and the Nickelodeon Family Suites by Holiday Inn, actually provide a childproofing kit—this can include doorknob covers, electrical outlet covers, and drawer latches.

- It's easy to make your own childproofing kit, using masking tape or, preferably, duct tape (caution: masking tape is easy for kids to remove). The tape is used to seal windows and latches, especially sliding doors, and to put together your own buffer for certain sharp areas like a table corner where you don't have bumpers. To cover electrical outlets, use the appropriate plastic outlet covers or the tape itself.

- When you check into a room, get down on your hands and knees and literally crawl the room at your child's height so you can actually see those hazards. In the bathrooms, always check the water temperature, because kids can easily get burned when you turn that faucet on.

- Don't forget that all babies also need passports.

More Travel Tips
For Airports and Train Stations

- Always arrive early. It's better to pace around the airport or train station with your baby than run down the corridor in a panic or—horrors—miss your flight or train.

- When traveling with a baby under age two, the "plus baby" often gets left off the reservation. Always check ahead.

- Print out your boarding pass ahead of time. That's one less line to worry about.

- Use curbside check-in if you need it. Or find a porter right away. This is especially useful at large Amtrak stations, as porters can pre-board you and the baby.

from KATHIE LEE GIFFORD

Don't travel with your kids in their best new clothes. Regis had given Cody this adorable little outfit. We were in the lounge at American Airlines and Cody promptly projectile vomited all over himself—and the lounge. It was so gross there was no salvaging the outfit, and it just killed me to throw it out!

> Ask to board early. If you're traveling with your husband, let him board first so he can get the carry-on bags organized.

> Children under two fly free on domestic flights, but there is a 10 percent surcharge on international flights. If you can afford it, purchase a seat for the baby, because even a very tiny baby can get heavy after a few hours. If you can't, ask to be seated in the middle row, where you're more likely to get an extra seat.

> Travel off-peak whenever possible, as in most airports the midday flights are the least crowded, tend to leave closer to schedule, and are often cheaper.

> If you're renting a car, be sure to request a car seat instead of schlepping your own. Or use the wondrous Sit'n Stroll, which converts to a car seat.

> Strollers can be checked at the gate.

> If your baby is crawling, ask the flight attendants if it's okay for the baby to crawl up and down the aisles. Sure, crawling babies get dirty, but they're also moving around, not crying!

> We've all been on flights with babies who've cried the entire time. It's heartbreaking, because most of the time these kids are either sick or in pain and deserving of sympathy, not scorn (but it also drives you crazy). Flashing a sympathetic smile to the harried mom might not stop the crying, but it will certainly make her feel less miserable.

> Try to time babies' naps and feedings so they're fed either right before takeoff or right after. If you can't do that, don't let them sleep until the plane takes off.

> Always pack bathing suits and swim diapers. A great way to decompress after a trip is to take the baby in the pool for a nice, warm swim.

For Road Trips in the Car

> Attach a mirror to the car seat, so you can see the baby.

> If your baby is having a meltdown, remember what Mary Ann's mother always said: "If the baby's crying, at least the baby's not choking!"

> When your baby decides to scream for thirty minutes, crank up the music. If you can't pull over, do *not* pull over. Turn the music up even higher and sing along.

> Use car shades to block out the sun.

> Attach a portable mobile onto the car seat handle. Mix the toys up so your baby doesn't get bored, or try giving a brightly colored, noisy new toy while strapping the baby in.

> Ditch the cutesy cooler for a larger one when you know you're going to be in the car for a few hours. That leaves plenty of room for extra breast milk (in case you're at the wheel and can't deliver the goods in person) and baby foods like fruit and applesauce packs. Healthy food also helps to keep the fast-food runs to a minimum.

PART TWO

Mommy Basics

CHAPTER NINE

Mommy Needs a Life, Too!

What can be more adorable than your friends and loved ones cooing over your new baby? Not a whole lot . . . *but.*

And here's what we mean by this big ol' *but:* It was lovely to get so much attention when we were pregnant. Okay, it wasn't so great when total strangers wanted to rub our bellies when we weren't in the mood to play Happy Bloated Genie Bottles, but that didn't happen all that often. The thing is, we *loved* the attention. We loved people asking about us. And then, poof! Good-bye, pregnant lady.

So, yeah, we got a lot of delicious care for nine months, and then, here's this precious bundle and it's not about you anymore. At all. Of course, that's as it should be, but the point is, care and concern for you can quickly shift over to the baby. It's easy to pretend that you don't have needs anymore. You might even be afraid to say that you need something, for fear of being thought selfish or uncaring of the baby's needs.

Because we often messed up on this topic, we can now act as your nag-o-matic voice of reason and tell you that it's okay to admit you need things and to ask for what you need. It's an absolute must if you want to enjoy both your baby and your life as a new mom.

WHEN'S YOUR "YOU" TIME?

There's no way you can do it all yourself—and no reason *why* you should do it all yourself. When you're new to the whole mommy experience, it's easy for guilt to take center stage. First there's your own self-inflicted guilt

("My baby needs me and only me 24/7!"), then society-inflicted guilt ("Your baby needs you 24/7! What do you mean you're going to the gym?"). Before you know it, you're stuck in a daily routine of baby care, baby attention, and self-neglect. Even though you may be ecstatic as a new mom, you can also feel very lonely at the same time.

Alicia: You can't do it all. When my sister, Kathryn, a stay-at-home mom, was pregnant with her second child, her son Logan was quite energetic. When I spoke to her, I always asked, "When's your *you* time?"

"I don't have any," she'd say.

"Well," I said, "if you work in an office, you get bathroom breaks, a lunch hour, and days off—so if you're working as a full-time mom you need breaks, too." I suggested that our parents babysit more often so Kathryn could have time to herself, without explanation or justification. Luckily, they were happy to comply.

> tip: *If you don't have your parents nearby to help out, ask a friend or hire a babysitter. A lot of new moms tell us they are uneasy about hiring a sitter before the baby is several months old, but I always tell them that not getting away from the baby will be much, much more expensive in the long run. As in the price of your sanity.*

> tip: *We also did trade-off time with another mom. She'd watch both kids while we went to an exercise class or baby-free time, and then we'd return the favor when she needed it. If you're anxious about doing this at first, time these trade-offs for when your baby has just gone down for a nap, and do it for only a short period.*

Alicia: When I was on maternity leave, sometimes the only "me" time I got was at night, when my husband returned home from work. Even though I was past the tipping point of tired, I would force myself to shower, get dressed, and go out. Often, I'd see a movie by myself, but mostly I met other new moms to chat over dinner.

Forcing yourself to get out is absolutely necessary, but if you feel you have too much on your plate to party, an afternoon of running errands— alone—at Target can be just as rewarding. Something about pushing super-sized shopping carts (sans baby's cries) while lingering in the aisles is very therapeutic. Find what recharges your batteries.

THE JOYS OF A M.I.N.I. PRESENT

Baby showers are joyful occasions, but by the time the second or third child comes along, moms usually have all the toys and gear a baby needs. Sure, another few dozen onesies always come in handy, but we've got a better idea: the M.I.N.I., or Mommy Immediately Needs It, present. It's an ideal way to encourage new moms not to neglect themselves.

Mary Ann: After my sister-in-law had her second daughter, I gave her a $50 Starbucks card and told her that it didn't matter when she went, but she had to stop in there every day for at least half an hour to chill out. By herself, or with someone—it didn't matter. Just no kids. This was time she needed to grab a book or just sit and stare into space, which is what new moms spend a lot of time doing anyway.

M.I.N.I. Present Suggestions

> Gift certificate for pampering: facial, haircut or styling (super-duper brownie points if the hair stylist makes house calls), makeup application from a professional makeup artist, manicure or pedicure, massage, even a bikini wax when new moms are up to it.
> Any kind of absolutely non-essential gift that new moms would love to have but are unlikely to buy for themselves: a bottle of perfume (fragranced body lotion smells just as good and is less costly), bath oils, brand-name moisturizer, soft leather gloves, a funky hat, scented candles, a gorgeous flowering house plant that's easy to care for and hard to kill if mom forgets to water it.
> Movie passes, exercise passes, or the ultimate gift: an IOU for babysitting.

WELCOME TO THE JUNGLE—MEETING NEW MOMS

The moms you meet can be lifesavers.

Alicia: The second my mom left (after staying five weeks with us), I panicked. Who was I going to talk to? My husband was busy at work, and for some reason wasn't particularly receptive to my phone calls always ending with "So when are you coming home?"

I didn't have any friends with babies in New York, so I knew I had to find them. Luckily, there are mommy lunches where for a fee (mine was thirty bucks) you attend a lunch, and the organizers match you with other moms whose babies are close in age to yours. You introduce yourselves and start chatting, and from there you make plans to meet. The group alternates meeting at the various members' homes for lunch, or at some other convenient time (such as at Mommy and Me classes).

There are any number of ways to find mommy groups in your area. Start with the Internet: urbanbaby.com, Yahoo, and Craigslist. You can also check your local YMCA, community center, or church or synagogue, or simply ask friends and acquaintances who have recently become mothers.

It was often hard to do this—and I realized there were a number of reasons why. When you're not feeling good about yourself, when you have a baby you still can't handle in public, and then when you're thrown into a room with thirty other moms and told to "chat". . . that's daunting. But for all the messy moments, there were plenty of payoffs.

Mom groups were just about the best thing I could have done for myself (and Jack). Boy, was I busy. I joined two different groups, and we would pack the blankets and meet in Central Park for picnics, and then we'd walk and walk, chatting and laughing and trying to imagine waking up with Angelina's flat tummy the next morning.

As long as you have a mommy friend (or friends) you can call on the spur of the moment, and ask to meet for a walk or trip to the library or the mall in, say, fifteen minutes, your day is immediately going to improve. Even better, out of the fifteen moms I hung out with over those months, six of us are still tight, and it's incredibly satisfying to know that our kids will all grow up together.

> tip: *If there aren't any mommy groups in your area, take the initiative and start your own. If you're a working mom, you can almost always find other moms at the local playground or library on weekends. Force yourself to be outgoing, smile, and approach a mom and start talking. All you have to say is, "Hi, your baby is adorable. How old is she? What's her name? My baby's name is Jack, and boy does he love to sleep in the stroller." Or ask about local pediatricians, teething, or which store is having specials on diapers—anything baby-related and not too probing. Don't expect to hit it off with everyone; making new friends is hard work and often takes a lot of persistence (something often in short supply when you're a new mom). But the sooner you start making new mommy friends, the easier it is.*

Mary Ann: I spent several months in Tulsa with my family, as well as traveling for the rest of my maternity leave. By the time I got back to New York, it was much harder to find new mommy friends. I soon realized this had been a big mistake, but luckily my babysitter was super-outgoing and quickly made Spanish-speaking nanny friends. I then became instant friends with the parents, and still am to this day.

> Host the first mommy get-together at your home. You need nothing but a couple of toys for the kids, some snacks for the moms, and you're set.
> If you live in an area where you need to drive most places, alternate meeting spots. Rotate the lunches or get-togethers at different houses. Meet outside when possible, so you can walk around. Fresh air is a must.
> Malls are great for meeting and walking. Don't take your credit card and then you won't be tempted to shop.
> Some areas have mommy meeting groups that convene at a nice bar or restaurant at the witching hour, after baby's nap yet before daddy gets home from work. The women have a cocktail with several other moms, and then go home and get the evening going.

KEEP A JOURNAL FOR YOUR BABY(AND YOURSELF)

Writing things down in a baby book or a journal/diary can be time-consuming, but it can also be incredibly therapeutic. Not only will you be creating a memory book that you and your child will adore, but writing down

CHERISH THE MEMORIES

This is my mantra to new mothers. You think you'll remember the treasured moments—the first step, first word, first solid food, adorable moments. Trust me: After another child or two, it all blends together. And think about all the brain cells that we lose in childbirth. Those definitely do not return.

My children are now teenagers, and they ask me for baby stories all the time. I look at them and think, "Okay, hmm, you were the best sleeper . . . no, maybe that wasn't you . . . could have been your brother." I don't know what to say. How I wish I could pull out the memory book.

Whatever you write doesn't have to be beautifully written. Just jot the memory down. You will cherish it in later years. —Debbie Kosofsky your worries as well as your joys is a good way to confront and understand what's bothering you.

MANAGING MATERIALIST MOMS

Just when you've found the perfect (barely used, but still not brand-new) non-designer stroller (on Craigslist) that your baby loves, someone you barely know will walk by pushing a spanking-clean brand-new Bugaboo (with every possible accessory) and flash you a superior smile.

Yep, you can't avoid them. The Materialist Mom Competition Club (MMCC) starts as soon as your baby's born (What? You haven't registered with that trendy preschool?) and quickly escalates as soon as you take the baby out of the car seat (What? You didn't pay another $300 for a state-of-the-art car seat system, handcrafted sheepskin cover, and hand-painted dangly toy?) and lovingly place him in the stroller.

The MMCC is something you need to protect yourself from, because once they're done comparing (especially your lack of designer labels, tsk-tsk), Materialist Moms often morph into Super-Competitive moms. They'll want to compare all their babies' milestones with you. Don't go there. We've both ended friendships when all the moms did was talk about how great their little Suzy-Q was, and how smart, and how off the charts, blah, blah, blah. Often, these moms have left high-powered jobs and merely transferred their competitive nature to their babies. But raising a child isn't a competition, and it's no fun to be around any of these moms.

Alicia: Let me explain about the MMCC and the strollers—it's because a stranger will see the stroller before seeing the baby inside. At mommy lunches, Materialist Moms immediately sized each other up by the look and size of their strollers. It's kind of funny, because some of these moms take the MMCC very, very seriously.

> **from JEAN CHATZKY**
>
> It gets very difficult to resist the competitive urges, particularly if you live in a place where people tend to compete on this level. But I think it helps, especially as your baby grows older, to close ranks as a couple and a family unit. When the baby is pre-verbal, start talking with your spouse about the things that are important to you; for example, if you want to go on a wonderful vacation this summer you'll have to economize now.

Dealing with Competitive Moms

By RUTH PETERS, Ph.D.

TODAY Contributor and Clinical Psychologist

There are two easy words to help you deal with super-competitive moms: *Consumer Reports.* Educate yourself as to the top-rated products so you can make the most informed decisions, knowing that your $100 car seat is just as safe as the $500 model.

And know that in the psychology journals I've read, studies have shown that buying expensive gear is very nice, but by the time kids are six it all evens out. Whether you've had endless Mommy and Me classes or Baby Einstein DVDs, a kid is going to be the kid he or she is, and your part is to nurture nature. The attention and stimulation you give your baby is what counts, not the price tag. To me, empty Tupperware and a wooden spoon is a lot more engaging than expensive toys.

If the competitive conversation and bragging gets to you, ask yourself why you're sitting next to a mom like that in the playground and suffering in silence. Some of your friends who have more financial resources than you do may not realize what they're saying, but if you let them know how their banter makes you feel, good friends will knock it off. Those who don't, well, it then becomes your issue if you stay around them. Before you give up on these friends, tell them that their comments make you feel as if you're not trying hard enough, and that you're certain it's not their intention, and take it from there. Sometimes you do need to let go of friends, as hard as that can be to do.

> **tip**: *If you're getting to the point where you're resentful and envious, make a Count Your Blessings List. List things like: I have my health, my husband's a good guy, my baby slept for four hours straight and I didn't get barfed on today. It helps you keep perspective on what's really important and what's best about your life and loved ones.*

THE VIRTUAL COMMUNITY OF CYBER-MOMS

If the weather's too crummy to go outside or you think you look crummy because you're just too tired to spackle on the concealer, going online can be a lifesaver. All you have to do is Google your area, or log on to www.ivillage.com, or find a local chat room where you can ask questions about family-friendly activities.

Online chat and message boards can be unbelievably helpful. No matter what question you have, it's highly likely that someone else has already asked it (which automatically makes you feel like less of a dunce). No matter what time of night you're up, some other bleary-eyed mom is going to be up too, for exactly the same reason.

Alicia: As an added bonus, these message boards are highly entertaining. Some nights when I couldn't fall back to sleep after a late-night feeding, I'd log onto www.urbanbaby.com. People are willing to share, in writing, what they can't or don't want to say to others. Press any hot-button issue and you'll read a firestorm of emotions.

Another diverting site is www.truemomconfessions.com. It's a fun place to see moms relieve their guilt about a wide range of topics, from feeding babies questionable foods (*"I give my kids pepperoni as snacks and they love it. I just realized that I don't even know what animal it comes from!"*) to wanting a little vino (*"I want a bottle of wine all to myself tonight. . . . Sure, honey, go for a movie with your friends. Have a great time!"*) to just about anything. It's a real kick in the pants, yet it's somehow quite soothing to know that we're not alone as worrywarts about our parenting skills.

> **tip:** *If you're worried about revealing your own name, create a virtual identity on a server like yahoo.com or gmail.com. Anonymity can be very freeing. Just be aware that the protection of anonymity gives some moms license to become cyber-bullies. You'll need a thick skin about comments; even the most innocuous comments or questions can get major blowback. Don't take it personally.*

If there's a topic, you can find a Yahoo group for it. Do a search at the Yahoo groups home page and you can find thousands of supportive and knowledgeable moms, posting regularly on a huge range of topics. Don't forget your own interests. If you have a hobby or something you really love, you can find a group about it.

These groups can be a tremendous source of information if you have any specific problems you want to discuss in detail. It's often easier to talk about difficult subjects when you have the anonymity of e-mail than it is to sit down with a friend face to face. Sure, the online community isn't the same as your real community, but we've made lots of "virtual" friends who are kindred spirits.

Make sure that you don't give out too much personal information. There are a lot of identity thieves and crazies out there. Anything on the Internet can be searched for and read when your babies grow up, so divulging any potential embarrassments or private information could backfire in years to come.

BEAUTY TIPS FOR NEW MOMS

> Buy a really expensive designer lipstick in your favorite shade. It'll last for years, because you're never going to use it.
> Use whitening strips on your teeth. If you have a bright white smile, you'll smile more and it will make you feel better.
> Keep taking prenatal vitamins, and drink lots of water.
> A crisp white T-shirt goes a long way. Save your stretched-out old ones to wear when you're feeding the baby, or cut them up into dust cloths.
> A manicure or pedicure is a really nice treat. You can sit in the salon with the baby in the carrier while you get the pampering you deserve. Be sure to find salons that are either eco-friendly or have a good ventilation system.

Put Your Best Face Forward

By EVE PEARL

TODAY Makeup Artist

I've talked to so many new moms who feel guilty that they're taking even five minutes to spend on themselves and not their babies. But to feel your best, it's important to give yourself at least five minutes to treat your body and your skin properly, whether you're raising one child or an army.

Five-Minute Maintenance Plan
for New Moms

The goal is to maximize what products you use and how to apply them. Think multifunctional—cosmetics that hydrate while protecting your skin from the sun, nutrient-packed lip products, colors that can be used on skin or eyes.

1. You must moisturize. For daytime, use a moisturizer with an SPF of at least 25. This is by far your most important step of the day.

2. Since very few new moms get enough sleep, concealer is a must. A concealing eye treatment allows you to hide under-eye circles while treating the area to a mini-makeover with vitamins, minerals, proteins, and antioxidants.

3. Brighten your eyes instantly with a couple of swipes of mascara. Use a non-waterproof formula for easier removal.

4. You might not have time to catch a tan (nor should you ever go out without sunscreen), but you can look sun-kissed with bronzers. A little goes a long way. Apply only to areas where the sun would naturally hit your skin—the apples of your cheeks, around the edges of your forehead, a touch on the nose, and a touch on the chin.

5. Your lips also need hydration and attention. Try glosses with nutrients inside to moisturize while adding shine, and maybe some delicious flavor, too.

Baby Products That Work
for Mommy, Too

> Chubs baby wipes are alcohol-free and hypoallergenic. Using them is one of the best tips I learned on TV and movie sets. These wipes will actually remove most stains (deodorant, food, et cetera) quickly. I can't live without them.
> A toothbrush and Vaseline will exfoliate and plump up your lips.
> Eucerin lotion over lips provides soothing therapy and holds lip color.
> Vaseline added to any shadow can make a gel blush or lip stain.
> Honey and baby oil combined and rubbed on the body will make it incredibly soft. Be sure to rinse it off before leaving the bath.

- Milk will add a smooth texture to the body; try adding some to your next bath.
- Epsom salts ease muscle aches and swelling.
- Lemon, lime, honey, and yogurt can lighten age and sun spots. Mix the juice from one lemon, one lime, two tablespoons of honey, and two ounces of plain yogurt. Massage into desired spots at least once a week.
- Sweet almond oil will moisturize extra-dry skin, helps lashes grow, and can remove makeup. It also soothes sunburned skin.
- Dab a small amount of extra-virgin olive oil on your hand and rub it into your face. Removing makeup with a wet washcloth will leave your skin feeling smooth and silky.
- I love Aquaphor cream and use it all the time. It's great for every part of your face and your body—you can put it on your cuticles, feet, hands, or on your lips at night. If your face is getting chapped, put it on there, too.

About Stretch Marks

Stretch marks are like cellulite. They drive you crazy, but there's not a whole lot you can do about them.

Mary Ann: I used the Clarins Tonic Body Oil Treatment, and while it's very expensive, a little goes a long way. The trick is to put it on immediately after taking a shower (while your skin is still wet). Alicia used Molton Brown Ginger Lilly nongreasy body oil. It isn't a product associated with pregnancy products, but it worked for her.

Hair Tips for New Moms
By DEIRDRE STADTMAUER
TODAY Hair Stylist

Hair grows in phases. While 90 percent of your hair is in the growing phase at any one time, 10 percent is in the falling-out phase. During the course of pregnancy, hormonal changes prevent normal hair loss. Many women will enjoy thicker and fuller hair during pregnancy, but then, after delivery, all of the hair that didn't fall out during the pregnancy will come out, and your hair can appear thinner than usual. Within six months your hair should be back to the normal growing phase, so don't fret about this temporary condition. By keeping hair on the longer side, the short-term increase in hair loss may be less noticeable.

Hair loss during pregnancy could also be the result of poor diet. Mineral deficiencies can also cause your hair to become dry and fragile.

Tips for Keeping Hair Looking Its Best for the First Year after Pregnancy:

> Biotin is needed for healthy hair. Some foods rich in biotin are brown rice, oats, lentils, green peas, sunflower seeds, and walnuts. Other hair-healthy foods include cold-pressed virgin oils, whole grains, yogurt, fresh fruits, and vegetables.
> Shampooing hair two to three times a week is sufficient. It's a fallacy that you need to wash your hair every day, even if it's oily. Your natural oils are good for the hair and scalp. Too much washing disrupts natural pH, thereby creating more oil. Feel free to rinse your hair between washings, and add a very small dab of conditioner on the ends.
> Look for nourishing ingredients in your shampoos: biotin, vitamins C and E, jojoba, and coconut oils. Conditioners containing chamomile, marigold, ginseng, and coconut oil keep hair healthy, too.
> Massage your scalp with essential oils such as lavender to increase blood flow.
> Avoid rough treatment, tight ponytails, and excessive brushing.
> Be gentle when combing wet hair, as it tends to be more fragile. Use a wide-tooth comb, and start combing from the ends up toward the roots to avoid breakage.
> Try to let hair air-dry. Avoid excessive blow drying and using other heated appliances. These are especially damaging if your hair is dry, brittle, or falling out.

Try not to fret about the amount of hair that comes out of your head. I have dark hair, and I had what looked like a small bird's nest in my tub drain after every shower. I was so worried that I had some sort of hair follicle disease until I finally stopped shedding six months after having Lucy.
—Alicia

Haircuts

Whatever cut you choose, keep it simple. You will have very little time for primping with the arrival of your new baby.

While many expecting mothers cut their hair short while trying to find a more manageable style, short hair can be harder to style. Invest in a good cut that will require minimal styling. This doesn't necessarily mean an expensive cut; the best way to find a good stylist is to ask women with great cuts who does their hair. Be realistic about your hair texture. If your hair is very fine, look at women with similar hair, as that'll give you a better idea of the skill of the stylist.

Faces tend to get fuller during pregnancy, so you can minimize this by having either bangs that go across your face or a soft wave around your face that cuts down on the fullness. Try to keep blunt lines, or go for a few soft layers around the face—not too much unless you're expert at doing your hair. Keeping length allows you to put your hair back in a clip or a loose ponytail, and longer hair can make your face look more slender.

Hair Color

While there may be no conclusive evidence that coloring your hair while breastfeeding will harm your baby, in order to be completely safe, consult your doctor or avoid coloring completely. Some of the worrisome toxins used in hair dyes are para-phenylenediamines (PPDs), lead, coal tar, and toluene. Placed directly on your scalp, these chemicals can enter the bloodstream and therefore may affect your milk supply. While there's no such thing as completely organic hair dye, there are safer ways of coloring your hair:

> Use henna, which is plant based and chemical free. While henna won't harm you or your baby, the downside is that it does not cover gray or lighten your hair.
> Choose highlights or low lights. These are good options because the chemicals are placed on foil, not directly on the scalp. Be sure to tell your stylist to keep the chemicals away from your scalp.

Style Tips

By LLOYD BOSTON

TODAY Style Editor

Sure, you might be too tired at first to even think about changing out of your pajamas, but with a little planning, you can have a post-baby wardrobe that's not only stylish but versatile and practical. Here are my style secrets to make you look slimmer:

Rule #1: Your size is your size.

Buy the size that fits, not the size number that you *think* you are—or hope to be. If your clothes fit properly, you will look put-together and stylish.

Rule #2: Layering slims if done right.

Most women think that layering can add bulk, but the opposite is true. The more layers, the lighter the fabric. A lightweight sweater vest in black, worn atop a thin, crisp white shirt, can make you look leaner. Add a belt over the sweater to create the shape of a waist. It doesn't have to be on your natural waist; it's not functional, just to taper.

Rule #3: Love the empire waist.

From tops, to dresses, and even coats—this will make your legs seem a little longer beneath an item that cinches just beneath the bustline.

Top Three Essentials

1. Layered T-shirts in a gauzy weight

Pair a short-sleeve tee over a long one in fun, unexpected contrast color combos (pink over yellow, orange over turquoise—have fun).

2. Feminine cargo pants

Not your husband's! Invest in versions in juicy colors (mango, kelly green, sky blue) and feminine fabrics (linen, washed cotton, seersucker), with a flare leg. The pockets are great for mom essentials, too.

3. Sabrina/Kitten heels

These are shoes with tapered heels no more than an inch and a half high. They're sexy while remaining functional if you have to dash.

Mommy Basics

Two Musts for Any New Mom

1. Foolproof pajamas you can answer the door in

Instead of your old standby (dare I say flannel PJs with sheep or ponies?), look for loungewear from Asia. Your local Chinatown, Koreatown, or East Indian sari shop is a stylist's hidden gem. From long, hip-hiding caftans to silky drawstring pants gorgeous enough to wear to a dinner party, you'll find chic treasures in these shops at price points that won't break the bank. Add satin slippers, and your sleep time will be just as stylish.

2. Yoga pants for casual wear

New moms adore sweat pants for good reason—they need comfort and flexibility while on the go. To solve this style conundrum, I prefer yoga pants to sweats. You'll find that most good-quality yoga pants have the following details: a looser elastic waist that sits slightly lower on the hip; a flared leg, instead of the traditional gathered sweat-pant leg that can make hips look larger and ankles look thicker; and a snug fit around the hips, which can make you look leaner.

Choose yoga pants in rich colors like dark chocolate, navy, eggplant, or black. This way, you can add a bright top in the summer that is a bit dressier (imagine a silk empire-waist top in cream paired with any of the above). Partner with a ballet flat in the same color as the pants.

If yoga pants are not appropriate, look for fun nonmaternity pieces with slimming properties.

Top Two Style Prescriptions

1. The wrap top

The best versions taper just beneath the bustline. You'll lift up the "twins" and secure the midsection.

2. A tapered jean jacket

This secret weapon can hide a multitude of sins and keep you looking both young and age-appropriate at the same time. Choose the darkest denim wash, or white. No need to button it—leave it cracked, and don a dark tank or T-shirt beneath.

Best Accessory

Big bag, small hips

This may sound silly, but proportion plays a mean role in the look of your body. That chic, huge hobo bag of the moment can double as a diaper bag—and make your hips, butt, and thighs look a little smaller when next to it.

Top Three Unexpected Choices for Comfy Fun Shoes

These are especially helpful for moms on the go, pushing those strollers for miles.

1. Espadrilles

French women swear by them. Grab them in navy, black, or tan first. Then sample fun, primary colors to add a lift to jeans or chinos. Awning stripes are fun too.

2. Classic sneakers from *your* childhood

Converse, Keds, Jack Purcell's, and Pumas all come in cool colors, fabrics, and designs today—making your simple capri pants look cute. Some brands come in faux laceless styles that have a secret elastic inset for easy slip on and off.

3. Bold ballet flats

Whatever you would normally choose in a ballet flat is what you should now avoid. Select a wild accent that will add pop to easy clothes. My top choices are faux animal prints, patent leather, tweeds, herringbones, metallics, and even day-glo suedes.

SOMETHING THAT LOOKS GOOD ON EVERYONE?

Hands down, the overall winner for just about any body type is a wrap dress silhouette. Some women, like petites, may need a touch of tailoring on the length, and others may need a body shaper worn beneath—but with a little fix here or there, this dress is timeless, elegant, and easy for travel (business or pleasure). Add a knee boot for a long, lean finish, or pair with sexy sling-backs for candlelit nights with your better half.

Black is the first choice to invest in, as it can go from desk to dinner in a flash. Buying prints in bold colors, especially stripes in a chevron motif, can also fool the eye toward a leaner you. Matte jersey is the best all-around fabric choice to fit and forgive.

Mary Ann: I lived in a sexy black, sleeveless jersey maternity dress by Old Navy when I was pregnant, and postpartum, too. It was so comfortable to wear. Plus it was easy to breastfeed from and it made me feel (a little bit) like a sex goddess even when sex was the last thing on my mind!

Your body definitely never quite goes back to what it was, but I made it a priority to stay in shape while I was pregnant. But what's always important to me is that beauty starts from within—so make sure you feel good about yourself and your body and you're half-way there.
                                                          —Natalie Morales

CHAPTER TEN

I Can See My Feet Again: Getting Back in Shape

Forget those celebrities who have astonishingly flat tummies two months after giving birth. Think of them as freaks of nature (with personal trainers, nutritionists, stylists, makeup artists, and unlimited budgets, not to mention an air-brusher who touched up their varicose veins), not role models. Your top priority is not to look like an Oscar nominee but to take great care of your baby while regaining your strength and energy.

Some of your pregnancy weight gain is genetically programmed, which means there isn't a whole lot you can do about it—except eat sensibly and not look at pregnancy as a nine-month all-you-can-eat buffet. If you didn't eat healthfully during your pregnancy, there's no time like the present to get back on track.

IT ALL STARTS WHEN YOU'RE PREGNANT

Mary Ann: I've been athletic all my life, and when I was twenty-six I trained hard enough to fight in the first Golden Gloves boxing tournament for women (if I do say so myself—I was *buff*!). I make smart choices about what to eat, but even I ate more that I should have for my first pregnancy. I think my weight gain was close to thirty-five pounds, and on my small and used-to-be toned frame, that was a lot.

It's never great to gain too much weight when you're pregnant, as it puts you at risk for gestational diabetes and other health issues. Plus, it's harder to lose that weight after giving birth. But you shouldn't obsess about every ounce either.

I walked everywhere. New York is ideal for walkers, but you can walk no matter where you live. Getting into the habit of walking before the baby is born will help you lose weight after the birth.

Alicia: I've never been a boxer or had abs of steel, but I've run four marathons and take care of myself. My morning sickness was so strong that I lost eight pounds before I started gaining weight. I ultimately gained twenty pounds with my first child and twenty-four with my second. My husband was so worried about my lack of weight gain that he'd try and force calories on me. It was kind of funny that he seemed more concerned about the health of his baby boy than he was about me!

WHO TOOK MY BREASTS AND WHAT ARE THESE?

Alicia: There's a little shop in Manhattan called Upper Breast Side (a takeoff on the Upper East Side and Upper West Side neighborhoods), and I wandered in one day when I was about eight months pregnant. An adorable older saleswoman, with a measuring tape lassoed around her neck, took one look at me through the glasses sitting on her nose, smiled, and said, "Honey, strip down and show me your boobs."

Now, this is not something you'd normally hear, but given the circumstances, I was happy to oblige. She took one quick look, smiled again, and announced, "You're going to be a double E when you have the baby."

My jaw dropped open. "No, I'm not," I protested. "I'm huge already!"

"Honey," she replied, "you ain't seen nothing yet."

So I gave her the benefit of the doubt, tried on some bras that were positively humongous, and bought them anyway, thinking, nah, this can't possibly happen to me—until it did. Sure enough, when that milk came down, I was a giant EE.

As someone who's amply endowed anyway, this was a shock. A day after my C-section, my breasts were their normal size, and the next morning I woke up and they were right under my chin. I had two soldiers, standing at

from ▶ DR. TANYA BENENSON

Eating for two is a convenient excuse (and a wonderful one) for us women to eat. However, most doctors recommend only approximately 300 additional calories depending on your pre-pregnancy body weight. The goal is to eat healthy food and gain the proper amount recommended by your doctor.

attention, waiting for their next assignment.

As soon as I stopped breastfeeding, I had a bra burning ceremony for those ratty ol' double-E bras.

Mary Ann: Pre-pregnancy, my breasts were pretty much a perfect, perky, full size B. Post-baby, they became huge, monster boobs, so I did what any smart Oklahoma woman does with her newfound boobies—I flaunted them!

BELLY SUPPORT—THE BEAUTY OF BODY SHAPERS

Mary Ann: As soon as the baby was born, a lot of weight came off. When I started breastfeeding, I experienced major cramping. Have the Motrin standing by, because it *hurts*. But I endured it, knowing that all the cramping was my uterus contracting back to its normal size and helping my stomach get smaller. I would use this time to do my Kegel exercises, because you want to help your va-jay-jay get back in shape, too.

Still, what lots of your friends with kids won't tell you is that you're going to walk out of the hospital still looking like you're six months pregnant.

Enter Spanx, a modern version of your mom's (or grandmother's) girdle. The wonders of modern techno-fabrics make Spanx much more comfortable, especially as your stomach muscles are a mess after giving birth—and boy do those Spanx help suck everything in. There's even a pregnancy Spanx for moms-to-be, which sucks everything in but allows your belly to be free (it's not good to constrict the baby in any way, even if you want to fit into your party dress).

Of course you need to follow your obstetrician's advice about when to resume doing any stomach exercises. If you have a C-section, it'll be months (for Alicia it was three months). In the meantime, Spanx will be your belly's best friend, and looking more sleek around the middle will help you feel like your old self again.

LIVING WITH YOUR BELLY

My otherwise wonderful hubby crossed the line one day when he referred to my post-baby pooch as "muffin top." Still, it made me think. Plenty of fast-food–loving teens show off theirs, so why shouldn't I? After all, my pudge of honor was a sign of what I'd created, and probably a lot healthier than some kiwi celery diet!

If we teach by example, my future teenage daughter will one day thank me for it. —Robin Sindler

Mommy Basics

GETTING YOUR BODY BACK

Your body has undergone nine months of monumental changes, so you have to be realistic about getting it back into its pre-baby shape. Once we'd been given the go-ahead from our doctors, a slow and steady program toward fitness, with lots of walking, was the best way to go for us. We knew that post-partum exercise isn't just something your body needs—your mind needs it too.

Alicia: I had to be patient during the six weeks post-C-section, during which I was advised to avoid all strenuous activity, because my body needed to heal. I decided that the best thing for me was to walk with my baby. Boy, did we walk. I often walked a mile and a half down to my husband's office to meet him for lunch. It was terrific exercise and I was back to my pre-baby weight in no time. In fact, I was smaller than my pre-baby weight during my maternity leave because I was eating right and exercising. I was thrilled!

Mary Ann: I've been exercising all my life, but with the demands of my job and my family, it is really hard for me to find the time each day to do the kind of routines I want to do. So I've had to compromise. Weather permitting, I ride my bike to and from work, and I often take an extra loop around Central Park on my way home. Yes, my kids and husband want to see me, and yes I'm hungry for dinner, but that ride sure feels great. It's fifteen short minutes that helps me clear my head after a long day, gets my heart pumping, and keeps my leg muscles firm. I'd go bonkers without it!

> I'd close the shades and turn on the Health and Fitness Channel (I'd Tivo "Body by Gilad") and do the workouts. It was great, because I could slot these in when the baby was sleeping. —Amy Robach

> My idea of exercise was reaching for a piece of cheesecake. I danced because of my shows, played tennis, and was a very active person, but I was never someone who went to the gym. I gained twenty-three pounds with Cody, and by the time I was pregnant with Cassidy I understood the benefits of exercising. I exercised all through my pregnancy with Cassidy and was in better shape at forty giving birth to her than I was at thirty-six with Cody. Two days before I had her, I was walking on my treadmill, and two weeks after my C-section I went right back to walking on the treadmill. —Kathie Lee Gifford

Nine Months On — Nine Months Off

By JEN WILSON

NBC Senior Fitness Specialist

You've just delivered your very own baby joey, and disappointingly he or she has left behind the pouch. Now what? Let me start with what's important:

1. You're BEAUTIFUL . . . STUNNING, even!

2. You've just persevered through an intense and utterly awe-inspiring event.

3. Last but not least, the world in twenty years could be a very different place because you were important in the life of a child.

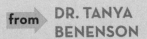

from DR. TANYA BENENSON

EXERCISE:
VAGINAL vs. C-SECTION

If you had a C-section, you'll have to wait longer than after vaginal delivery to start some of these exercises. You have an incision that needs to heal. Walking is a good start, but avoid lifting anything heavier than your baby. The general rule is to wait until your six-week check-up to start anything more strenuous than walking. Talk to your doctor about when you can start exercising and what you can safely do.

Now that we've achieved our motivational quota for the day, let's get to the benefits of exercise, aside from physical health and weight loss:

> **Exercise helps regulate your emotions.** Not only are there physiological changes you can't control, but your emotions are likely all over the place thanks to the enormous changes in your life. Exercise works wonders for stress reduction and will aid in regulating your hormone levels. Even better, there's scientific proof that the endorphins produced by exercise can have the same effect on the body as opiates.

> **Exercise helps rid your body of postpartum aches.** The exercising you're going to be doing postnatally will be low impact, slow, and probably on the floor. The light stretching and strengthening I recommend is designed to help you regain strength and optimum muscle length. When you strengthen what's weak and lengthen what's too tight, aches will dissipate because you're reteaching your body how to hold itself.

> **Exercise helps regulate water retention/flushing.** Postnatal sweating is common, so it's great to know that adding sweaty exercise to your day will give it an outlet.

Before you start, be sure your physician has given you the all-clear. Then move on to "Jen's Basics," which I use with all my postnatal clients. The beauty of the Basics is that all but one can be done on the floor next to the crib while your baby is taking a nap.

Basics #1: Get Moving Again

This could be simply walking up and down your driveway, walking around the block with your stroller, going for a swim, or using cardio equipment at your gym. Whatever it is, you want to make sure that it is low impact and low intensity. Start out slowly. Try walking for five to ten minutes. If that feels okay and you're still able to have a conversation, then bump it up to fifteen to twenty minutes. After the four-to-eight-week mark, as long as your physician gives the okay, you can increase your intensity. Running is okay, too, if you were a runner before or during pregnancy. A week after delivery is *not* the time to start training for a 10K!

Basics #2: Strengthen Your Pelvic Floor

This one you can do all day long and no one will know or care. But don't let that diminish its importance, as you already know how important those Kegel exercises are. If you don't believe me, sneeze, laugh, or cough with a full bladder. Now your pants are wet and we've got a whole other set of issues to fix. Your pelvic floor has been stretched and poked and prodded beyond all recognition. Doing three to four sets of fifteen Kegel exercises, holding for five seconds each time, will retrain the muscles of your pelvic floor and also aid in healing by increasing blood flow to the area.

Basics #3: Strengthen Your Abdominals

Your abdominal muscles, no matter what shape they were in pre-pregnancy, are now stretched beyond optimum length and are weak. This provides the framework for potential issues and injuries if not corrected as soon and as safely possible. If your diastasis (that space above your belly button between your recti muscles) is more than two finger widths, start with modified head and neck raises. If you've had a C-section, wait for your physician's approval (approximately six weeks). If your diastasis is narrower than two finger widths, you can begin with crunches, pelvic tilts, and leg slides.

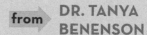

from DR. TANYA BENENSON

VAGINAL DISCHARGE

Lochia, the vaginal discharge after birth, should change over several weeks from bright red to pink to white. If your discharge increases without slowing down with rest or changes back to a red color, this may be a sign you're overdoing it. Contact your doctor if these symptoms don't improve with rest.

Basics #4: Protect Your Back

The number-one complaint I get from new moms is "MY BACK IS KILL-ING ME!" The muscles of the back and the structure of the spine tend to be extremely temperamental, which is why when you lift something today the same way you did before you had the baby, you can't move. New moms are in the precarious position of having the muscles that would normally help protect the spine (the abdominals) hanging over their belt. You're going to need to do low-impact strengthening for your para-spinals (muscles of the low back that line the spine) and light stretching. When stretching, be careful not to overstretch. The effects of the hormone relaxin will have a loosening effect on your joints and ligaments for approximately four months after you deliver.

Basics #5: Push-ups

For the foreseeable future, you're going to be lifting five to ten pounds all day every day. And if you feed that little glutton as much as he or she wants, that weight is going to increase. Push-ups are the perfect upper-body exercise. It uses every muscle safely, and it's quick.

EXERCISES WITH DATES OF WHEN YOU CAN SAFELY COMPLETE THEM

You must consult your physician before beginning any exercises, and adhere to what's been recommended.

Kegels

Tighten the muscles of the pelvic floor as if to interrupt urine flow. Hold for five seconds and release. Do three to four sets of fifteen repetitions.

Wall Push-ups

Stand away from the wall so that you have to lean into it. Place your hands shoulder width apart, tuck your pelvis under, engage your abdominals, and lower yourself toward the wall. Be careful to keep your back flat and not to drop your belly toward the wall. Begin with ten and work your way up to forty per day.

Head and Neck Raises

While lying on your back with your knees bent and feet flat, wrap your

	Post-Delivery: 2 Weeks	2-4 Weeks	4-6 Weeks	6 Weeks & Beyond
Kegels	✿	✿	✿	✿
Wall Push-ups	✿	✿	✿	✿
Head & Neck Raises	✿	✿	✿	✿
Pelvic Tilts	✿	✿	✿	✿
Bird Dog		✿	✿	✿
Torso Twists		✿	✿	✿
Bent-over Rows			✿	✿
Crunches			✿	✿
Leg Slides			✿	✿
Floor Push-ups			✿	✿
Cat Stretch			✿	✿
Hamstring Stretch			✿	✿
Child's Pose			✿	✿
Plié Squats				✿
Scaption Raises				✿
Hip Bridges				✿
Hip Abduction				✿
Hip Adduction				✿

arms across your abdomen so as to hug yourself. Slowly, lift your head off the floor, leading your chin to your chest. Be careful not to lift your shoulders off the floor. Begin with ten and work your way up to forty per day.

Pelvic Tilts

Lie on your back with your knees bent and your feet flat on the floor. Take a deep breath and arch your back. Next, exhale while tucking your pelvis so you press your lower back flat into the floor. Hold for fifteen to twenty seconds, then release. Do one to two sets of ten to fifteen reps.

Bird Dog

Start on your hands and knees with your hands directly below your shoulders and your knees directly under your hips. Next, lift and fully extend your right hand while lifting and fully extending your left leg, making sure to keep your elbows and knees completely horizontal. While lifting, make sure your pelvis is tucked under and you are tightening your abdominals. Complete ten lifts, then switch to the left hand and right leg. Complete ten lifts on that side. Perform two to three sets.

Torso Twists

Do these with a medicine ball, a gallon of milk, or a heavy book. Plant your feet shoulder width apart and make sure your kneecaps are in line with your middle toe. (Don't have your knees bowed out or caved inward.) Soften your knees, tuck your pelvis under, engage your abdominals, and slowly twist to your right side without moving anything below the waist. Then twist back to center. Watch carefully to make sure you don't rotate through the hips or pivot on your toes. Do two to three sets of ten on each side.

Bent-over Rows

Grab a dumbbell, a jug of milk or juice, or a pack of diapers. Place the other hand on your knee, bed, or the arm of a chair and bend over from the waist. While keeping your back flat, pull the weight up to chest level and lift your elbow back toward the ceiling. Do two to three sets of twelve to fifteen for each arm.

Crunches

Lie flat with your knees bent, feet flat, pelvis tucked, and hands behind your head. Slowly lift your head and shoulders off the floor while pressing your lower back flat into the floor. Start at ten and work up to forty per day.

Leg Slide

Lie flat on the floor with your knees bent and your feet flat and together. While pressing your lower back flat, slide your heels away from you until you start to feel your lower back lift. At that point, slide your heels back toward your glutes. Start at ten and work up to forty per day.

Floor Push-ups

On the floor, make sure you're on your knees with your ankles up, your hands should be about shoulder width, and your butt should not be up in the air. You want to try to keep a straight line from your knees, through your hips, to your shoulders. Then drop your chest toward the floor until you have approximately a 90-degree bend in the elbow and then back up. Throughout the full range of motion, you want to make sure your pelvis is tucked under and you are tightening your abdominals. At first, do as many as you can without losing form, working your way up to two or three sets of twelve to fifteen reps.

Cat Stretch

Start on your hands and knees with your hands directly under your shoulders and your knees directly under your hips. Take a deep breath while arching your back up as high as you can and drawing your chin into your chest. Exhale while releasing your spine back down to a neutral position and extending your chin upward. Do two to three sets of ten.

Hamstring Stretch

Grab a towel and lie on your back with one leg fully extended on the floor. Place a towel over the bottom of your other foot and extend that leg straight up. Press your knee as flat as you can to feel the stretch. Hold for twenty to thirty seconds.

Child's Pose

Start on your hands and knees with your knees together. Slowly sit back onto your heels and lay your chest forward onto your thighs while outstretching your arms overhead. Your hands and forehead should be on the floor.

Plié Squats

Place your feet wider than shoulder width with your toes outward. Tuck your pelvis under, engage your abdominals, keep your chest up and your shoulders back. Squat while keeping your knees in line with your toes, then return to standing position. Do three sets of ten.

Scaption Raises

This exercise is for the shoulders and rotator cuff (deltoids and supraspinatus). Grab dumbbells, bottles of water, or cans of soup. Lift your arms diagonally to shoulder height with your elbows flat and thumbs to the ceiling. Then lower them back to your sides, slowly and controlled, with your elbows staying flat. Do two to three sets of twelve to fifteen reps.

Hip Bridges

Start on your back with your knees bent and your feet on the floor. Press your hips up off the floor as high as you can, trying to attain a straight line from your knees, down through your hips, down to your shoulders. Continue to lift, lower, and squeeze your buttocks, starting with ten reps and working up to forty per day.

Hip Abduction

Many times lower back and knee pain can be attributed to these muscles being too weak. Start lying on your side with your knees flat and your heels flexed. Lift your top leg 30 to 45 degrees while keeping your toes and knees forward and not toward the ceiling. As you get stronger, you can add ankle weights. Do two to three sets of twelve to fifteen reps.

Hip Adduction

This exercise is for the muscles of the inner thighs (adductors brevis, longus, magnus, et cetera). Start lying on your side with your top leg bent and crossed over the bottom leg. Lift the bottom leg with the knee flat and foot flexed. Do two to three sets of twelve to fifteen reps.

Weight Loss: Top Twelve Tricks
By JOY BAUER, M.S., R.D., C.D.N.

Registered Dietician and Founder, Joy Bauer Nutrition

1. Think positive.

Successful weight loss is 50 percent attitude. Decide you're going to lose weight permanently and you will do it!

2. Consider the buddy system.

Some people do better if they have a friend, spouse, therapist, or *someone* they can talk to about successes and setbacks. Ideally, this person is unconditionally supportive. If you thrive with a little help from your friends, go ahead and ask for their help and guidance.

3. Out with the old, in with the new.

Go through your cabinets and fridge—and toss or donate the junk food. Also, be sure to get rid of your *personal* trigger foods. These are the foods that once you start eating . . . you can't stop. Instead, stock up on produce, lean meats, low-fat dairy, and whole grains.

4. Don't forget to eat.

Within ninety minutes of waking, start the day with a smart breakfast. Then, continue to eat every four to five hours throughout the remainder of your day. You'll keep your blood sugar levels stabilized, which helps control hunger and cravings. For most people, this means eating a well-balanced breakfast, lunch, afternoon snack, and dinner.

5. Preplan your meals and slow down your eating.

Take ten minutes the night before to plan out your food for the next day so you won't impulsively grab high-fat, calorie-loaded food during your busy day. If you're mentally prepared with a food strategy, you'll be less likely to stray to bad foods.

Then prepare yourself for eating. Taste your food. Savor the texture. Put your fork down between every two bites and sip water during your meal. This is not the time for multitasking. Avoid mindless eating while rocking the baby, checking e-mail, watching television, or doing other distracting activities.

6. Keep sugarless gum on hand.

Sugarless gum gives you a hit of flavor, keeps your mouth busy, and cleans your teeth when you can't brush.

7. Shock your tongue.

Hot and spicy flavors encourage slower eating. Hot (temperature-wise), low-calorie beverages can also help you feel satisfied and hydrated. When you're bored, it's possible to nurse a hot cup of skim latte, green or herbal tea, or diet hot cocoa for much longer than it would take to eat a snack.

8. Drink two glasses of water before meals.

Within thirty minutes of every meal, guzzle two glasses of water. This will help meet your daily fluid quota and remind you to follow through with smart food choices at the upcoming meal. Perhaps it will also take the edge off your hunger, but most important, it will keep you thinking about your plan. Thirst can mimic the feelings of hunger—if you wait ten minutes after drinking water, you may find you don't want to eat at all.

9. Be patient with yourself.

There is a phenomenon well known among weight loss experts: When people who are dieting slip up and overeat, they often decide that the entire diet is broken and continue to overeat for days. By then, all their hard work may have been undone. If you find yourself in this situation, be as kind to yourself as you would be if your friend confessed a small slip-up. All humans make mistakes. Learn to give yourself a little forgiveness.

10. Get enough sleep.

This is a real toughie, but during sleep, our bodies rest and regenerate so we can be clear-headed enough to make wise food choices. Furthermore, sleep deprivation causes an imbalance in certain hormones, including ghrelin (which causes appetite) and leptin (which decreases appetite). When we don't get enough sleep, our levels of ghrelin go up (leading to weight gain) and levels of leptin go down (so we are hungrier). Don't think of sleep as downtime, but as another important facet of your nutrition plan.

11. Donate your "fat clothes."

Losing weight is a major accomplishment. As soon as an item of clothing is too big for you anymore, give it away. Don't keep it in your closet as part of your "just in case" wardrobe. It is easier to backslide if you have bigger pants to slide into.

12. Move it and lose it!

Commit to thirty minutes of daily exercise—anything goes. Take a walk with your baby in the stroller, join an exercise class, jump rope, follow a workout video, or ride your bike.

Joy Bauer's Program to Knock Off Leftover Baby Pounds

This surefire weight-loss regimen will help you burn fat while boosting your metabolism and energy. It's loaded with fiber, vitamins, minerals, and antioxidant-rich foods. You'll get a blast of daily nutrition *plus* feel full and satisfied while you lose weight. Be sure to drink plenty of water—aim for nine-plus cups each day—and take a daily multivitamin for backup. Make it a prenatal if you're nursing.

My daily "do-it-yourself-menus" have been calculated at approximately 1,400 to 1,600 calories. If you're nursing, don't go lower than 1,600 calories. And good news: You don't have to give up your favorite treats, since this plan is based on my 90/10 food strategy. That's 90 percent healthy and 10 percent fun. *Bon appetit!*

90 Percent Healthy

1 serving of high-quality STARCH with each meal

(3 total servings for the day—use whenever you'd like)
One serving = 1 slice whole-wheat bread (or 2 slices reduced-calorie bread)
$1/2$ cup cooked brown rice or whole-wheat pasta
1 small whole-wheat pita bread (70 calories)
$1/2$ large whole-wheat pita bread
$1/2$ medium baked white or sweet potato
$3/4$ cup whole-grain breakfast cereal (120 calories or less)
$1/2$ cup dry plain oatmeal
$1/2$ whole-grain English muffin
$1/2$ cup peas, corn, starchy beans (e.g., kidney, chickpeas), acorn/butternut squash

2 daily servings of fresh FRUIT (can be eaten with meals or snacks)

One serving = 1 medium piece of fruit, 1 small banana, $1/2$ mango, $1/2$ papaya, $3/4$ cup berries, or $1/2$ cup fresh fruit salad or grapes

Unlimited VEGETABLES throughout the day

One serving = 1 cup raw or $1/2$ cup cooked. However, you should count peas, corn, and potatoes as starch (see above).

Lean PROTEIN with each meal

Appropriate portions: 3 to 5 ounces lean meat/chicken/fish/tofu
1 cup skim milk, nonfat yogurt, or 1% reduced-fat cottage cheese
1 to 2 ounces nonfat/low-fat sliced cheese
1 whole egg + 2 egg whites
$3/4$ cup cooked beans or other legumes

Limit the FATS at each meal

Portions:

1 to 2 teaspoons olive oil

1 tablespoon regular salad dressing

2 to 4 tablespoons low-calorie salad dressing

1 to 2 tablespoons nuts

1 tablespoon peanut butter

1 tablespoon healthy spread (light cream cheese, soft-tub trans-fat-free margarine, guacamole, reduced-fat mayonnaise)

10 Percent Fun

> Each day you have the opportunity to plug in ONE treat of 150 calories or less. This helps satisfy cravings and removes the deprivation often associated with dieting.

> You may choose to skip the daily fun food, and instead enjoy an additional serving of one of the following: high-quality starch, fruit, protein, or fat.

Fun Food Examples

1 oz dark chocolate

1/2 cup fat-free pudding

1/2 cup low-fat ice cream, frozen yogurt, or sorbet

1 low-fat ice-cream pop (less than 150 calories)

7 cups light popcorn

1 oz baked chips

1 oz pretzels

4 licorice sticks

1 cup natural applesauce

small bag of soy crisps

10 strawberries with 2 tablespoons reduced-fat whipped topping

baked apple with 1 teaspoon sugar and cinnamon

frozen banana

BEAUTIFUL MINDS

Your body isn't the only thing you'll be concerned about—your brain is most definitely in a different place. Just when you think you're starting to get it together—the baby's starting to stick to a schedule, you're sleeping better, your tummy is no longer hanging down to your knees, you don't have zits anymore—you realize you put the car keys in the freezer and the shopping list in the diaper pail.

Yep—you've got Mommy Brain!

Mommy Brain is that confused state, partly due to sleep deprivation and partly due to out-of-whack postpartum hormones, that can strike at any time, but most often when you're running late and then of course you can't remember where you're supposed to be going or who you forgot to call to say you're not going to make it on time.

The only good thing about Mommy Brain is that all moms know exactly what you mean. Since they're suffering from the same condition, they're much more likely to be sympathetic next time you drive away from the supermarket with all the groceries on top of the car.

Alicia: When Mommy Brain struck, I became even more dependent on writing everything down. Otherwise I knew I'd forget *something*. So my list grew from a few scraps of paper into a three-ring mini-binder with a datebook that has become my faithful companion wherever I go. I just stash it in my purse, and it contains all my many lists for home, personal, work, and miscellaneous things.

To make things even more streamlined for my family, I have a big white dry-erase board calendar at home. I list all the classes and doctor's appointments, days I might be out of town, play dates, and anything else that's relevant, so we all know everyone's schedule—and so do my husband and babysitter. To avoid any confusion, I also list the doctor's phone number on the date of the appointment and the phone numbers for whoever is hosting the play date, so it's all up there and impossible to miss. The dry-erase markers make it easy to change and wipe down every month, as long as I remember where I put them.

Mary Ann: What helped me with Mommy Brain was reading the *New York Times* every day. Okay, I skimmed. It still counts—and was a nice way to stay engaged with the big world that was still rotating even though my own little world had temporarily shrunk when I was on maternity leave. It also helped me have something to talk about with my husband over dinner.

CHAPTER ELEVEN

For Better or Worse: Partner Time

And baby makes three . . . Relaxing at home with your partner and sharing the bliss of watching your delicious little baby grow is one of the most wonderful feelings.

But let's get real. For many moms, husbands can get very lost amid all the craziness of their baby's demands. They're used to having our attention, and then all of a sudden the baby comes along and we're just not as available as we used to be.

It's not that dads aren't willing participants—it's that they often need a lot more time to adjust while moms have already figured things out. And they might find it hard to admit that they're feeling as overwhelmed as you are, since they've been thrust into a brand-new world where moms call most of the shots, especially if they're breastfeeding.

Here's how to give your partner his own map to navigate the adjustment.

TALK, TALK SOME MORE, AND STRATEGIZE ABOUT HOUSE RULES BEFORE THE BABY IS BORN

Parenting as a team starts when you're pregnant, and it's crucial to sit down together at a time when neither of you is unduly stressed and talk (and then talk some more) about what your goals are. You want to be on the same page as much as possible—and to feel comfortable talking about anything and everything—*before* the baby is born and you're running on empty.

An easy way to strategize about parenting is to draw up house rules. You and your partner should draw up your own lists, then compare notes and figure out what will work best. House rules can range from simple, such as who takes out the trash; to more complicated, such as who's going to do the food shopping once mom goes back to work; to very tricky, such as what to do if the baby gets sick a lot and will need many more doctor visits than anticipated.

Think of these house rules as fluid and flexible, as obviously they'll evolve over time and will become much easier to agree upon and manage. You can even set a trial period to see whether or not a particular rule works.

Mary Ann: My husband loves to work out, so I'd make deals with him. If he worked out during the week, I went out with my girlfriend, sans baby, on weekends.

SAMPLE HOUSE RULES

1. Mommy does the feeding.
2. Daddy does the laundry.
3. If Daddy can't do the laundry that week, Mommy gets to buy a whole new set of onesies because baby needs clean clothes. We're not slacking off on the feeding, burping, and bathing of the baby. Daddies shouldn't slack off on the laundry.
4. Daddy does the diapering when he's home.
5. Once Daddy gets home, Mommy gets to spend thirty minutes doing whatever she wants without the baby—sleep, eat, watch *Dirty Dancing* for the umpteenth time . . . whatever. All moms need some time away from the baby.
6. Daddy is responsible for providing two dinners each week, and only one of those two can be take-out.

DADS ARE OVERWHELMED JUST AS MUCH AS YOU ARE

Mary Ann: When Zurielle was born, I thought she was a little blob. My husband, Alexander, thought she was the most beautiful thing he'd ever seen; he was just so thrilled and happy and filled with emotions unlike any he'd ever experienced before.

But Alexander didn't grow up in a large family like I did, so he was really scared about handling the baby or touching her belly-button stump, and he freaked out when she squirmed while getting dressed. I had to say, "Honey, babies don't break because daddy can't put on the diaper correctly, so go ahead and take your time and just figure it out."

I have to be honest. Although Alexander loved Zurielle to bits, it was really hard for him to make a deep connection at first because he wasn't getting a lot back. I was breastfeeding, so although he was a tremendous help with diapers and burping and cuddling, it was mostly about me taking care of this baby glued to my breast.

Finally, when Zurielle was about five months old and sitting up on her own and smiling a lot, he got over the feeling that she might just split in two if he handled her incorrectly, and life got a whole lot sweeter.

IT'S NOT "BABYSITTING" WHEN DAD WATCHES THE BABY!

Here's one of our pet peeves: Dads who get nice pats on the back when they "babysit."

Sorry, but staying home to watch your own child is not babysitting; it's *parenting*. So please refrain from gushing over any dads who watch the baby. It's their job, too. In fact, it's a lifetime commitment.

tip: *If your husband comes to you and says, "The baby's crying," you have our permission to reply, "So pick him up and deal with it."*

KEEPING YOUR RELATIONSHIP ALIVE WITHOUT TALKING ABOUT THE BABY

Alicia: My husband and I love each other dearly, but even in the best of marriages there are times when communication breaks off, and when that's happened we've figured out a way to talk it out. As long as there's talk throughout the day about how we feel, then things will be okay. That made me super conscientious that Mark and I had to make baby-free time for ourselves.

Mommy Basics

What works for us is to talk and e-mail throughout the day—as long as there's communication that's *not* baby-related. This can be a comment about a movie or some news about a friend—anything that you know your partner will like to hear about.

I have to confess that this became much easier to do once I went back to work, where I felt like we were equals, both missing our children but both happy to be at jobs we love. Still, I definitely needed to improve my conversations with him while I was home. So I gave myself a little homework on discovering alternate ways of communicating with my hubby. I'd go online, catch up with family stories, and plan couples nights out with our friends. Sure, I'd still call with the occasional "When are you coming home?" but I was able to pepper in more substantial stuff on the back end.

For many moms, *everything* becomes about the baby. My philosophy is that when my husband and I are out with friends, I don't want to talk about my own baby's poop, so I don't want to talk about your baby's poop unless it is just the funniest story that you've heard in your entire life. Yakking with mommy friends about it is another diaper altogether.

> My husband and I got closer after we had kids. Yes, there might have been some angry words exchanged, but for the most part we fell so much in love with our children and the idea of having them be a part of us. Having babies forced us to put our thoughts into another person whom we both loved.—Amy Robach

FIGHT NIGHT—TRYING NOT TO STRANGLE HIM

All couples fight. It's part of any marriage. But it's the amount of fighting and the savageness of what's said that can kill even the most loving relationship. Add a crying baby, sleepless nights, cuckoo hormones, and thirty extra pounds hanging down to your knees, and we defy anyone not to snap once in a while.

If you find yourself quivering with resentment after your hubby calls you, lounging on freshly laundered sheets in his expense-account hotel room, while back home the baby just spit up all over your bed, you really have to talk about it. You can't slam the door or stomp off into another room to ignore what's troubling you, or you'll just end up even more hurt. And you can't go to bed steaming. You'll sleep badly, if at all, and wake up tired, making it easier to get hurt and upset by the most innocuous of comments.

Now is not the time to scream any of the "YOU NEVER . . ." kinds of statements that might be true but are not the reason why you are angry at that precise instant. Instead, count to twenty taking very deep breaths—this stops you from being able to scream—and then say, "Let's talk about it."

Mary Ann: I would get so angry at my husband for something that he did, and then as soon as I'd sit down to talk to him about it, and actually hear the words coming out, I'd realize how irrational I was being. I had to admit I was upset because he had freedom and I didn't. In addition, I grew up with parents who fought constantly before divorcing, so I am hyper-aware of how destructive fights can be and have worked very hard to keep tabs on this in our relationship.

Alicia: Fights are going to happen. They're inevitable, but it's a slippery slope. Just try to remember what you started fighting about, because nine times out of ten you'll completely forget what triggered the fight in the first place.

TEETERING ON THE EDGE OF A MARTYR COMPLEX

Mary Ann: Moms are not the only people who can take care of a newborn. If you go back to work, someone other than you will be applying the diaper cream, so get used to it sooner rather than later. Even if your husband always forgets to use diaper cream, either give him a gentle reminder or do it yourself later. Just don't criticize him right after the fact or he'll feel inadequate and decide not to bother at all.

Don't forget to spell out who does what. Don't wait for your husband to say, "I see you're trying get dinner ready and you're changing the baby and now you're feeding the baby, my love, and the baby's still crying—what can I do to help, oh goddess of mine?" Instead say, "I need to finish dinner. Please take care of the baby."

Dealing with Your Husband's Needs
By GAIL SALTZ, M.D.

TODAY Mental Health Contributor and Associate Professor of Psychiatry, New York Presbyterian Hospital

All human beings want some kind of nurturing and caretaking, and even when you are the primary caretaker of your new baby, it's important to think about how your partner feels, too. This doesn't mean you need to attend to his every need. The attention you give could be as simple as saying, "Hey, you look hot today," or "Thank you, darling, for making me that cup of tea. I really appreciate it."

Tell each other what kind of gestures are truly appreciated (foot rubs, running a bath). Sometimes just coming up behind your hubby and rubbing his neck for a few seconds can make a huge difference, as that small gesture acknowledges who he is and that you haven't forgotten him, even if you are dying to say, "Oh just grow up and stop being as big a baby as the baby!"

I'm not saying you're not going to have thoughts that your partner is driving you crazy or acting like a baby, and I know how hard it can be to put one more thing on your daily to-do list, but no relationship can exist without some maintenance.

Both moms and dads are afraid of what they're going to lose when a new baby comes along. Men are often afraid they won't have any time for themselves anymore, and that life will be just drudgery instead of an easy, enjoyable time together. Remember that you're still a couple, and that if your hubby takes out the garbage because you wanted him to, he's doing it not just out of obligation but because he loves you.

On Dads and Delegating
By RUTH PETERS, Ph.D.

TODAY Contributor and Clinical Psychologist

It's very, very common for moms to take full responsibility for all baby care from the minute they walk in the door at home, and for dads to get the feeling that they can't do it exactly right, so why do it at all. It's called learned helplessness. And if that happens, moms have only themselves to blame.

So if I had one thing to tell first-time moms, it would be to accept less than perfection from their husbands. If the diaper is on backwards, it doesn't really matter. It's much more important *not* to allow learned helplessness to occur, and to let dads feel good about what they can handle, because they do want to participate as much as they can. If dads are "trained" from the get-go, they'll help out more.

If you admit that you've created this situation, first, stop blaming your husband, and then, if you want something done only your way then do it yourself—but stop nagging. There are two methods to address learned helplessness: sneaky and open.

For the sneaky method, use situations in which you have to leave home for a while, either for your job or for some other reason. Or you could have two things to do at once, and then dad *has* to chip in. For example, say, "I need to cook dinner now, so I need you to bathe the baby." He'll bathe the baby, you will not comment on how he does it, except for offering praise, and then bathing the baby will become dad's regular duty.

Or you can try the "open" method, which is to sit down together and confess that you're done with whining and nagging, and you're sorry, and that hubby isn't a big enough part of the baby's life, and that's not good for anyone. Get creative now so that you're setting up a lifetime pattern of interactive behavior with dad and the baby. Let him do his own special thing with the baby, such as taking the baby for a walk every Saturday afternoon, or whatever he suggests.

Part of the problem with learning how to delegate is that a lot of people don't know how to begin the conversation, or that they need to have the conversation in the first place, instead of calling their mom or girlfriends to complain.

What you need is a checklist, a sort of mental map or guide of what duties there are and who's going to be in charge of them. The ideal time to start discussions is before the baby arrives, not in the heat of the moment when the baby's been crying for two hours and you haven't slept in three weeks. Sit down with some paper and figure out your options. Obviously you'll have to wing some of it, depending on your baby's needs. A colicky baby needs more attention, a mellow baby less. But you can still create a plan by asking yourselves, if we're not breastfeeding, who'll do the feedings? Who's in charge of diapers? Who does the grocery shopping?

If you follow the checklist from day one, you'll always know who's meant to do what, and this will help you avoid fighting over petty things.

CHANGE THE HOUSE RULES WHEN YOU GO BACK TO WORK

Whether you go back to work two weeks, two months, or two years after the baby is born, sit down with your partner and draw up the new house rules. When both of you are working, it's even more crucial to divvy up the duties and be specific about it.

It's best to sort out a schedule for whoever is responsible for dinner. Perhaps you can offer to take care of three meals during the work week while he takes care of two. Even if dinner is no more exotic than scrambled eggs or pizza, at least you know you aren't in charge all the time and don't have to hurry home on those nights when you aren't cooking. If your work situation changes—a huge project or travel assignment comes in unexpectedly—draw up temporary rules, and then change them again when this period is over.

Helping Out, and Finding "You" Time
By MATT LAUER

I'm never there in the mornings, which is both a good and a bad thing. It's bad because you always like to be there when the baby wakes up, and good if the baby tends to be cranky when he wakes up. But I'm there for bath time and always have been, since it's a very important time in my household.

Jack was a tough one to get to sleep, so I also helped out a lot with that. I spent a lot of time driving that baby around. So bath time and sleep time were when I would try to give Annette the most assistance I could.

I learned that family time is more important than goof-off-and-play-golf-with-your-buddies time. I have to work to find time with my friends, and there are still a lot of moments when I miss the days when I could jump on a plane in the winter and go play golf somewhere for a weekend. I don't do that anymore, because I can't justify leaving my family for a weekend when it's not essential.

But I've also learned that you cannot live on just work time and family time. You need time for you. I have my free time; my wife has hers. It makes you a better father and a more patient person, and I think in the long run it's a much healthier situation.

ON HELPING OUT
My father was a bus driver, so I grew up used to a tight schedule. I'm on a similarly tight schedule when it comes to my children. I keep their calendars and print them out and put them on a bulletin board. I also do the grocery shopping and cooking for the family.—Al Roker

Dads Do Get Better as the Baby Gets Older
By ANN CURRY

Husbands get better at child-rearing over time. I certainly had times when I was *very* frustrated because my hubby wasn't as intuitively programmed to jump up when he heard the baby cry or know enough to help me out. But as my babies grew older he really stepped up and became a truly amazing father.

Still, it was hard, even though I knew that my husband wouldn't be good at nursing because he didn't have the equipment, and he wasn't good at washing dishes because he'd never done them before we got married, and he wasn't that good at shopping because he always bought the wrong thing. But I forgave him, as he became unbelievably great once the hardest part of taking care of the baby was over. I know this sounds sexist, but that's how it worked for us. If I'd known when I was a brand-new mother that my husband's talents would shine several years later, I would have been a lot less frustrated and had fewer expectations. That doesn't help when you're falling over with exhaustion and the baby won't stop crying, but babies do get older and they do stop crying.

GIVE EACH OTHER SPACE

Alicia: As the rabbi said at my wedding, "You can't always be the flower. Sometimes you have to be the stem." Which means that if I'm taking extra "me" time, as I was when writing this book, I couldn't be upset if my husband went out with his friends on Friday night *and* Saturday night. It was his time to be the flower. My husband had fed the kids and put them down when I was working late, so it was his turn to have the nights to do what he wanted. And everything's fine.

tip: *Keeping score is for basketball. Don't keep a running tab of who did what, unless you want to be called for a foul or benched. A healthy give-and-take is an essential part of any good relationship. Make sure it's part of yours.*

When Counseling Helps
By RUTH PETERS, Ph.D.

TODAY Contributor and Clinical Psychologist

If you are feeling resentful (past the normal overreactions common to sleep deprivation); if you are holding a grudge; if you are obsessing about how unfair it is that your hubby's not helping; if you do not have a good support system with relatives; if you're so irritable and stressed that when your hubby gets home, all you do is dump a laundry list of what negative things happened that day and what he did or did not do, then counseling might be a good idea.

A calm mediator—not a relative—whose judgment you trust can help any couple deal with big changes or issues in their lives. My patients know that

Mommy Basics

neither the wife nor the husband can play dirty during our sessions. We have to talk it out, and not just bring up old stuff, because they know I'll stop it. I'll literally lob kooshie balls at people when they're being nasty—it shuts them up! A big part of the process is letting each party speak without interruption.

The best way to find a good therapist is word of mouth. Do not find a therapist in the yellow pages. After a few sessions, if you don't get good vibes, move on, because you need to feel comfortable with someone who will be discussing the most intimate parts of your life.

Not everyone can afford therapy (nor does health insurance always cover it). You might be able to speak to your pastor, but his or her primary duty is not couples counseling. If you can't hire a therapist, try e-mailing each other. You can edit your e-mails prior to sending, so take your time to write out your concerns. If the e-mail back ignores your point, then send another message, saying, "You may have a valid point [that's not an admission; it's a statement], but please address my issues first."

If your e-mail is particularly hard-hitting or angry, do yourself a favor and send it to yourself first, then read it a day later. That way you won't regret sending something in the heat of the moment that you wish you hadn't put in writing. Many e-mails sent to yourself are going to end up deleted, because you'll find a better way of handling the situation, or the act of having written it down defused it.

SEX AFTER BABY: NOT TONIGHT, HONEY— ASK ME AGAIN IN A YEAR OR TWO

Mary Ann: My midwife had warned me to avoid sex for at least six weeks after birth. "I'll tell you six," she added with a laugh, "but I suggest you tell your husband *eight* weeks, just to be sure."

Although sex was the last thing on my mind, by week eight it was certainly on my husband's mind. He tried his best to be gentle, but it was still crazy painful for me.

GETTING BACK IN THE GROOVE

> If you're breastfeeding, your hormones cut way down on the necessary lubrication, so make sure you have something on hand to help you along.
> If you're feeling bad about your body and haven't lost the baby

weight yet, trust us, your partner will not care one bit. He'll be happy getting *anything*!

> Watch what you say to your husband, as language is extremely powerful, especially when the topic is sex. If you say, "I'm not in the mood," make it clear why, being careful to note that it's not about him. Otherwise, he will take this rejection to heart and be very hurt. He may even think it's a direct insult.

Bottom line: You can't *not* be in the mood too many times. When you say it, your husband will be rolling over on the other side of the bed, unhappy and a little bit bruised.

Alicia: When we were sans children, Mark and I used to make whoopie in the morning, but we had to switch from a.m. to p.m. when baby made three. It was quite difficult to get back in the saddle after those first few months. I was overwhelmingly tired at the end of each day, and after that last feeding I was so groggy I was often asleep before I hit the sheets. But there were some nights I knew I needed to do whatever it took to wake up, like refreshing myself with a shower because I hadn't had a chance to do so all day and felt gross. Once you're out of the shower you'll feel like a new woman—trust me.

Don't worry if the baby is sleeping in the crib in your room when you and your partner are in the mood. The baby is not going to remember anything. Not only that, but lovemaking is what created this baby in the first place, and any display of affection is a lovely thing for your baby to start seeing early on. And as long as there's a crib, you don't have to worry about the door opening in the middle of the night and a little voice piping up, "Mommy, why are you naked?"

On the other hand, a definite buzz kill is when you're finally enjoying each other and, of course, the baby wakes up and starts wailing.

GET CREATIVE SEXUALLY

Your partner needs to understand that you just had something the size of a small watermelon travel through your birth canal. In other words: You're sore!

Sexual behavior doesn't always need to include actual sex. Be honest about what you feel comfortable with. A foot or leg or head massage, for instance, can be wildly sensual, and ask your partner to think about what he knows turns your brain on. If he doesn't ask what would make you feel good, now is your moment to speak up!

Realize that men usually love to be thrown off guard, so the more unpredictable you can be, the better. Tell him you're too tired and then pounce a few seconds later. Put on your sexy lingerie under your spit-up–encrusted bathrobe. Keep the lights on low and the candles flickering to greet him when he gets home.

SCHEDULING TIME FOR SEX (PROS AND CONS)

Alicia: As you know, I'm the girl with a list for everything, but lovemaking is the one thing I don't want to schedule, and certainly not write on the calendar on the back of the door! This does mean that we get interrupted by a crying baby a lot, or fall asleep, but I'm still a big believer that when everything else in your life is on a tight schedule, being spontaneous about sex is the way to go. And believe me, most of the time my husband has this on *his* mental "to do" list!

That's what works for me. It may sound unromantic, but lots of very busy couples I know actually thrive on setting a schedule for sex. It heightens the anticipation, and it's an acknowledgment of how important a good sex life is to any relationship.

Mary Ann: I agree with Alicia, but if you notice (after the doctor gives you the go-ahead, of course) that you are going a few weeks without wonka-wonk, it's time to make a date with daddy.

Sex and the Mommy
By GAIL SALTZ, M.D.

TODAY Mental Health Contributor and Associate Professor of Psychiatry, New York Presbyterian Hospital

Feeling sexual again is usually difficult for several reasons:

> First, you just had a baby come through that opening, so there's a lot of anxiety and apprehension about the first time and whether it will hurt. Even women who have had C-sections have pain, as there's tenderness around the cervix, plus breastfeeding can cause dryness, to say nothing of leaking or squirting from your breasts if you have an orgasm!

> Speaking of breasts, those sort of belong to the baby as feeding tools now, and it's hard to see them as sexual and your baby's bottle at the same time. For many women, the role of mother doesn't feel consistent with the role of sexy lover to their partner. They feel that with a baby at their nipples a good chunk of the day, or in their arms, it's "glued" to them, and they don't want anyone besides the baby touching them. I know it's hard for men to understand, but nursing is a somewhat sexual experience that's very intense. You're being sucked on and touched and it smells good and it can be very fulfilling and intimate. For you, not your partner.
> You're very tired, so sleep is much more desirable than sex.
> Your body has changed dramatically, and it takes a long time for muscle tone to come back and extra pounds to be lost, and that makes a lot of moms unhappy. To them, it doesn't matter if their partner says they're great and sexy. If you don't feel sexy in your own eyes it's hard to feel sexy, period.
> Hormone changes kill the mood.
> Because many couples have much less sex or no sex in the last trimester, husbands can be waiting with bated breath for you to be back, and that can add a lot of pressure. Dads often wonder what their role is, especially if you're breastfeeding, and a lot of them get relegated to the diaper changing, which is not really fun. So your husband may be looking for his place since he often feels very left out, and whatever nurturing you used to give him is now directed to the baby.

All this may make men more sexually hungry, but think of it more as a hunger for intimacy. Sex for men is not just about the sex act. It is really their intimacy with you. Denying sex creates a lot of anxiety, tension, and anger. It's important for new moms to realize that their husbands *are* looking for things that are not just sex—other important elements like physical intimacy and feeling safe and loved.

Try to give your partner the baby for a couple of hours before bedtime, as he needs to touch and cuddle the baby and you need a break from the baby touching you. It's good for everybody. This way, by the time he gets into bed with you he's not diving on you for any physical attention, although he'd still like to have sex with you. It also helps for you to take a bath before bedtime, to be alone with your own body and your own thoughts.

If you're not ready for intercourse and keep putting it off because you fear the pain, try inserting a tampon, alone, to see how it feels, without the pressure of a sexually aroused man near you. If it feels uncomfortable, you can tell him that there are other ways to please each other, and that other sexual acts might be what you want to do until you feel comfortable with actual penetration. When you're ready to have intercourse, it's better for you to be on top the first time to control how fast and how far, and to lessen any soreness.

On Getting Back into the Sexual Groove
By MEREDITH VIEIRA and NATALIE MORALES

Meredith: After childbirth, you come home with a donut and it's not from Dunkin. It's so unromantic! Then when you have to go to the bathroom, it hurts. Everyone says you're going to love being a mom but they never tell you how you'll suffer. You're going to have hemorrhoids.

I wasn't in the mood for a while. I felt our son, Ben, needed all our attention. "So you be the big boy here," I used to say to my husband. "Big boy!" Which didn't go over well. I wouldn't say we had a rocky time, but there were some tough conversations. You do have to make an effort, especially to spend time alone together, and that was something I had a hard time with. I worried something might happen every time I was away from my baby, but when I finally made the effort with my husband, it was worth it.

Natalie: I'm still trying to get back into the groove! It's hard, as you go from being a married couple who has sex a few times a week to scheduling it during your child's naptime once a week. It becomes a little bit of a chore for me, especially because my husband and I work a lot of different hours, so I'm usually exhausted when he's ready and raring to go. But we have had some amazing romps too. You just have to let the good times be the real incentive to get in the mood.

DATE NIGHT WITH DADDY

The more you get your life back to the way things were, the better. Date nights can be hard because you're so focused on the baby, and you can't help looking at your watch when your breasts start to leak because it's feeding time. But the sooner you get a routine going with your partner, the easier it is to keep it going.

Mary Ann: Alexander and I made a house rule that we'd go out together one night a week. We got a babysitter so we could have dinner, see a movie, or catch up with friends. We'd be home at a decent hour, but it was one night dedicated to the two of us. It was really necessary for us to have that time together.

About eight months after Zurielle was born, we took a weekend away alone. Me, my hubby, and my breast pump. It was not the most sexually fulfilling weekend ever, but once we got over that hump, we thought, hey, we need to get away like this more often!

> *My kids would be thrilled if there was a force field around the house and we never left. But if you don't leave, the kids are more likely to be unhappy when you do go out. In the last two years we have yet to achieve dinner and a movie. We can do either, but not both. When we go to dinner, halfway through we're too tired, so we go home and wait for the movie to come out on DVD!*
> — Al Roker

Keeping Romance Alive
By TIKI BARBER

The romance is the hardest thing to hold on to. As I got more and more desperate, it was the farthest thing from Ginny's mind. Romance, and by extension, sex, wasn't an assumed event as it had been before the baby was born. It became a courting ritual again. It took a lot of planning and "us" time, such as having date nights during the first couple of years, and as our kids have gotten older, "anniversary trips," where we're able to go away by ourselves for three or four days. We have been fortunate and blessed in this regard because Ginny's parents live with us.

Ginny and I definitely know how to have fun, and we realize that actively coordinating nights on the town with friends is not only fun, but necessary to keep us young and engaged. Our game plan isn't set in stone, but at least once a week we have dinner out with friends, and once a month we have an "out all night" event, which includes dinner, clubbing, or karaoke. Most of the following mornings are regretful, but the night itself is always worth it!

CHAPTER TWELVE

What No One Wants to Bring Up: Postpartum Depression, the Baby Blues, and Unwanted Advice

Having a baby is one of the most joyful experiences you'll have in your lifetime, but it's also one of the most stressful. But because having a baby *is* so joyful, admitting that you are struggling can be very hard. Not only are you constantly bombarded with messages about what happy families are supposed to look like, but you can beat yourself up with shame and guilt or fend off a surprisingly large amount of criticism if you aren't constantly brimming with baby love and enthusiasm.

POSTPARTUM DEPRESSION OR THE BABY BLUES? MARY ANN'S STORY

Mary Ann: Alexander and I were married for four years before we had kids. The first time we tried we got pregnant. I had a miscarriage, but three months later I was pregnant again. I was so sure I was having a boy that Zurielle was shock number one.

But that was only the beginning.

Shock number two came in the hospital right after she was born. I didn't feel any happiness at all. I had been ambivalent during my pregnancy, but all the books I'd devoured assured me that was normal, and that once my child was born I would feel love like I'd never felt before. When I didn't, I started to get worried. Instead of having great, gooey feelings about my beautiful new baby, I couldn't stop obsessing about how I'd had such a great marriage and had been on top of my game at work and then all of a sudden this wailing infant had taken away my independence. I felt like a total failure.

In retrospect, I think all of those hormones, coupled with the exhaustion from the birth, affected my brain, and this awful voice kept telling me that this baby meant everything I'd worked so hard for all my life would be over.

I checked out of the hospital much too early. The next day, we had to go to the pediatrician to get the baby tested for allergies. The doctor said the baby was perfect, but I felt he was really looking at me and saying, *But you're not and I'm going to take this baby away from you forever.* I was so paranoid that it was a miracle I didn't start crying right then and there. Of course, if I had, I might have gotten help a lot sooner.

A few days later, I was barely keeping things together, but I went into the office to fill out some paperwork. I ran into Matt Lauer and he said, "How are you doing? It's really hard, isn't it?" I said that it was, and he went on to say that he understood how difficult it was dealing with exhaustion, hormones, and everything else. And I said, "Truer words have never been spoken."

Little did he know that I was not well. I was having crazy thoughts that had started immediately after giving birth. That week after Zurielle's birth was especially hot. Our apartment felt like a greenhouse and my husband was always opening the windows. I'd walk by and think of throwing myself out, or worse.

So picture this: My husband, who had no idea I was falling apart, kept opening every single window, and we didn't have child guards yet, or screens. I'd shut the windows. He'd raise the windows until I'd scream, "Do not open this window!"

My mom didn't know, and my husband didn't know either, because I didn't want to admit that I was in such bad shape. Everyone was so happy about the baby. They would have been devastated if I'd told them I didn't feel the same way.

Three weeks after Zurielle was born, my mom had to return home to Tulsa. I bawled my eyes out. To make matters worse, my husband started traveling for work.

Feeling all alone and scared, I decided to go stay with my family in Oklahoma. I stayed in Tulsa for six weeks with my amazing brother, Robert, his wife, Carrie, and their three kids, because I was too paranoid to be left alone. I knew I wouldn't let anything happen, because I was accountable to my family and didn't want to go cuckoo in front of them. They protected me. They protected my baby. I needed an extra pair of hands, to have people hold Zurielle, to get some time to myself and resume a little bit of what I thought my life should be.

At the six-week mark, I said, fine, you can make it to the two-month mark. One day, I went to see *Anchorman* with Zurielle sound asleep in the BabyBjörn, and as I sat there, laughing my head off, I thought, *You know what? I can still do all the things I used to do; it's going to be okay.*

That turned into the three-month mark, then six months. As time went on I started having fewer psychotic thoughts and got more sleep, and then I was fine. Which is when I related what I'd experienced to my husband, who was shocked and felt terrible that he hadn't been able to support me or to realize how much I'd hidden my feelings. But that had been part of my problem. When I finally told my friends, they all said they never would have known. Even at my worst, I still was able to feed and care for my baby.

During my second pregnancy, I was stronger and smarter. I got the name of a good psychiatrist, I warned my midwives, and my husband and I prepared for the worst-case scenario. Only now I had a team in case I needed it. And when Arabella arrived, she was a much more mellow baby. It was like God was giving me a break because of what I'd gone through the first time.

tip: *If you think you may have postpartum depression, don't tough it out like I did. Get help. The consequences could have been severe, and I feel my daughter and I both suffered because I was too embarrassed to be honest with those who loved me most.*

My Postpartum Depression
By KATHIE LEE GIFFORD

I had postpartum depression with Cody, but I had to go and put on a show and my audience didn't deserve that. Regis didn't deserve that. I've been a professional since I was twelve. The cliché that the show must go on is true, because I took only one sick day in fifteen years. I didn't look particularly good at six a.m. when I went to work, but while many people think of me as someone who shares everything in life, I always kept some things private that I did not feel comfortable sharing.

It was worse at night. I would nurse Cody, put him back to sleep, and just cry my heart out. During those long nocturnal hours I would quote the Psalms and pray. I would eventually fall asleep with a prayer on my lips and I'd wake up the same way. I couldn't take any medication because I was nursing, but I'd rather pop a prayer than a pill anyway. The depression lasted for several months, but ultimately this time-tested solution worked better for me than any prescription could.

Signs of Postpartum Depression
By RUTH PETERS, Ph.D.

TODAY Contributor and Clinical Psychologist

Postpartum depression is very common and should not be a reason to feel shame. An analogy I like to use is, if you had diabetes, or if you fell and broke your leg, wouldn't you get help? Bear in mind that you won't be much good to yourself or your baby if you don't seek help as soon as you notice any signs.

Note to dads or partners: If you notice any unusual changes or behavior that's not quite right, you need to be proactive and bring your wife or partner to a doctor.

Warning signs: You can't get out of bed, or if you do get out of bed to feed the baby, you may bring the baby into or near the bed for the next four hours; sleep disorders (too much or too little sleep); eating disorders (eating too much or too little); and what I call the "Blue Funk." The Blue Funk is a cloud over your head, preventing you from finding joy in life. You're not smiling, you're not enjoying your baby or the things that usually give you pleasure.

If you are suffering from any of the above, go to your gynecologist or family practitioner. Antidepressants can be very helpful, but they take several weeks to become effective, so do not wait if you or your loved ones think you may be depressed.

On Postpartum Depression
By GAIL SALTZ, M.D.

TODAY Mental Health Contributor and Associate Professor of Psychiatry, New York Presbyterian Hospital

Most women have some form of mood changes after giving birth. These come primarily in the form of postpartum blues, occurring anywhere within the first two weeks after giving birth and not lasting longer than two weeks. It could be that you feel blue, or irritable, or one minute you're elated and the next minute you burst into tears over nothing in particular. This kind of moodiness is thought to be due to fluctuation in hormones (estrogen and progesterone) as well as sleep deprivation, adjustment to your new role, and the stress that brings. These blues should be very fleeting.

One in ten women will go on to have much more serious postpartum depression that can occur anywhere from several days after giving birth to up to a year afterward. This depression is also thought to be due to a combination of a drop in estrogen and progesterone, sometimes a sudden drop in thyroid function, chronic sleep deprivation, and major upheaval in the family structure. You'll know this is true postpartum depression if you're having more than two weeks of feeling hopeless, helpless, worthless, and guilty (guilt being particularly associated with this type of depression). Other warning signs are difficulty sleeping, trouble breastfeeding, and loss of appetite.

Like Mary Ann, many women endure these feelings in silence. They feel terrible about themselves, wondering why they should be feeling this way and what this means about *them*. But this depression is triggered by a combination of shifting hormones coupled with an imbalance of expectations and reality. So many new moms expect life to be like the baby magazine with the cute infant on the cover. They've seen friends gushing and cooing over their own newborns, or spent nine months thinking about how wonderful being a mom will feel without factoring in the poop and vomit and sleepless nights, and how they'll feel about their role change into a new world of total responsibility for another human being.

Maternal ambivalence is totally normal. It's the degree to which you are accepting of this ambivalence that can lead to depression. Feeling ambivalent about the massive changes in your life never means you're a bad mother. It means you're a normal mother. Postpartum depression is particularly incongruous because there's such a myth that joy and utter happiness equals good mothers, so feeling bad equals bad mothers. That just isn't true.

How to Get Help

Be blunt with your obstetrician or midwife. This professional should let you know that if you have any symptoms or need to talk within the next several weeks after giving birth, you should give him or her a call to take a cursory history and see whether the symptoms are severe enough for a referral to a psychiatrist. If you have postpartum depression you should be evaluated, but don't assume you'll need medication. Some medications come out in such small amounts in breast milk that you still can breastfeed. Anti-psychotics, however, are not in this category. Mild forms of postpartum depression may respond without the need for medication, simply by allowing you to talk about your feelings. Getting

LOVE AT FIRST SIGHT?

Love at first sight doesn't happen for every mom. It's okay not to be immediately overwhelmed with love for your baby. This doesn't make you a selfish or uncaring mom. It makes you a mom who just needs a little bit more time to adjust. Our good friend Betsy shared some insight on this. She summed it up like this: "Did you love your husband instantly? Or was it something that had to develop over time and you had to nurture?"

family support and as much sleep as you need is hugely important, so try to arrange for someone to help you with the nighttime feedings.

You should also talk to your spouse, or a trusted friend if you're single, because what you really need is support—somebody to step in and cover for you so you can get long stretches of sleep. Shutting out your spouse can make you feel even more isolated with your feelings, so your spouse, your obstetrician, and perhaps other loved ones may step in to help, too. From my perspective, it's very helpful to visit a psychiatrist who knows about postpartum depression with your spouse so that he can hear and understand how this isn't just about you, and that this situation is all too common. It's awfully scary for your spouse to hear you say, "I'm thinking I want to throw the baby out the window," and much less scary to have a psychiatrist explain that lots of women have these thoughts.

A more serious form of postpartum depression is postpartum mania, which is actually the first sign of bipolar disorder. Bipolar disorder often surfaces in the late teens and early twenties, and hormone fluctuations, stress, and lack of sleep can exacerbate it. The mania may appear as a "high" state—not necessarily joyous, but expansive and grandiose and feeling on top of the world. But it's more likely to make you highly irritable and agitated. Treatment usually involves talk therapy, antidepressants, and hormone treatment if necessary.

Men Can Get Postpartum Depression Too

Postpartum depression in men is not hormonally driven, but stems more from the dramatic changes in their role and lifestyle. Becoming a father drives a man to feel protective and as the primary provider, but that doesn't leave room for him to feel anxious or fragile without the support of his wife, who is busy with the baby. It's much harder for men to open up about these totally normal worries.

Often, when women are depressed they get weepy and sad, but when men get depressed they can get angry and irritable and jealous of your relationship with the baby, because it's difficult for them to express the feelings of sadness. If you have an irritable and angry husband who's picking fights and you're wondering what the heck is going on, be aware that underneath the anger is someone who's sad and afraid. It can be very useful to visit a therapist to get affirmation that his anxieties are not bizarre or abnormal. And you can do your part by allowing him to help out with the baby, to develop a loving bond with the baby, and to give him special time with you as well.

"WHERE'S THAT BABY'S HAT?"
DEALING WITH UNSOLICITED ADVICE

What to wear, what not to wear, how to hold the baby, how to feed the baby, what to buy the baby, how to let babies cry it out, how to comfort them—all in the span of one endless elevator ride with a bunch of snoopy strangers in your office building!

When this started to happen, we were taken aback. Either we couldn't think of the right thing to say or we automatically felt that we were doing something wrong, even when we knew we were right and the "critic" was wrong.

All the *TODAY* show moms were a huge help for our criticism management. Being able to come in to work after a long weekend with the in-laws, or with people asking you questions you didn't need to answer, and to share (okay, *vent*) with our co-workers helped diffuse much of the hurt feelings. Believe me, there's been a *lot* of commiserating! And once you realize how often unwelcome advice is dished out to all new mothers, it makes it much easier to bear.

We learned how to let comments go in one ear and out the other, because most people aren't trying to be mean or critical. They want to be helpful; they can just be clumsy or stupid about it. How can you take seriously such comments as "Give your baby formula—it will help him sleep through the night." "Put rice cereal in the bottle." "Put brandy on the baby's gums to soothe teething." "Babies don't get enough food with breast milk alone." "Your baby should always be wearing socks, even if it's 100 degrees out"?

Being able to accept such advice graciously, and then discard it without feeling defensive, is an excellent way to gain confidence in your own parenting skills. At the end of the day, you're the mom, and you are going to have to trust your own judgment and be your own advocate. Working moms in particular are going to have to brace themselves for a slew of comments from those who say you should be a stay-at-home mom, and how dare you want to go back to work!

All you can do is try your best. Know that you're going to make mistakes, and there will be occasions when your decisions are going to be wrong, but most of the time what you want to do is just fine—and nobody's business.

The best advice I've been given and what I relay to moms-to-be is this: Whatever people tell you, no matter what the advice is, nod and smile, and then do what feels right for you. Remember, it's your child, and you are the child's mom, and whatever you do will be the best for your baby.
                                                    —Cecilia Fang Wu

DEALING WITH RUDE COMMENTS USING THE SMILE-AND-WAVE TECHNIQUE

You're dripping with sweat as you stroll down the street during a heat wave. The streets are practically melting, and your baby is flushed and cranky even though all she's wearing is a cotton onesie.

Naturally, someone will come by and say, "Why isn't your baby covered up?"

When you're taken aback by a snarky comment, your brain can turn to mush, because it's such a shock to hear anyone being less than loving about your beloved baby. You don't know what to do. Should you respond? But then, just because someone else is rude, you don't want to be rude, too, or engage that person in any way.

An easy solution is the Smile-and-Wave Technique. You don't have to say a word. Just smile, wave, and walk away.

If you do want to say something, plaster a big smile on your face and say, "Thank you for sharing, have a nice day!" Wave good-bye, and walk away.

If the comment has been particularly egregious, like "Why don't you people stay home with your baby instead of dragging it out to dinner to disrupt us?" (never mind that your baby has been blissfully asleep since the minute you walked in the door)—you can smile and wave while saying, "Why do you want to know?" and then walk away. Trust us, only the most thick-headed nitwit won't get the message.

YOU CAN'T CHOOSE YOUR RELATIVES: DEALING WITH PARENTS, GOOD AND BAD

Speaking of advice, there's the tricky issue of your family. Dealing with rude strangers is often a breeze compared to dealing with your relatives.

Mary Ann: Since I've had kids my relationship with my mother has gotten much, much better. Like all kids toward their parents, I harshly judged her but now I think, my God, she must have been completely exhausted! No wonder she was, well, snarly when I'd get scared and wake her up in the middle of the night. She was just utterly worn out.

Alicia: If I had a nickel for every time that we walked into my in-laws' home, no matter what the weather, and heard Jack's grandma lovingly ask, "Why isn't my grandson wearing any socks? It's too cold for him not to be wearing socks," I'd be writing this from my retirement home in Hawaii (where we would never need socks!).

tip: *One deflecting technique that works well with relatives is to call in the experts. For example, say, "Thank you very much for that information, but I talked to my pediatrician and he said XYZ, so I'm going to try this for now." Chances are pretty high that even the most interfering of relatives will not feel the need to challenge an M.D.*

FINAL WORDS OF ADVICE

1. Don't get upset about all the details. *Let things go.* Everything does not have to be perfect. It's okay to have a house that's less than spotless. Instead of cleaning, spend the same time playing with your baby. You will never regret it.

2. It's okay for your babies to know you are human, too. As a mom, you don't have to know all the answers and you don't have to be right all the time. You will learn as you go. There is no one way to do this. (This will be especially important as your babies grow older, as you'll need to let your children win some battles. They will be stronger for it.)

3. Hugs and kisses are some of life's biggest rewards.

4. Laugh with your babies. Let them see you giggle. Nothing is more delicious than the sound of a baby's laughter!—Debbie Kosofsky

PART THREE

Worktime Basics

CHAPTER THIRTEEN

Making Your Job Work for You

We both knew we'd go back to work after we gave birth. As a result, our kids are growing up knowing that our jobs are a vital part of our identity and our lives. Sure, they're thrilled when we're home on weekends (if we're not on the road), but when Monday rolls around and Mommy has her work clothes on, they're fine with that, too.

While you're pregnant, bear in mind that you might have conflicting feelings about returning to work. Once you're a mom, your baby will define you in a very different way. You're not just a mom—you're a *working* mom.

FIGURING OUT YOUR MATERNITY LEAVE

While you're pregnant, ask your Human Resources department if you're at a large company, or your boss if you're at a small company, about their policy on maternity leave. Make sure all the proper channels are followed and departments notified so a good schedule can be worked out for everyone.

It's essential to know your rights, because it's illegal to fire an employee solely due to pregnancy.

RETURNING TO WORK

Alicia: I wasn't emotional on my first day back. I trusted my sitter, plus it was kind of exciting to go back to work knowing that I had a family at home. But that was day one. The rest of the week was harder, and I had to

deal with the *Oh no, I'm not there for my baby, woe is me!* feelings. I couldn't help myself from wondering how many milestones I was going to miss. But then I realized that even if Jack took his first step with the babysitter, when I got home I might not be seeing the first step ever, but it would be the first step for *me*. And that's what mattered.

Mary Ann: I took a long maternity leave. I felt guilty not going in to the office every day, and I worried I'd get sidelined once back at work, with diminished responsibilities—or worse, that I'd be forgotten about entirely. It was so refreshing to come back and have everything be familiar. I made it clear to my bosses that I had no problems going right back to what I'd been doing, including all the traveling. Sometimes I'd get in at the crack of dawn to do my morning segments, then cycle back home and be at the breakfast table before my kids even woke up, and then we'd all eat together before I went back to the office.

FINDING THE STAMINA WHEN YOU GO BACK TO WORK

Sure, you're back at work, but chances are pretty good you're still buying the groceries, managing the household, and making sure there's always a stash of toilet paper, diapers, and wipes. And that's on a good day!

Alicia: I was thrilled to be back at work, but once I got into the heavy hours, crazy mornings, and juggling schedules, I heard myself saying, "What did I get myself into?" Factor in the learning curve with you and your husband when you're trying to figure out how to get your work schedules in synch, such as who gets home first to relieve the sitter when you both have to work late. It takes time to figure it all out.

I slept all the time those first few months back at work. I would come home, feed the baby, and pass out. I don't even think I shared more than a few sentences with my husband. It was a very difficult transition period. But after you get through it, your energy picks up. Definitely give yourself license to order in a few more meals than you usually do during those first few weeks back.

Mary Ann: There can be bad days, of course. I may have had a fight with my husband and then the baby puked all over me and I hadn't even gotten dressed yet, and then I did something wrong at work, and then I got filled with pangs of mourning for my old life, when I had more money and time and could go hang out with my girlfriends whenever I wanted. It's really okay to have a good cry if life stinks right now. Take your time crying and then move on.

When Your Dream Job Becomes a Nightmare
By MEREDITH VIEIRA

I was going to take six months off, and then I was offered my dream job—the only job that I can honestly say I coveted as a journalist—to work on *60 Minutes*. I was offered it the week before my baby was born. It was like having two babies, and I realized I was fighting myself from the moment the offer came in. I didn't want to turn down the job I'd always wanted, but damn, the timing was terrible.

When I was negotiating the job at *60 Minutes*, I had Ben by my side, clutching my index finger. That was the only way I could keep my priorities straight. I told myself to remember who I was *now*, and not get sucked in. It was working, I thought. For the first two years I agreed to do ten stories a year, instead of twenty. That seemed doable.

About a week into the job I realized it wouldn't be fine, as there were so many pressures at work and at home. Being a new mom, I wanted to be with my baby *and* my husband *and* get this right the first time, while trying to juggle an equally demanding new job. I was trying to be everything for everybody, and as a result I never felt totally complete. I cried a lot when I was at home. I cried a lot when I was on a story.

Because I had a hard time juggling, I didn't hang around to schmooze with the boss as others did. I became one of those employees who did their job and then left for the day. That really wasn't the mindset of the show and the culture there. So my boss and I started to butt heads almost from the beginning in a subconscious way. I'd wanted this job so badly, but my comfort level was never quite there. When I was called to go overseas to do a big interview, my stomach was in knots. I knew in that moment my gut-check, which I always believed in, validated the decision that I wanted more kids more than I wanted to be on *60 Minutes*.

I'd already had four miscarriages before Ben, and another one before getting pregnant with Gabe. I kept Gabe's pregnancy quiet until I was asked to do a story that involved flying—the one thing my doctor forbade me to do. I had to tell my boss on the phone that I couldn't do it. There was a silence on the other end of the line, and then he said he had to get somebody else to do the story. I knew it wasn't going to work out, and I left. I had been nervous all the time up until then, but the minute I made the decision, it was as if the proverbial weight was lifted.

I think you have to set your priorities and stick with them and believe in yourself. Shortly after I left 60 *Minutes*, a woman came up to me and said, "Aren't you setting back working women?" and I thought, if I didn't leave, I'd be living my life as a lie. What is *that* saying to women? We need to be able to make our own choices and feel comfortable with whatever works best for our needs and our families.

BREASTFEEDING AND PUMPING BREAST MILK AT WORK

If you want to keep breastfeeding once you go back to work, you need to figure out how to pump discreetly. Sorting out a schedule can be tricky. It's not as though you can stand up and announce you're off to the Boob Boardroom.

Mary Ann: After I pumped, I stashed my bags in a tote in the fridge. But then someone told me it was against OSHA rules to have any kind of body fluid placed in a public refrigerator. So I purchased a mini-cooler and kept it under my desk.

If your boss is unsympathetic about your need to pump, try to compromise. Be open about how much time you need, and where. Obviously it will be difficult to pump in the company break room at lunchtime, but it should only take ten or fifteen minutes to get the job done at some other point in the day. If it says in your company's guidelines that they have to provide a place, they'll find you a place. Not taking no for an answer coupled with a little persistence will make it clear to your superiors that you're serious about pumping. If you're willing to discuss alternatives, such as staying in the office longer to make up for your pumping breaks, chances are it will never become a problem. And you can remind them, and yourself, that breastfeeding is a temporary situation.

We hope that as more working moms continue to breastfeed once they go back to work, more companies will make their employees less embarrassed or worried they'll be fired, which is illegal. You can remind them, too, that a breastfed baby tends to be healthier, which means fewer out-of-office days.

Breastfeeding and Work
By JOAN ORTIZ, R.N., B.S.N., C.L.C.
President, Limerick Workplace Lactation Program

> Some states have a law requiring businesses to provide a private, clean, safe room other than a bathroom stall for women to use on their breaks and at lunchtime for expressing their milk. For more information, go to www.llli.org/Law/LawBills.html.

> Preparing ahead of time for your return to work will help lessen anxiety. Start pumping at least two to three weeks prior to your return date, so you'll have more than enough milk stored for the first day or so. You want your body to think of the pumping as another feeding, so pumping at the same time each day is helpful. You usually have more milk in the morning, so it's best to pump after your first feeding in the morning. You can expect to get about one to two ounces from pumping after a feeding, so if you pump once a day three weeks prior to returning to work, you should have at least twenty-one ounces for your first full day back at work. After pumping, put the fresh milk in the refrigerator. Once it's cooled, it can be combined with chilled breast milk from a previous pumping, then frozen in the amount that your baby is most likely to take for a single feeding (usually between three and four ounces).

> Don't be discouraged if your first attempts yield very little milk. Regular pumping usually results in ample yield in one to two weeks.

> Milk may be stored in rigid plastic baby bottles. Label bottles with the date, time of collection, and any unusual food consumed. This will help you determine if any foods cause your baby to become fussy or gassy. Milk may be refrigerated for use within forty-eight to seventy-two hours. Freeze any milk not used within two days.

> At work, try to pump every three hours or on your breaks and at lunchtime for fifteen minutes. Pumping consistently at around the same time each day will help maintain your milk supply and keep you comfortable. Your goal is to pump the amount of milk your baby is taking while you are at work.

> Feeding your baby before you go to work, when you get home, and as much as your baby would like when you are home in the evening will help maintain your breastfeeding relationship with your baby. On the days you are home with your baby it is best to breastfeed, as this will help increase your milk supply.

> You'll be tired during your first week back at work, and your milk supply may go down. Keep dinners simple, and allow your baby to nurse as needed. Stress can also have an effect on your milk supply, so you'll need a backup plan. It's okay to give formula. Whether you only feed breast milk or do a combination of breastfeeding and formula feeding, know that you're giving your infant a great start. Finding a balance so you can enjoy your baby and family is most important.

> Items to pack when you go back to work: a picture of your baby; your breast pump, power cord, and tote; tubing and breast cups; four to six bottles for pumped milk; a small container of dishwashing soap; labels with your baby's name and a place for the date; the labeled expressed milk to leave with your day care provider (if dropping your baby off); extra nursing pads; extra breast pump supplies; water bottle and healthy lunch/snacks; lap cloth to protect clothing when pumping and to dry breasts; and a storage cooler for milk.

MAIDS A'MILKIN'—WHEN YA GOTTA PUMP, YA GOTTA PUMP!

You can pump anywhere—and sometimes you have to.

Alicia: When I was covering fashion week at New York's Bryant Park, my assignment was to shoot the editor-in-chief of *Glamour* magazine at six different fashion shows. Imagine being a lactating mom, with several extra pounds still lingering, watching super-skinny models walk the runway.

Naturally, after the first show I started to feel horribly engorged, and I just had to relieve myself. With breast pump in hand, I excused myself and went searching for the restrooms. Fashion people pee in pretty potties, right? Wrong. The tent bathrooms at Bryant Park were downright nasty, and I was not about to sit in a stinky port-o-potty for twenty minutes while producing the milk my daughter was going to drink.

So I did what any other manic mother with leaking breasts would do. I shared my embarrassing situation with a bald, muscular fashion tent security guy wearing a tight black tee. In a very deep voice he said, "Look, lady, no more details. I get it already," and rushed me into the big fashion tent so my big boobs could be relieved. The place was stark, decorated in only black and white, with strobe lights brighter than the sun. He even blocked the entrances for me while I was in there and dimmed the lights. Who says chivalry is dead?

Mary Ann: Take your hand pump with you everywhere. They're great to use when you're in a traffic jam. Plenty of working moms have plugged their electric pump into their car's cigarette lighter and gotten going. Now, that's multitasking!

ENOUGH WITH THE BABY TALK ALREADY

If you have lots of doctor appointments, or you're out a lot with a sick baby, don't go back to the office and think your co-workers will welcome you with open arms. This is particularly true of your colleagues who are childless, or whose children are grown. They don't get maternity leave, and they still have to cover for you, often for many months. They're much more likely to have a little resentment. Can you blame them?

Offer to help these colleagues out, too. Although you might be dropping with exhaustion, they might think you just came back from a long vacation, and listening to you go on and on about your baby's first tooth . . . it gets old in a hurry. You aren't a bad mom because you don't talk about your baby at work all day long. In fact, you're a professional who's at work to get the job done.

CONFLICTING FEELINGS ABOUT BEING BACK AT WORK—WHEN YOU'RE NOT CRAZY ABOUT YOUR JOB IN THE FIRST PLACE

Having a baby triggers a lot of self-examination about every aspect of your life—and especially about work. "Why do I need this job?" you'll doubtlessly be asking yourself. "Why do I have to stay here? Sure, I need the benefits, but what are the alternatives so I can spend more time with my baby?"

Even if you love your job, returning to work as a new mom can be difficult. Or you might find that while you still like your job and your colleagues, that it pales in comparison to the joy you get from your baby. Is it possible to make changes without losing your position or the much-needed income?

We've found that the best solutions have come from moms who were willing to compromise and get creative. Some stayed at work; some worked less; some asked to be transferred to other locations near family, where they'd have more support from family members. Others with the financial resources were able to quit, but still planned to find another job once their babies were old enough for school.

TO WORK OR NOT TO WORK

> One technique that often helps is to draw up a list of pros and cons about your job. Whether it's the people you work with, the perks, a short commute, or extra vacation time, there must be something about that job that makes you go to it every day. If there isn't, you need to marshal your resources and start investigating other job opportunities.

> Draw up a budget to figure out how much you need to earn to cover your overhead plus extras for savings or emergencies. (For more about money management, see the next chapter.)

> If you're open and honest with your Human Resources department and/or your boss, there may be some sort of negotiation that you can make, and you might be surprised at how willing your employer is to help. It's certainly more cost effective for them to keep you aboard than to hire and train a replacement.

> See if you can make a lateral move to a different department or for a different boss.

> Perhaps you can change your hours to lessen the commute or give you more flexibility. One co-worker explained that she could work only four days a week and asked whether they could figure out a way to make this work, and a great compromise was reached.

> Ask if you can telecommute, so you can work at home when the baby's asleep. Be aware that if you do work at home or take a lot of work home with you, expectations can rise that you're on call 24/7. Set good boundaries if you do telecommute.

> If you're having problems with your boss, this is not the time to clam up about it. It's the time to communicate more. Tell your boss exactly how you're doing something and how you plan to imple-

ment any strategies in the future. Make it clear that you do not spend your days at work trolling eBay. Document this information in writing. The more your superiors know about how hard you're working, the better you'll feel about yourself, and the better you can to get your job done.

> If your company has an HR department, get an ally there. Their job is to be problem solvers. Find a way to say, "I'm not getting along with my boss. How can we make this work? My boss doesn't think I'm doing enough because I'm a new mom, but I disagree."

> If you're honest about unforeseen problems, such as a sick child, most employers should cut you some slack. Honesty is the best policy. If you just disappear in the middle of the day hoping that you won't be missed, think again!

> Know your rights as an employee. If you're being mistreated or sidelined because you're a new mom, document it, then go to HR or consult online to find out what your rights are.

Conflicting Feelings About Going Back to Work
By ANN CURRY

I went back to work after four months and it was too soon, so I do regret not staying on a longer maternity leave. The peace I made with my decision was to switch from being a correspondent just before I decided to have a family to becoming a news anchor, so I wouldn't have to travel so much. This allowed me to give some certainty to my children, who were born two years apart, that I would be home more. But it also meant I had to be on the air at 5 a.m. I'd leave in the middle of the night while they were sleeping, with their dad in the next room. He gave the first morning feeding with a bottle of breast milk, and then I came home and put them to bed. I didn't sleep during the day because they were mostly awake, and I didn't sleep during the night because they were up and down, up and down, and as a result I was unbelievably exhausted. I used to feel my heart flutter because I was so sleep deprived, but this was what I needed to do to be with my babies.

All of us are faced with the same problem of not having enough time, of feeling guilty, of wondering whether we can still be good at work while being so physically knocked out that we're sitting on our bottoms not knowing if we can get up. What helped me was realizing that doing my job well *was* taking care of my kids, because if I do a good job at work, I can provide for them and also contribute something to the world we all live in.

The other thing I realized was that I could *not* do a good job if I did not give 100 percent to my job when I was at work. Unless my child is sick or there's some other issue, I rarely think about my children when I'm in the office. And when I get home, I don't think about my work.

Another thing we started when our kids were babies was that even if I was exhausted after being on the go since four o'clock in the morning and working late every night, we always sat down for a family meal.

You just need to do the best you can under the circumstances. I also think that you compensate for not being there all the time by your intensity and your ability to communicate about how really precious your baby is when you *are* home. What gets me through my most stressful moments at work is picturing the faces of my son and daughter when they were babies, looking up at me. To them, I became a warrior. That helped make me able to do this job and to be more confident as a person, because in their eyes I was the most important person in the world. I was *invincible*!

Prioritizing My Life
By KATHIE LEE GIFFORD

Your career should be the way you make your living, but your family should be the place you live your life.

If you can find a way to do so, you will never, ever, ever regret putting your family first. When Cassidy was a baby I got a call from Julie Andrews and her husband, Blake Edwards, asking me to take over for Julie one night a week during her run of *Victor/Victoria* on Broadway so she could rest her voice. I had lunch with them, and Mary Poppins was asking me to do something I'd dreamed about my entire life.

Still, I agonized over it because I was so busy with my TV work and my daughter was so little. And then I took a deep breath and told Julie, "I'm deeply, deeply honored that you would entrust this to me, and I cannot believe that I'm saying no to Mary Poppins, but my daughter will never be this little again and I have to say no." Julie looked at me and, morphing in front of my eyes into Maria Von Trapp, said, "Kathie, you'll never regret it when you put your children first. You'll always regret it when you don't. I had to make the same decisions when my children were young."

I wanted to be the kind of mom that my children want to be around because there's always laughter and happiness. It's not about money. It's about creating an emotional, creative, and nurturing environment.

STRESSBUSTERS AT WORK

> Nix the comparisons with moms who have more money, more this, more that. You don't know what goes on behind their closed doors.
> Don't beat yourself up if you make mistakes.
> The power of positive thinking is incredibly potent.
> Get out of the office and take a walk. Fresh air does a body good.
> Find a friend, share a laugh. Sometimes all you need is a little bitch session together about troubles with work or home for all to be good in the world again.
> Do deep yoga breaths to clear your head.
> Make lunchtime matter. Eat slowly. Enjoy the food. Try to spend twenty to thirty minutes with your close work friends. Most of us don't have the time to do this every day, but try to manage it as often as possible.
> If you live near home, use your lunch break to run in and give your baby a kiss.
> Problem solve. Don't dwell on how the problem started—think about how to fix it.
> Try not to procrastinate on deadlines. When you get a project, *do* it.
> If you're having a terrible day, grab your favorite picture, and tell yourself that you know how much you love this baby and this baby loves you, and at the end of the day this is what counts in life.

Getting Creative About Work After Baby
By RACHEL BURSTEIN

When I was hired at the *TODAY* show, I was already four months pregnant—and worried about how to mix motherhood with working every night until midnight and being on the road several days a week. So I spoke with my supervisor about taking a position in the booking department. With a phone and a computer, I could book guests from anywhere and still make it home for dinner and bedtime.

NBC went for it, and it made sense . . . until I returned from maternity leave and realized how much I missed the creativity of producing segments. So I went back to my bosses and asked if I could start producing again. It meant a much more erratic schedule, one closer to the one I thought I no longer wanted. But I think being a working mom made me realize that if I was going to be spending time away from my baby, I wanted to like what I was doing. I am very fortunate to be in a job where there are options, since so many working moms don't have flexibility or the chance to love what they do.

Someone recently asked me how many hours I see my daughter each day, and I instantly felt that mommy guilt rush through my body. But I think I'm setting a good example for her that I can be her mom and still have an identity and the career that I worked so hard to build before I had her.

Deciding Not to Return to Work
By CLAUDIA DAVID HEITLER

I feel like I had the best job in television, or maybe even the best job anywhere, ever. I booked interviews and produced for Matt Lauer, as well as for the show in general. I had a backstage pass to the events and people shaping our nation. But covering so many tragedies (school shootings, plane crashes, and 9/11, for example) made me increasingly aware of how resilient, but also how fragile, life can be. Ironically, my amazing job made me want to just be at home with my family.

I had concerns about dropping out of the workforce, but one of my mentors told me that being a hard worker and a team player is more important than having a specific skill set. My fingers are crossed that this applies when it's time for me to go back to work in whatever capacity that may be.

So I left feeling good, but I soon felt like I had fallen off the face of the earth. Just weeks before I had been working on stories with Prince Albert of Monaco and Rudy Giuliani, and I was missing the high you feel when a story airs live for six million people. My mind also hadn't slowed down, and I continued to think of story ideas. The fact that my former bosses would respond to my pitches probably saved me in those first few months.

When Arlo was one, I freelanced part-time for *TODAY* from home for a short while. Part-time work, though it seems win/win, can be very challenging. You are giving 50 percent to two things that require 100 percent of you. I ended up taking work calls at Gymboree play classes with loud children's music in the background, ordering a lot of take-out, and putting Arlo in front of the television more than I would have liked. I remember conducting one phone pre-interview with Arlo hanging onto my leg.

When I got pregnant with Lois, I focused fully on being at home, though I recently turned in a fourteen-page newsletter for their nursery school featuring the federal bailout and the Lyme Disease controversy. Nonetheless, staying at home was absolutely the right decision for me and my family.

WORK-RELATED TRAVEL AWAY FROM HOME

Travel is a huge part of our jobs. Sometimes it's really nice not to have to deal with the day-to-day child-rearing . . . to just get on a plane and focus on work. Some moms may think we're terrible for thinking this, but as much as we loathe the lines and the taking-off-your-shoes at security and cancelled flights, traveling on assignment is still an adventure. That's how we look at it, so we still have fun doing it, even though it's not all fun and games.

Child care while you're out of town is usually the hardest issue to deal with. There's dealing with who's going to take care of the baby, and either juggling the schedule with your partner or finding extra help if you're a single parent. If you don't have family nearby to help out, then you'll have to make your own family. Single moms we know rely on a tag team of babysitters, friends, and other moms. As long as there are more hands than kids, your baby should be okay.

You can also calm any anxiety you have with phone calls, instant messages, and/or a quick workout in the hotel gym. The baby is not going to remember you left for several days on a business trip.

CHAPTER FOURTEEN

Babies Cost a Bundle: Financial Planning

When Alicia's grandmother left the hospital with her little girl, the bill was a whopping $15.

What will $15 buy you now? A jumbo bag of diapers, if you're lucky. And how many diapers is your baby going to go through? Hmm. Let's see. Oh, maybe about eight thousand!

Babies are *expensive*.

They're also more precious than all the gold in Fort Knox, of course, but while your love may be priceless, your MasterCard bill may not be. Babies are so expensive, in fact, that you can go into sticker shock before you've bought your first pacifier. And we're not talking luxuries, like the latest stroller beloved by celebrities (and so huge you can't even get it through your front door). No, we're talking about the supplies you simply have to have—such as diapers, clothes, food, and formula (if you're bottle-feeding), stuff to clean up the mess, a carrier, a stroller, a car seat, a high chair, toys, books, enough detergent for the 47,652 loads of laundry you'll be doing during your baby's first year, and some pain reliever for when you get a headache balancing the checkbook and wondering where all the money went.

Then, just when you're getting a handle on your budget, you'll get your first day care bill.

START SAVING TODAY

It's wise to start tightening your belt long before the baby is born. There will be unforeseen expenses (more than you can imagine), such as frames for all the ultrasounds, colorful flats and flip-flops for your ever-expanding feet, and late-night ice-cream runs.

GET A LOCKBOX

If you don't use a safety deposit box at your bank, get a lockbox for your paperwork at home. You can find one at most home improvement stores. It should be fireproof.

Keep all your most vital paperwork and information in the lockbox. This should include your passports, social security cards, insurance policies, any other legal documents, credit cards and/or list of all credit card numbers, any vital medical information, school vaccination records, passwords for various accounts, and jewelry that has been appraised.

If the lockbox is heavy, keep all the paperwork in a binder inside. In case of a fire or emergency, all you'll have to do is grab the binder and go. Be sure you know where the key is, and give a duplicate to a trusted friend or family member.

Top Ten Financial Planning Tips
By JEAN CHATZKY
TODAY Financial Editor

1. Don't be afraid to discuss finances.

We don't like looking at numbers. And so we don't do an assessment of what our next stage of life is actually going to cost, whether it's having a baby or moving into a bigger house or retiring. That's a huge mistake, because only once you know what something is going to cost can you start to make conscious changes.

The best way to get over your fears of having "The Conversation" is to schedule it. You *can* do it, if you just do it.

Pick a nonconfrontational, non–stressed-out time when you know you and your spouse are going to be in a decent frame of mind, set a time limit (perhaps fifteen minutes the first time), and then start talking. You and your partner should make a list of the things you want to discuss in this conversation. Don't get angry. This isn't an argument but a simple conversation so you can see where you stand, because the misconception is that when you marry somebody you will automatically start to want the same things in life. In order to have the same financial goals, you have to get them out there for discussion. And realize that when you fight about money, you're really fighting about power, and to see who's the boss in your family.

I'm a big fan of using a financial advisor as a sort of short-term therapist. Pay for an expert to sit down with you for an hour or two to give you pointers on what you need to know and where you need to focus. Then you can schedule another session three months later.

2. Figure out what you need.

With or without an advisor, once you're pregnant or have the baby, start assessing. What are you looking at in medical expenses this year, and where is that money going to come from? When the baby gets bigger, will you have to move, and when's the right time to do that? Do you need to start saving now to afford the down payment? And should you be working on your credit score so you can actually get a mortgage? And how about your car? That two-seater Miata was great, but there's no room for a car seat. So start thinking now about what everything is going to cost and when the right time is to make a transition.

You need to get real about the numbers. It might sound scary, but it's actually freeing. A lot more freeing than not looking and just being scared by the fact that there's potentially a huge number looming!

This is especially important if you're thinking about staying home, working part time, or telecommuting. My advice is always to road test your options . . . *financially*. If you want to stay home, try living on one income from the time you get pregnant. Not only will that show you whether you can actually do it, but it gives you a nine-month cushion of the other banked income, which you can then use to pay for new furniture or to start a college savings account or whatever you want to do. A financial road test shows you very quickly whether you *can* quit completely, or whether your partner is going to have to gear up and earn more money.

3. Start saving and stop spending.

If you have any goal, saving automatically is a fabulous idea. Moving a set amount from your checking account to your savings account is the best way to accumulate money.

Parents need to rein in the overwhelming feeling that babies *have* to have a lot of things, because they don't. It's up to parents to model the kind of behavior that they want for their kids. That means having a clear sense of what your goals as a family really are. Spending is out of control when you haven't thought about priorities. You have to want something more than you want the designer clothes or new car.

4. Lessen your debt load.

The best way to lessen a debt load is to come up with a systematic approach to getting rid of it. It's just like saving for a goal, except the goal is paying off the credit card. The return on investment is your credit card interest rate, so it's a guaranteed return that you're not going to get anywhere else.

Use that as an enticement, because there's nothing fun about paying off a credit card. Pick the one with the highest interest rate, put all your extra cash against that card, and pay the minimum on all the others. Don't be shy about calling credit card companies and asking them to lower your rate. You'll be surprised how often this works.

When you're looking for extra cash, go through your expenses, line by line, and figure out where your money is going. Unless you keep a detailed list every day, it's hard to know where your cash disappears most of the time. It's not cappuccino, despite what some financial experts want you to believe. It's all of the other random places where you spend money irregularly—dry cleaning, birthday presents, dinners out.

Spend a full month tracking where every single penny is going. It's a real eye-opener! Once you have that information, you can use it to make choices about where you'd rather spend the money, and use that to cut some expenses. Once that card is paid off, retire it. (Don't cancel it, because that negatively affects your credit score.)

Paying off some of your debt is not a free pass to go shopping, as you have to take the extra money that you had been coming up with to use against the debt and funnel it into savings. You want to build up an emergency cushion, and beyond that to start investing in other ways to fund your future.

5. Have an emergency fund.

Everyone faces financial emergencies. The transmission might go out or the roof might start leaking or the baby might need special medical attention, which is why having an emergency fund, which is three to six months' worth of living expenses for basic needs—rent, food, transportation, insurance (not clothing or entertainment)—is so important. Those living in a one-income household need six months rather than three, because if that person loses a job the financial results can be catastrophic.

Cash savings is the only thing that keeps you out of credit card debt. When you don't have cash you put it all on the credit card, which starts a cycle of indebtedness that can last forever.

Don't forget to replenish the emergency fund, or you can be in worse trouble when the next emergency arises.

6. Don't forget to fund your retirement.

Many people are not saving enough for their retirement. You need to fully fund your retirement and take advantage of all the tax savings in a 401(k) or IRA. Find out if your employer is matching dollars, as that's where you're going to get the bigger tax benefits from the government.

As for 529 plans for your child's college education—yes, there are some small tax advantages, but they're nothing like what you're going to get for funding your retirement. That's a notion that can feel selfish, as if you don't want to help your kids. But there will be ways down the road to help them, which may include putting money into a 529 once you've satisfied the retirement contributions you're able to make, or helping pay off student loans after college, since the debt assumed by the student is cheaper than that by the parent.

The other thing to look at is a Roth IRA, which is very flexible, as you can withdraw money from it to pay for college. If you can fund a Roth, it's a way to take the burden off your conscience and still fund your retirement, since if you don't use it at all you can just let it grow.

7. Single Moms and Money

About 95 percent of us are going to be single women at one point in our lives, and for any single parent it's crucial to have protections—not just life insurance but disability insurance, because if there's no other wage earner and you're disabled, you need something to fall back on. Along with your will, you need a health care proxy and a designated power of attorney, because your baby is counting on you.

You also need a programmatic means of saving money, because women still earn only eighty-one cents for every dollar that a man earns, and because you may end up taking some breaks from the work force to either care for your baby or care for a parent. Single moms need to put a lot more muscle behind it, and make sure that the money is continuing to grow. I know that the stock market is a very scary place for many, and couples can get around this if the wife invests conservatively while the husband takes more of the investment risk (or vice versa), and it balances out. But if you're single, you have to make sure your asset allocations are truly age appropriate. If you don't know what you're doing or if you feel unsure, there are target-date retirement funds (mutual funds that essentially rebalance themselves toward your retirement date). They're brilliant and they work, so I would recommend looking into them.

8. Having babies later creates different financial pressures.

If you have your baby when you're forty, that baby will be going to college when you're sixty and approaching retirement. If your eighty-year-old parents are still alive and need your financial assistance, you'll be hit with a triple whammy of financial obligations.

Of course, many moms who have babies later are more set in their careers and have some savings built up, which is great. But it's really important to keep funding those savings even if you take time off from work. Married moms can put money in a spousal IRA and still make a retirement contribution every year. You've got to maximize the good years you have.

9. Use a financial planner.

If you're considering using a financial planner, look for somebody who is licensed and has a clean record—and who passes your gut check. Planners should be willing to give you a short introductory session for no charge, so you can get a feel for each other. If you feel intimidated or don't like his tie or her hair, then go with your gut and find someone else. You'll be discussing private information and you need to be at ease.

The most important thing about a financial planner is that you can talk with that person honestly and openly, which means admitting when you have screwed up with your money. I know how hard that is, as a frequent complaint I hear from financial planners is that while their clients don't lie, they withhold information, so the planner doesn't get the full financial picture and can't do a good job. So you need to find somebody whom you feel as comfortable with as you feel with your gynecologist!

Financial planners do not get unrestricted access to your accounts. Some can trade on your behalf, but if they do, you need to read through your monthly statements carefully.

10. Acknowledge that you must make financial decisions.

The most important thing that you can do is acknowledge that as a parent, you have to make financial decisions. As a new mom you're thrust into this new level of responsibility, and these things just have to get done.

What so many people do, though, is gather information until it gets so overwhelming that they can't find the perfect answer, and so they don't do *any-thing*—which is just about the worst way to make decisions. Whether it's picking a guardian or deciding which bank to go with, realize that there's a level of "good enough" that's going to be just fine when you are a very busy person. Make the decision, and live with it. If you decide it's wrong, changing it should be easy. But *not* deciding is a *really* big mistake.

tip: *Keep a separate account for yourself. If you're used to earning a good wage and having spending money, it can be surprisingly off-putting (if not humiliating) to have to ask your partner for money when you're home on maternity leave.*

PROTECTING YOUR MOST VALUABLE ASSET

Financial protection becomes so much more important with a new baby. Most adults in America don't have a will, because they don't want to have to make the decision about who their children's guardian will be. But if you have five brothers and sisters, you don't have to tell all of them, only the one you've picked as the guardian. Make sure to get permission.

You also need a living will; a durable power of attorney for health care in general; and life insurance (term life insurance unless you're independently wealthy). You should also consider disability insurance.

—Jean Chatzky

CHAPTER FIFTEEN

Child Care that Works When You're at Work

FINDING THE RIGHT CHILD CARE

One of the biggest sources of concern for all working moms is child care. There are pros and cons to every method, and there is no one right or wrong way. If you have a variable schedule with lots of travel, a nanny or babysitter may give you the flexibility you need. Is there a day care center on your way to work, making drop-off and pickup convenient? Or does a neighbor provide day care in her home?

However you start researching child care in your area, bear in mind this can be a lengthy and often frazzling experience, especially if the only day care you like has a two-year waiting list, or the nanny you finally decided to hire got poached by another family. Doing due diligence is a must. You can't be worrying about your baby's safety and well-being while you're at work.

Once you find the best situation, you can relax, knowing that your baby will be happy, thriving, and well-loved. Besides, don't you think it's about time that your precious little bundle of joy spits up and slobbers on someone else besides you?

ABOUT NANNIES

When it comes to nannies, Mary Poppins doesn't exist. But you can come pretty close, as long as you have realistic expectations.

A nanny is the most important person in the world because she's taking care of your children, so you need to ensure that you really like her, your baby likes her, and that you're able to communicate easily and freely when there's anything to discuss.

A good way of figuring out whether you should hire a nanny is to go through a simple checklist. If you want your baby to get one-on-one attention; if you have crazy, abnormal work hours and need someone to arrive early and stay late; and if you don't mind someone seeing your scatterbrained schedules and your sink loaded with grime-encrusted dishes, then a nanny might be for you.

HOW TO FIND A GOOD NANNY

We both found our nannies through word-of-mouth, which is how most of our friends did, too. Put the word out several months before you'll need to go back to work. Craigslist is also a good source for babysitters, as long as you thoroughly check references.

If you live in a large city, there may be agencies who vet nannies and other household workers, and as you're paying them a fee, you can interview as many nannies as they have available until you find one you like.

When you're interviewing a nanny, these questions should be helpful:

> Do you have references? How did you get along with your previous employer?
> What was your reason for leaving? (Many nannies switch jobs when the babies become old enough to go to preschool or elementary school, so this is normal.)
> Do you have flexible hours, and if so, how late can you stay on weeknights?
> Can you work weekends?
> What are your commitments to your own family? If your nanny has small children of her own, how are they being taken care of? What if one of them gets sick?
> How do you plan to get to work every day? How long will your commute be and what kind of transportation will you use? Do you have a valid driver's license? (Applicable only if you need her to drive the baby to activities.)
> What are your ideas about child-rearing, spanking, discipline, and dealing with other babies who might be bigger and pushier?

- Do you know CPR? (If not, you should pay to send her to a course at your local YMCA or Red Cross chapter prior to starting work. While you're at it, it's a good idea for you and your husband to take a class, too.)
- Are you available to work overtime? Be sure to ask about the overtime, vacation, and sick days that she expects. The more upfront you are with one another, the better work relationship you'll have.

Trust your gut. The nanny might come with glowing recommendations, but you still have to click. If you don't like the nanny during your initial meeting, will you like her better in a month? If the nanny seems evasive, or too good to be true, or just *off* somehow, you might want to keep interviewing. On the other hand, we have friends who hired a nanny within one minute of her starting to talk—they just *knew*!

We had the wonderful Christine as our nanny. She came from a large family we adored. Christine cannot be in a room without a dog or baby instantly licking her face or wanting to be held. She's just that kind of person. So my advice is to hire a person who is full of joy. Now that my kids are grown, Christine is still working for me as vice-president of my production company. And my kids still prefer her!

—Kathie Lee Gifford

Scheduled day care was absolutely not an option, as my husband and I both work and travel constantly. But I would have loved to have had the option to put my baby in a place where he could have had more social interaction with babies his age. As a compromise, I signed up for classes instead, that either the nanny or I could go to.

I interviewed over thirty nannies, through an agency and by word-of-mouth recommendations. I asked everybody! As it turns out, word of mouth worked best for me the first time around.

—Natalie Morales

TIPS FOR HAPPY NANNIES/HAPPY BABIES

- Make your needs known. Explaining what you expect your nanny to do in addition to watching your child must be made clear prior to hiring her.
- Whatever your house rules, make sure that your babysitter knows them.
- Find out the going pay rates in your community by asking your friends. Don't expect to have a great nanny if you don't compensate her accordingly.
- Sit down with your nanny every six months to discuss anything important (such as schedules, or things going on in her life). This is also a good time to do a mini review.

Needing to Work / Needing Child Care

By ADA FAMULARI

TODAY Program Manager

When I became pregnant in 1987, I was thirty-three and worked for a small company. In preparation for the birth, I squirreled away my entire allotted vacation (all three weeks of it). The company had no paid maternity leave, so my only source of income after the birth would be from disability and paid vacation.

Derek was born in February 1988. I had exactly seven weeks to find child care and get back to work. As I did not have a true partner in my marriage, everything was left for me to figure out. My mother was working full time, while I was living in the suburbs of Long Island, where every mom (except me) stayed at home. I was so stressed out, and I mentioned my worries to a neighbor. She said, "So don't go to work, stay at home." But I *had* to work.

I knew I wanted my child cared for at home. I didn't know where to start my search, and I was terrified of the day I would have to leave my baby with a total stranger. Four weeks before returning to work, I placed an ad in a local paper and asked around at local churches. Soon, I had a long list of names and started to interview potential candidates. The questions I asked were: How long did you stay at your last job? Why did you leave? Do you have references? Tell me about yourself.

Fortunately, my story has a happy ending. I did find a babysitter who became part of our family. She helped raise Derek, and two years later, Blake. She stayed with us for twelve years, and to this day we remain friends. She cared for my children and loved them as if they were her own, and for that I am forever grateful. As for my boys, they've grown up to be amazing young men.

MANAGING THE MOMMY GUILT—
EVEN IF YOU FEEL GUILTY

Ah, yes, the guilt trip—the longest journey you'll ever take to work!

All working moms know that their caregivers spend more waking hours during the work week with their babies than they do. We both know how heartbreaking it is the first time your baby wails in distress when your nanny leaves for the day. When that happens, it's very hard not to think you're a failure as a mother, or that your baby loves your nanny more than you.

We prefer to think of our situation as a rotating universe, with our work environment, husbands, caregivers, and us. All the grownups are interchangeable, whether or not the babysitter has to stay late and put the baby down because we're out of town on assignment, or our husbands have to feed the babies breakfast, or we're with the babies all weekend long—our orbits are all equal. And we firmly believe that within the big scheme of life, having all these orbits is just a great thing for the babies. They have more grownups to spread the love. It makes them more emotionally resilient when they learn to deal with new personalities, a skill that will help them when they get older, have more playdates, and go off to school.

On Guilt
By AMY ROBACH and ANN CURRY

Amy Robach: Ten weeks after giving birth, I went back to work as a reporter in Washington, D.C. I didn't have a lot of options, as I needed to pay my mortgage. The day I got back was the first day of the war with Iraq, in March 2003. And I was assigned to Pentagon duty, working from 2 a.m. till 2 p.m., in a secured building where cell phones didn't function. It was tough. When I got home I would be so tired, but my first baby had colic and was a crier who didn't like to take naps. There were moments when I had to put her in a crib, go into my room, and just bawl, because I'd had no idea it would be this hard.

Mommy guilt will always be with me no matter what. But I do believe I am teaching my two little girls that there can be fulfillment in a lot of different ways, that staying at home is not for everybody, and certainly not for me.

I still spend a lot of time with my kids, and on my weekdays off it's just us—there's no sitter, and my husband is at work. And on weekends I get half-days home with my family. It's the hardest for me when I have to travel—I try not to, but I cry every single time I go to the airport. It's so embarrassing!

Ann Curry: Oh gosh, the guilt was so out of control, so constant, it took my breath away! I just didn't feel that I had a break, because our babies need as much as we can give them. Even if you're there every single minute, they still want more.

I think your brain needs to tell your body and your heart that you created a safe place for your child, and that now you're going to forge for the things your child needs. So just know you're not alone. All mothers go through this. There is really no getting rid of the guilt feelings except by knowing that your baby will get used to what you created, and it will get easier as the baby grows older.

I cannot tell you that the first years are easy, and you don't want to just get though them. You want to *remember* them, enjoy them, smell that baby and love that baby and enjoy that baby till you're exhausted and tearing your hair out, and at that point there'll be a whole new set of challenges.

So I can't tell you anything that will make the guilt go away, but you can learn to live with it by remembering that what you're doing is valuable. The really sad part about all this is that women who are remarkable at their jobs can't accept that they deserve a break, and praise, because they feel they need to be *more* than what they are already. I mean, look at what you're doing. You're raising a wonderful baby, doing your job, and contributing to your community. You're a wife, a friend, all those things, and yet you're still putting yourself last and not saying WOW, great job! What's that about?

Erase the Mommy Guilt
By DR. NANCY SNYDERMAN
TODAY Medical Correspondent

Do you still blame your parents for everything they didn't do right in your life? I hope not! So if you let your parents off the hook, it's time to start forgiving yourself now, too.

For example, I have one adopted child and two biological children. I'm a big believer in breastfeeding, especially due to the immunological pluses and the bonding experience, but that said, my bottle-fed adopted baby never had an ear infection, yet my two breastfed babies did have them. Did I feel guilty about that? No. But it's seemingly a trend that the breastfeeding moms versus the bottle-feeding moms, or the stay-at-home moms versus the working moms, are pinned against each other in a mutual dance of guilt.

Relax. This too shall pass, and it's really not anything to feel bad about. Trust me on this—there are much bigger things to deal with as your baby grows older. You might not believe it at the time, but the first year is really nothing to worry about in the end.

EMERGENCY CONTACT LIST

Be sure to make an emergency contact list and put it in a prominent place in the house—on the fridge, near the front door, or by the telephone.

> List all the numbers for you, your husband or partner, and/or friends or family, along with the local police precinct, your pediatrician, and poison control. Make sure everyone who'll be looking after your baby knows where the list is and who all the people are.
> Program all essential numbers into your cell phone(s), too. A great shower gift to request is for one of your friends to do this for you.
> All families need an emergency plan. In case of a large-scale emergency, you can't count on cell phones to work, so figure out a designated meeting place.
> Always keep a landline in your home with at least one extension that isn't dependent upon electricity to work. It's extremely scary to be unable to make a phone call during an emergency.

WHEN YOUR MOM IS YOUR BABYSITTER— AND SHE'S DRIVING YOU CRAZY

If you're lucky enough to have your mom watching your children, treat her the same as if you were paying a professional sitter. That means with respect for what she does, and especially for her schedule. Showing up chronically late without calling first or expecting your mom to drop all her own activities if you want to go out, is not going to make for a happy family.

But even if all other aspects of your mom's babysitting are wonderful, the big sticking point can be when you have different ideas about taking care of the baby. Your mom might be more of a strict disciplinarian, or have specific ideas about what to feed the baby, and you might feel she's totally wrong and way out of line. Now is not the time to keep silent about what you believe is best for your baby. Find a time to talk (without accusations), and explain why you believe what you do. Perhaps you can get support from your pediatrician, whose advice is much less likely to be questioned.

That said, if you're depending on a parent (or other family member) and there's a lifetime of issues between you, it may make everyone's lives easier if you let the smaller things go and save the battles for something more important. If your mother gives your child Cheetos when you asked her not to, it's not going to make the child a junk-food junkie—time with Grandma is much more important than always eating ideal food.

Mary Ann: The first time Zurielle ate pasta, my mom let her wash it down with Dr. Pepper. (Yes, she was still a baby!) I didn't realize it had happened until I went to pick Zurielle up and saw her trying to grab the soda can. "Mom," I said, "Why is Zurielle jonesing for the Dr. Pepper?" When she replied, "I gave her a sip," I will spare you what I said. We stopped that bad habit fast.

ABOUT DAY CARE

Good day care gives babies plenty of attention and stimulation in a fun and loving atmosphere. They are also exposed to a wide range of other babies and personalities, teaching them early on how to get along and giving them playmates who often become treasured childhood friends.

Day care can give moms with a fixed working schedule the peace of mind they need. Our own company has a day care center nearby. If you work for a large corporation, be sure to check out all their benefits prior to giving birth.

DAY CARE CHECKLIST

> Do you have a license?
> What kind of insurance coverage do you have?
> Do all the caregivers have CPR training?
> Where is the fire extinguisher?
> What is your emergency plan?
> What is your illness policy? Can babies come to day care if they just have a runny nose? What about a fever? How long must they stay home after having had a fever?
> What are your hours? Look for day care that offers some flexibility in their hours. Even if your work schedule is fixed, there will always be traffic jams and other things that pop up, causing unavoidable delays.

> There should be a separate sleeping area, away from the more noisy play area.
> See if there's a wide range of activities and playthings for the babies.

On Child Care

By LINDA MASON

Chairman and Founder, Bright Horizons Family Solutions

It's a misperception that having a baby at home with a caregiver is the best way to go. Dr. Terry Brazelton is on our advisory board, and he made a comment I love. He said, "Babies, unlike adults, thrive on multiple lovers." If you think of traditional cultures, babies are never alone. We know that babies are very social. They thrive on activity and being held, and they develop a more secure sense of the world when more than one adult loves them. In good child care centers, babies develop a sense of community; they know that this is their world, and that all the teachers in the room adore them. And of course this creates a wonderful community for parents too.

There are many positives about child care:

> In good centers, the caregivers are trained in early education, are supervised, and work in teams, so there's always someone looking over their shoulders should the need for assistance arise. As new moms often feel lost about how to take care of their babies, having experienced, trained caregivers is a huge plus. They can show you strategies on putting the baby down, soothing, feeding, and nursing.
> If the center is close by, you can visit your baby and continue to nurse when you go back to work.
> One of the earliest developmental centers in the brain is the language center; it's very important for babies to be bathed in language, which takes place in high-quality centers.

Here are some more tips:

> Whether you have onsite care or not, you next need to talk to parents of other infants, as word-of-mouth is the best way to get child care recommendations.

> The most important element of any child care program is the individual caregiver who'll be taking care of your child. High turnover is a red flag. We've learned how crucial consistent care is, and the importance of caregivers who look in the baby's eyes and talk to the baby while feeding and changing.

> You need to ask if you can sit in the classroom where your baby will be and observe the caregiver. If a center is reluctant to permit that, it's another red flag.

> Trust your gut. Ask yourself if you'd feel comfortable having your baby in the arms of this person.

> But realize, too, that babies don't need exclusive one-on-one care. Look for one teacher for every three to four babies. This works, as each baby is on an individual schedule: one is sleeping, another exploring, while the caregiver is holding yet another.

> The center should be spotless and well lit. As babies explore their environment on their bellies, the baby room should be a no-shoe environment, with soft carpeting and soft, age-appropriate toys, should have no hazards such as sharp corners, and should be clean and hygienic.

> The staff should work with you on joint strategies to keep your baby happy.

> We do take a lot of photographs but we don't like video streaming, as clips can be taken out of context. Child care facilities should have a completely open-door policy, in which parents are encouraged to come in and out all day so they can see their baby whenever they want.

> One of the unavoidable negatives with child care is that babies are exposed to mild illness. On average they're sick about twenty days during their first year in group care, whether it's child care or kindergarten. The flip side is that babies develop an earlier immunity to future illness.

> Other negatives are the cost, as high-quality child care is very expensive, and that many centers with fixed hours might not be an option for those who work long hours.

> There is no one right choice for every family. What it comes down to is finding high-quality care within whatever options you have, whether it be a fantastic nanny, a neighbor, or group child care. And be willing to pay for quality care. There is no better investment of your money than in the early years of your child's life.

GETTING TO WORK WHEN YOUR BABY GETS SICK

What's a working mom to do when the baby is too sick to go to day care? The only solution—and this is a tough one—is to have backup. And sometimes a backup for the backup. Here are some suggestions:

> Make an arrangement with friends who are stay-at-home moms, working moms with more flexible schedules, or even childless friends with flexible schedules, to have them babysit when your baby is sick (but not sick with something as contagious and potentially dangerous as the flu). Have these friends on standby for emergencies. Offer to reciprocate whenever possible.

> Have a regular nighttime or weekend babysitter on standby who may have daytime hours free. If the sitter can come in the afternoon, you may be able to get in to the office later in the day to catch up on some work.

> Enlist your husband or partner to help out too. You should never have to worry about jeopardizing your job because your hubby refuses to deal with his cranky boss. Try to alternate taking the time off, if at all possible.

> If your baby is sick often, speak to your boss or HR department about working out a strategy to cover lost days. If you are proactive about tackling this issue before the baby gets sick again, chances are better that any absences will not be dealt with harshly.

Determine whether the baby's sickness is "real" or just a cold or other mild illness. Determine whether the crisis at work is an actual crisis or someone else's crisis. If the illness and crisis are both real, your baby comes first.

—Melissa Lonner

COPING STRATEGIES FOR SINGLE MOMS— BACKUP FOR THE BACKUP

If you don't have a live-in partner, a sick baby can be a total nightmare. Not only do you have to worry about missing work, but you have to cope with worrying about the baby too.

It's even more crucial for single moms to have backup for the backup. Find friends, family members, or other babysitters to rely on. You'll need to recruit these people as backup in case your baby becomes too sick to attend day care or if your nanny gets sick or takes vacation time. You might even think about having an arrangement with mommy friends so you can rely on them when a child care crisis develops.

On Being a Single Mom

Going back to work when Joshua was only seven weeks old was hard, because although he was with caregivers I knew and trusted, nobody's going to treat your child the way you would treat him. And I needed to prepare the bottles and make sure he had enough clothes for the day, diapers, blankets, and everything else. Sometimes I truly thought that I was going to lose my mind and would have to quit my job, because it was so difficult to manage everything and get back into my routine while worrying about being late for work and whether I'd forgotten something.

Without my parents' help, I probably would have gone crazy. I wish my mom were here today, and what I often tell people is that they don't know how good they have it when their parents are still around. They may not be in your life every day, but just to know that they'll be there if something happens to you is such a relief. Your parents might not be able to help out all the time but when they do, it helps a lot. That's what kept me sane. And my mom would show me what worked after being with Joshua all day . . . little things like patting his bottom a little bit before he went to sleep to keep him calm.

When you're a single parent, be prepared to have no alone time for yourself. No matter how much you try, it's just not going to happen. So I got used to taking my baby with me wherever I went, whether on errands or to get a haircut. Whenever my mom had time she would try to squeeze in babysitting so I could get the laundry done or catch up on some reading or take a nap.

Thank goodness I had an exceptionally understanding supervisor. We had an agreement that as long as I got my work done, we'd figure out the other end. When you have somebody backing you up during times of intense stress, it means the world.

So my advice for single moms is to be financially equipped and make sure you have reliable people and a good team around you. Try to find some balance in your life. If not, you'll quickly get seriously overwhelmed as I did, like on all those nights spent crying that I couldn't do it anymore, that I wanted to just give up and forget about everything and run away with my son.

Fortunately, I was blessed with a baby who rarely got sick. Maybe God looked at me and said, "You've got enough to worry about besides having a sick child!" I ended up going back to my parents' home with Joshua for a while when I could not afford my own place anymore. I didn't want to do that at first, because I felt like I had gotten pregnant on my own and had lived on my own, but my mom was there for me. It also lessened my stress at work, as I knew Joshua was safe instead of worrying that I'd get calls all day long from incompetent babysitters. That also helped me tremendously as I could start saving, and I was able to get my own place a few years later and settle down while being more financially equipped than when I first had him.

—Vanessa Rowson

I'd been told that newborns only sleep and eat and poop. Well, my baby girl, Jenna, definitely ate and pooped, but no one told me that she'd barely sleep more than twenty minutes at a time. I didn't shower; I never knew if I could. My husband didn't want me to keep the diapers or toys downstairs since the baby's room was upstairs, so I would go up and down all day long. That was just a part of what pushed us apart. It wasn't a wonderful marriage to begin with, and having a baby proved our incompatibility.

So I had nobody to help me. I was dealing with this tremendous guilt about my marriage and, in retrospect, was having postpartum depression, though I had no idea what it was. Although Jenna rarely cried, she would just look at me and I would say, "What am I not giving you?" I didn't yet realize that she was just soaking it all in—something she still does twenty-one years later! Worst of all was waking up in the morning, thinking "Oh my God, here we go again," and I didn't realize that the feeling was more fear that I was alone with a tiny baby than anything else. Now, I know a lot of it was hormonal, but I did not know how to manage what I perceived were my inadequacies.

Eventually, when Jenna was three months old, I remember talking to somebody at a baby shower about all these feelings, and everyone chimed in that they'd gone through that too. As soon as somebody validated my feelings, I realized that I was fine and normal, and from that night on I became the best mother in the entire world.

Sure, money was often tight, but I never looked at money as an issue when it came to having children. There was nothing that I would want for Jenna that I couldn't afford to have, but I didn't want a lot because it wasn't important to me—I had my daughter, so I had everything I needed.

It's the best gift in the world to create another human being, and for me there's nothing better than having love from a child. So as far as the fears, the advice, the gimmicks, or the gadgets, that's all crap. Just love them unconditionally and take from them what they have to give you, and you can't go wrong.

—Leslye Fagin

CONCLUSION

by Matt Lauer,
Natalie Morales, Ann Curry, and
Mary Ann and Alicia

Matt Lauer: My parents were big believers in letting their children know that they would always be there for us if we needed them, and that we had an emotional safety net. My dad in particular was the kind of guy that you could always rely on. If I had a horrendous thing happen, the first person I would ever think to call was my dad. I could vent to him, and share great highs and great lows with him, too.

There's a wonderful sense of security that goes along with knowing that your parents love you unconditionally, and that they will not judge you. They might have an opinion about what you have or haven't done, but that will not shake the core of their love and affection for you. That's really important. I tell my kids that I love them, and I don't say it as a throwaway phrase. I look them in the eyes, and tell them this in quiet moments in the car or in bed at night when I join them for a snuggle. I never want them to doubt for a second that they have a wonderful foundation of love, and I think they'll feel comfortable turning to me no matter what, knowing that I will never turn my back on them. That's the biggest lesson my dad taught me.

Watching your babies accomplish little things, and seeing the look on their faces when they get something and are proud of themselves, makes you soar. I don't think there's any pride that's as great as the pride you have in your children. Seeing my children grow and blossom is the most rewarding thing in my life. Forget work, forget anything else. Raising my children is just about as good as it gets.

Natalie Morales: Know that your child is going to consume your entire being, especially in the beginning. So you have to remember who you are as a person, and as part of a couple. The best gift you can give your children is you showing them that you're a strong, confident, hard-working but loving parent, and that you're putting as much effort into their care as you are into every other aspect of your life. When you do that, you're giving your babies the same confidence in life that you have.

And take time to enjoy those great little moments. Sometimes it takes a snapshot to remind you of all those little moments and how fast they go—but at the same time you may not be appreciating them along the way because you are so stressed, you're working so hard, and you're consumed by what is going on with your partner. It's easy to forget to just enjoy your baby.

Ann Curry: I'd say the best advice I could give is that you should be consciously reassuring yourself on an hourly basis that you can give your baby exactly what she needs. Tell yourself that you can love this child and raise this child well, no matter what.

Let your baby show you how to be a mother. I'm not saying don't be disappointed if your child is acting up; what I mean is that if you listen, you will hear who your baby is. And when you look into your baby's eyes, seeking the truth about who she is, she'll know you're looking right back at her, with all the reassurance and love in the world.

Mary Ann and Alicia: Being a parent is a series of trials, tribulations, tears, laughter, and love. It's an all-consuming responsibility, and we don't profess to be perfect at it. All we can do is try our best and show our children unconditional love. Being a parent is the single greatest thing either of us has ever produced.

INDEX

Index